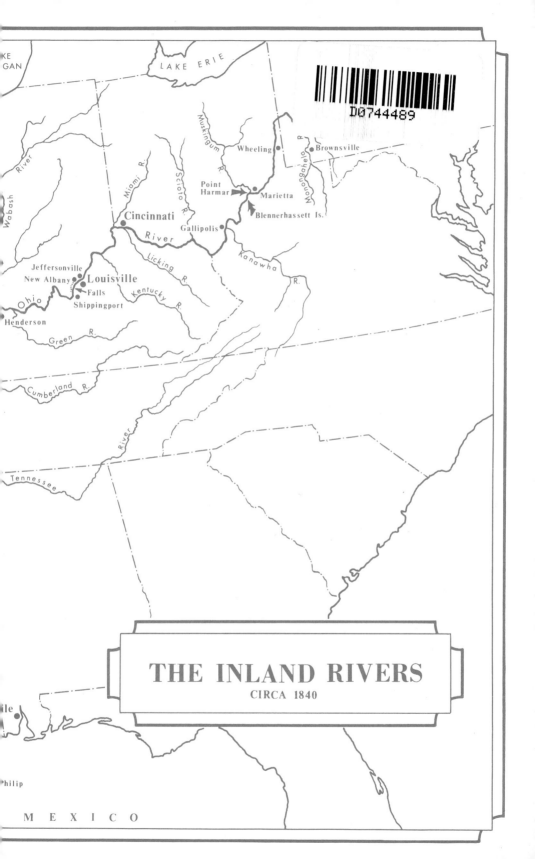

THE INLAND RIVERS

CIRCA 1840

Conquering the Rivers

Henry Miller Shreve

Conquering the Rivers

Henry Miller Shreve and the Navigation of America's Inland Waterways

EDITH McCALL

Louisiana State University Press
Baton Rouge and London

Designer: Albert Crochet
Typeface: Linotron Caledonia
Typesetter: G & S Typesetters, Inc.
Printer and Binder: Vail-Ballou Press, Inc.

The author wishes to thank Lloyd Hawthorne for the
drawings at the beginnings of the chapters.

LIBRARY OF CONGRESS CATALOGING IN PUBLICATION DATA

McCall, Edith S.
  Conquering the rivers.

  Bibliography: p.
  1. Shreve, Henry Miller, 1785–1851.   2. Naval
biography—United States.   3. Inland navigation—United
States—History—19th century.   4. Steam-navigation—
United States—History—19th century.   I. Title.
VM140.S57M35   1984   386'.092'4 [B]   83-12054·
ISBN 0-8071-1127-9

To those who assured me I was not
alone in feeling this book should be
written and who, when difficulties
and discouragement came, urged
me on to its completion

Contents

Illustrations

Conquering the Rivers

Introduction

The United States in 1810 was like an adolescent boy following a rapid growth spurt, somewhat overwhelmed and not knowing exactly what to do with a changing body. The land between the Appalachians and the Mississippi River ceded by England in the Treaty of Paris in 1783 was as yet only sparsely settled when in 1803 approximately 828,000 square miles more became United States territory. This additional tract, known as the Louisiana Purchase, pushed the boundaries far into the nearly uninhabited western plains and mountains. By 1810, in all that vast domain west of the Appalachians there were only three states—Kentucky, Tennessee, and Ohio. Even in early land acquisitions east of the Mississippi, many thousands of acres were as nature had developed them, untouched by the ax or the plow of man.

But one had only to observe the stream of flatboats, arks, keelboats, and other assorted craft afloat on the Ohio River to see that this situation would soon change. There were pioneering settlers nosing into every navigable waterway, seeking a choice piece of fertile land upon which to build a crude cabin and begin the task of making the chosen acreage productive. As with the growing boy, the potential of what maturity would bring was becoming apparent in the development of the "West" of those days.

But then, as today, a transportation system was vital to productivity and economic growth. And this was the major problem of inland America. It would be many, many years before the land between the Appalachians and the Mississippi River could be crisscrossed with even the poorest type of highways and even more years before the trans-Mississippi region could be so traversed. Railroads, even along the populated Atlantic seaboard, were still twenty or more years into the future.

Fortunately, nature had provided at least the basis for a solution to the transportation problem in the form of a ready-made waterway network. Traversing all of inland America, in the form of a colossal distorted cross, was the Mississippi-Ohio-Missouri river system. With its multitude of navigable tributaries, it made accessible much of this huge, potentially productive land area. By 1810 these rivers were already proving their

1

value. The newly cleared tracts of land along the Ohio were producing more than the families living upon them could consume, and crude riverboats were transporting increasing amounts of goods to market each year. Frontier settlement had pushed its way to a few miles west of the Mississippi River, and many small communities were developing. Embryo marketing cities were boasting of their growth—Pittsburgh, Cincinnati, Louisville, and the westernmost of them, St. Louis. All sent shipments to the oldest inland city, the seaport of New Orleans.

Each city and most small communities were built along riverbanks. From the towns and from landings between them, rivercraft were loaded and poled out into the current, the principal motive power to downstream markets. Their cargo consisted principally of products of the pioneer farms, such as apples, live poultry, barrels of pork packed in salt, and more than a few barrels of whiskey, cider, and brandy. There was also a minor amount of manufactured goods, most of which came from Pittsburgh. The manufactured items included bar and cast iron, nails, tin and copper wares, and glass. Most of the cargo went the full journey downriver to New Orleans, where it was sold for local use or for reshipment via oceangoing sailing ships bound for the American eastern seaboard cities or for European or other more distant ports.

Few of the rivercraft could return upstream. Most were boxy flatboats, impossible to move against the difficult Mississippi River currents or even the less turbulent waters of the Ohio. When their cargo was unloaded, these crude boats were broken up to be sold as lumber. Upriver transportation was limited to craft shaped for less water resistance—the keelboat and similar vessels. For growth, inland America was much in need of a two-way flow of goods, especially for development of its rich potential for manufacturing.

Even the keelboat was brought upriver only by means of long and arduous labor. It was manned by a crew of the "half-horse, half-alligator" men of legendary fame. But the muscle power of even these toughest and strongest of boatmen was strained to force the boat—often literally dragging it—against the unpredictable currents of the Mississippi. A Pittsburgh-based keelboat could make but one round trip to New Orleans per year in the months the northern rivers were open, bringing cotton, sugar, tea, and other goods to the people up the rivers. The number of keelboats attempting to serve the growing inland population was far from adequate. Obviously, the sooner the inland rivers could be navigated by steam-powered boats, the better for the welfare of the entire vast region and especially for the growth of cities.

In 1810 people were hopeful that steamboats would soon appear upon the Ohio and Mississippi rivers and possibly would even make their way into the wild Missouri. Since 1807, Fulton's first crude steamboats had been plying the rivers on the Atlantic seaboard. But in all the thousands of miles of inland riverways, no steam-powered boat was as yet operating, although the steamboat was hailed as the great hope for the development of inland America. The news in 1810 that a steamboat was under construction at Pittsburgh was greeted with tremendous enthusiasm.

The boat's construction was planned and financed by Robert Fulton and his partner, Robert R. Livingston, who had enabled Fulton to build his eastern steamboats. Fulton and Livingston planned from the start of their undertaking to use the first steamboats as tests for practicality, with the intention of building steamboats for the area where Livingston had long been aware that there was the greatest need—the western waters. Their success in the East assured, the partners backed construction of the first steamboat to be launched in the Ohio River, setting up a boatbuilding yard at Pittsburgh. This steamboat was to serve the route between Pittsburgh and New Orleans, with other steamboats added to the line as rapidly as they could be built.

The *New Orleans* was duly launched in the fall of 1811. People were wildly enthusiastic as they witnessed demonstrations of the steamboat moving upriver on the Ohio under its own power. Among those most enthusiastic at the news of the coming of the steamboat to the Ohio was a young man of twenty-six who had already become successful as a merchant-navigator, Henry Miller Shreve. Captain Shreve, owner and operator of a keelboat traveling the route between Pittsburgh and New Orleans, realized from firsthand experience that the steamboat was vitally needed to replace the keelboat. The sooner he could be in command of one, the better he would like it. He had learned a great deal about steam power, watching all developments as steam engines were taking over the work of water power in American industry. He welcomed the news of the building of the *New Orleans*. Steam power would end the demeaning human drudgery of bringing a keelboat upstream. Furthermore and of great importance, it would make river transportation much more rapid. Yet, as

Shreve observed the machinery being set into place in this first inland river steamboat, he was skeptical that its low-pressure engines could master the difficult river currents of the Mississippi above Natchez.

The first months of operation of the *New Orleans* (which amazed the public by surviving a downriver voyage into the center of what may have been our nation's worst earthquake) proved that Shreve's skepticism was well founded. The long-awaited and much-heralded steamboat was unable to stem the Mississippi River waters above Natchez and could make no return voyage to Ohio River ports. The *New Orleans* was used to transport goods and passengers between the port city and Natchez, and did not attempt to go farther upriver.

This left the people of almost the entire inland river system in their old predicament. The distance from Pittsburgh to New Orleans via the Ohio and Mississippi was reckoned at about 2,000 miles, of which less than 325 miles had steamboat service. Although a keelboat could go downriver from Pittsburgh to New Orleans in about six weeks, the return time of travel was four and a half months. Even the voyage from Louisville, Kentucky, to Pittsburgh took a month by keelboat, and this was through a much easier river course than the waters west and south. The residents of the region above Natchez felt keen disappointment.

Disappointment was coupled with resentment toward the Fulton-Livingston company, which was based in the eastern United States. Westerners already felt that the United States government favored the easterners. The resentment was due to the granting to Fulton-Livingston the exclusive right to use steam-powered vessels in all the waters of Louisiana. For many years, the use of the port of New Orleans and trading rights there had been vital to the western economy. Now it appeared that although the Fulton steamboats were not able to function on the river system, no enterprising person who built a better steamboat would be allowed to use it to go down to the port city and bring back merchandise to the upper river areas. True, the Fulton group had begun construction of another steamboat at Pittsburgh, but the changes in its design from that of the *New Orleans* were minor; it was not likely to be more successful in difficult Mississippi River waters than was the first steamboat.

This was the opinion of many, including young Captain Shreve. Another concern to Shreve and many others in inland America was the threat that arose in 1812 when war was declared against England. The

British naval and military forces blockaded American seaports and threatened to capture New Orleans. The year 1814 was the time of greatest crisis in a decade fraught with problems. Satisfactory solutions were vital to the progress of inland America.

In addition to these problems that demanded immediate action was another of long standing—one to which rivermen had grown accustomed over the years. For centuries, floods and storms had deposited tree limbs and even whole trees, some of great size, in the rivers. Along with shifting sandbars, these underwater trees, or "snags," were a menace to river navigation, causing great losses in property and even in lives. Until these snags and other underwater hazards, plus the accumulations of driftwood that often formed large "rafts" on the river's surface, could be removed, travel by boat had to be cautiously slow. Even the potential for speed of a steam-powered boat would be of limited help as long as navigation was thus hindered.

It is remarkable that one individual provided answers to, or assistance in solving, each of these problems. That individual was Captain Henry Miller Shreve. He was a product of the western Pennsylvania frontier, reaching his majority in the early 1800s. Without political or financial backing, Shreve defied the Fulton-Livingston monopoly and fought it in the courts, succeeding in opening inland rivers to free enterprise. As he began this risky David-versus-Goliath venture, Shreve was also involved in the solution of the New Orleans problem, assisting General Jackson in his successful defense of the city in January, 1815. At that time, Shreve was in command of the *Enterprise*, the first steamboat to make the entire round trip from Pittsburgh to New Orleans and back. He used the steamboat to transport munitions and troops, under Jackson's orders. With the *Enterprise*, he ran a blockade against British cannons, the first time a steam-powered vessel was so employed.

Shreve's next contribution was to design and build a revolutionary type of steamboat, specifically for the inland rivers. In this endeavor, he persisted despite ridicule, heavy financial burdens, and a tragic accident. His *Washington* opened the way for the steamboat age. Before long, Shreve had a line of steamboats in operation and had designed the prototype of the "floating palace" of Currier and Ives prints. His steamboat inventions and improvements brought the solution to the upriver transportation problem.

Acknowledged as the father of the Mississippi steamboat, Shreve was willing to give up his profitable steamboat operations to attack the problem of river clearance of underwater hazards. He invented a "snag machine" that succeeded where earlier inventions had failed. Personally directing operations with this steam-powered vessel, Shreve served through several presidential administrations as United States superintendent of western river improvements. He capped his riverman career with an assignment deemed impossible of accomplishment—the opening of the Red River, long blocked with a huge driftwood "raft," about 160 miles in length. Here, too, he eventually succeeded despite major setbacks.

The story of the opening of the inland rivers is so interwoven with the life of Henry Miller Shreve that the two cannot be separated. Yet, few people are familiar with his name. The purpose of this book is to reveal in a combined narrative these two highly interesting phases of American history too long overlooked.

1 / **The Rivers Beckon**

In 1788 Colonel Israel Shreve, veteran of the American Revolution and a great admirer of his commander, General George Washington, led a wagon train of family and friends to western Pennsylvania. Henry Miller Shreve, his fourth son and ninth child, was not quite three years old at the time. The colonel's choice of a new homesite was important, for it would allow Henry to learn the ways of the rivers. And Henry Miller Shreve was to become the one person most influential in opening America's inland rivers to safe and rapid navigation.

Israel Shreve and his eldest son, John, had both served under General Washington for six years and had heard their commander-in-chief speak of his prewar travels and of the tracts of land he had purchased west of the Appalachian ranges. Washington's favorite claim was one lying between the Youghiogheny and Monongahela rivers in western Pennsylvania, and there he had selected a site on which a mill was constructed in the early 1770s. The mill was on a stream later named Washington Run, flowing into the "Yough," as the Youghiogheny was familiarly called. The tract was divided in Washington's survey into five "farms" and totaled 1,644 acres, reaching from the Yough to within five or six miles of the Monongahela. The Yough joined the "Mon" a few miles downstream, and the Monongahela joined the Allegheny to form the Ohio River about fifty miles from the Washington tract. Thus, the Washington land was adjacent to headwaters of the great inland river system. Before he formed his wagon train, Colonel Shreve had learned that Washington's lands, including the millsite, could be leased or purchased. He was determined that the millsite and adjacent farms would someday be his own.

Israel Shreve was forty-one years old and in poor health when he returned to his family just before the close of the revolutionary war in 1781. His own farmhouse in north central New Jersey had been burned to the ground by the redcoats as they marched through; his wife, Mary, and his children found refuge in the old Shreve family homestead, with Israel's older brother Caleb. The two-story brick house, with the date 1742 worked into the bricks on the east end, was on ground homesteaded by Israel's grandfather in a Quaker community just east of present-day Columbus, New Jersey. There, on October 21, 1785, Henry Miller Shreve was born.

Shortly after his return to Mount Pleasant, as the homestead was known, Israel regained his commission as a justice in his home area, but he never fully regained his standing as a respected member of the Society of Friends. His Quaker associates had demanded that he confess to wrongdoing in taking up arms in the defense of home and country. This the colonel and the other Shreve men who had served in the Continental army refused to do. This severing of old ties was among the factors that made Israel restless in the years after his return. When his son John decided to marry and go to the "forks of the Yough" in 1787, Israel's mind was made up. He, too, would go to the area he had so long dreamed of and find the Washington lands.

Not a man to make hasty moves or take risks with his family's welfare, Colonel Shreve arranged in advance to lease a log house that was being built a mile or two from John's cabin. From there, he would be able to check on the Washington mill and farms that interested him so much. The Shreves and several neighbors gathered in Caleb's main room in the Mount Pleasant house and planned an expedition. Israel was to be the captain. His brother William, who had also defied Quaker ethics to bear arms, decided to join the party, with his wife and two grown children.

When the emigrating group assembled on July 10 for their departure, there were twenty-nine people in all, of whom little Henry was the youngest Shreve and possibly the youngest in the party. Three of the six wagons belonged to Shreves, and three more to neighbor families.

Israel kept a journal of the trek, a journey made more difficult by rain, almost impassable roads up and over the mountains, wagon breakdowns, surly innkeepers offering poor food or none at all, and the illness and death of little Ann Beck.[1] As they struggled through the last muddy miles, Israel was cheered by meeting a fellow New Jersey citizen who reported that the house the Shreves hoped to live in was ready for them.

And so, early in August, 1788, young Henry Shreve arrived in the area that was to influence him so heavily. It was not truly an isolated frontier location, for families had been settling there for nearly twenty years, since Colonel James Burd had built a stockaded settlement at Redstone Old Fort (so named for an ancient moundbuilders' "fort"). The town that developed there was renamed Brownsville in 1785, but most people still referred to it as Redstone when the Shreves arrived to settle a few miles away in 1788. The boy Henry soon learned to love this area, which would be his home until he reached manhood.

Israel Shreve investigated the Washington lands almost as soon as his family had moved into the leased house. He wrote an optimistic report of what he found to his brother Caleb in December of 1789, stating that he had been in touch with George Washington via his agent and that the general was willing to rent the entire tract to his old associate from wartime days for a term of five years, with an option to purchase it. The Shreves would operate the mill as soon as it was repaired, with the adjacent farm, and lease the other "farms" to help meet the rental.[2]

When the family moved to the Washington lands, Henry was four years old. With older brothers to help their father in working the farm and the mill, he had plenty of free time to roam the meadows and woods, learning to trap rabbits and other small animals to add to the family's meat supply. He climbed the apple trees in the orchard and helped himself to the juicy ripe fruit as he picked it for his mother and sisters to preserve. He helped

1. Israel Shreve, "Israel Shreve's Diary and Letters," *Magazine of American History*, II (1878), 743–48.
2. Franklin Ellis, *History of Fayette County, Pa.* (N.p., n.d.), 710–11.

feed the grain into the mill hopper and lugged the full sacks over to the open door. He felt the warm sun on his shoulders as, with a big dog to help him, he drove the cows back to the barnyard for milking.

But most of all he loved to go down Washington Run to where it met the Youghiogheny River. There he found his true and lasting fascination. He saw the flatboats bringing heavy loads of bar iron and millstones from Connellsville, heading for the confluence with the Mon just a few miles to the north. Thence they would go down to Pittsburgh, the city that the boy vowed he would someday visit.

Along the banks of the Yough he talked with families who were camping there and awaiting the completion of a flatboat on which they hoped to float to a land of milk and honey, their own conception of a paradise where they would start life anew. Henry saw the families load their wagons, their animals, and their meager household furnishings aboard the finished crude flatboat and push off.

He asked questions of his half brother John, who eked out his living by occasionally going along as a hand on one of the merchandise flatboats that embarked from Brownsville on the Monongahela. These flatboats took wheat, bacon, millstones, and bars of pig iron down the rivers. Sometimes they also carried glassware from the works farther up the Monongahela at New Geneva. If they still lacked a full load, they took on more glass and ironware and perhaps some whiskey at Pittsburgh. Once John went all the way to Cincinnati; on another trip, his destination was Louisville, Kentucky, outpost of civilization along the Ohio. His longest voyage, taking him away from home for seven months, was the entire length of the Ohio and on down to New Orleans, a journey of two thousand miles.

Each time Henry learned that John was back home on his farm, not far from Colonel Shreve's, the boy hurried over to John and Abigail's cabin, now crowded with the children who arrived regularly. Henry would follow John about as he did his farm chores, perhaps lending a helping hand, but always asking questions, soaking in every detail of the voyages as John reported them. In his imagination, Henry was down the river with John, sharing in the narrow escapes from Indians or river pirates, helping push and pull the flatboat to get it unstuck from a sandbar or prevent its being overturned by an unexpected brush with a snag. He knew then that he, too, would follow the rivers. But he would not do as John did, making only an occasional voyage and coming home to farm. The rivers would be his entire life.

River fever possessed him. He was constantly in touch with the flow of rivercraft and the people who traveled on them, for the Shreve lands were not only near the rivers but were situated close to principal emigration routes of that day. A much-traveled route into this area was the Cumberland Road, an outgrowth of Braddock's Road, where Washington had come close to a premature death in the French and Indian War. This road entered Fayette County, in which the Shreves lived, from the east at the county's southeastern corner, just north of the Maryland-Pennsylvania line. Wagons could be ferried across the Youghiogheny at that location and in low-water times could ford the stream. The wagons then followed the road northwest, crossing Laurel Hill, one of the many Allegheny ridges, to go to Uniontown. The Cumberland Road continued on to the northwest about seven miles to Brownsville. This town was the nearest riverport to the Shreve home, not more than five or six miles over the narrow wagon trail that crossed Little Redstone Creek near John Shreve's cabin.

Occasionally, Henry would ride along with an older brother or his father to Brownsville, located where a high ridge ran parallel to the Monongahela and continued as a bluff along Dunlap Creek, a tributary of the Mon. The road entered the town along the Dunlap Creek bluff and then dropped down in a steep curve to the bench of land along the river. A person could see a long way from the bluff—across the Monongahela to a rolling countryside and the tiny new settlement that would become West Brownsville, to mountain foothills to the south and a more gentle landscape to the north. The river itself soon disappeared around a bend.

To the left, looking downward from the bluff, one could see Dunlap Creek flowing into the Monongahela and the new log bridge across the creek that provided easy communication between Brownsville and the small settlement of Bridgeport. Looking to the right from the bluff, the more distant Redstone Creek, where Brown's flour mill operated, could also be seen, but the activity of Brownsville centered about the Dunlap's confluence with the river. Down there lay the boatyards and the mooring places for the many rivercraft. The boy Henry always made his way eagerly down the steep, curving road to the riverbank.

Along the riverfront were a few rustic shops and mills to supply the boatmen and the boatbuilders. But the boy's eyes sought the riverboats sure to be tied at the landings. There were always flatboats and sometimes the crude, heavy hollow-log canoes known as pirogues. Henry always hoped to see, whenever he was in Brownsville, the arrival of a keelboat, with the bearded men of its crew in their tight trousers and red flannel shirts, shouting to one another and to the loafers at the landing.

Anytime Henry went to Brownsville or even to the Yough, he could see flatboats—crude, rectangular, shallow boxes with or without a roofed-over cabin. Flatboats were for those who had no plans to bring the boat back up the river, for this type of craft was too heavy and cumbersome to move against the river currents. The flatboat was the boat of the emigrants, bought or built at Brownsville or another river town at the end of a wagon trek over the mountains, to float downriver to new homelands along the Ohio. Flatboats were also used by merchant-navigators who loaded the products of the region on board to float down the rivers to market cities, often as distant as New Orleans. At the end of the voyage, with the merchandise sold and unloaded, the flatboat itself was sold for lumber.

But the keelboat was different. It was the finest type of inland riverboat thus far afloat on American rivers. As its name implies, it was constructed on a long keel to which ribs and planking were applied. (A large keelboat was often called a barge, but because of the modern connotations of the word *barge*, implying a box-shaped vessel, the term *keelboat* will be used here for all boats of this type, regardless of size.) The keelboat was so shaped at its ends that it could be moved against the current with a minimum of water resistance. Its whole structure was assembled with much greater care and with better lumber than a flatboat because the keelboat was expected to be useful over a period of three or four years, bringing merchandise back to its home riverport as well as taking it downriver. On a voyage from Pittsburgh to New Orleans and back, the usual time consumed was six months, for even this finest of rivercraft moved upriver very slowly indeed.

Young Henry's imagination was working in high gear when he chanced to get to Brownsville at a time when he could see a keelboat at short range and hear the talk of its crew. At other times, the most fascinating place in town to the boy was the boatyard at the mouth of Dunlap Creek. Sometimes a keelboat was under construction there, and always there were flatboats being built for emigrants and merchants. Near the boatyard he saw the long sheds containing the apparatus that twisted hemp into rope—the rope walk. A great deal of rope was needed by each group embarking on the river, to secure cargo and to secure the boat itself. Keelboats also required a long towrope, or *cordelle*, as the French boatmen had named it.

Moving up the street, the boy looked in at the glowing forges of the smiths. Several of them shod horses and also made household items of iron, such as pothooks, kettles, or door hinges. One had a specialty of making the square nails that the people up on the bluff wanted for their new homes of sawed lumber. There were a printshop and several stores where one could buy anything from dress calico to horse blankets, from pins to candle sconces; they also carried a good supply of the broad-brimmed gray felt hats favored by the Quaker gentlemen of the area. Business was augmented in these stores by sales to the emigrants, stocking up with coffee, tea, sugar, and salt for their long voyages.

If there was time, Henry would linger along the waterfront where the boats were sometimes being loaded. A specialty of the area was the shaped millstone, for a type of stone suitable for millstones was abundant nearby. When his older brothers would wait no longer, he would reluctantly mount his horse for the homeward trip. At the top of the bluff, he might turn in his saddle for one last look at the Monongahela, where the boxy ferryboat plied its way to the opposite bank, taking people and horses to the place where the Cumberland Road continued on its way toward that far-off city of Wheeling, on the Ohio River. A few travelers took their wagons that far now, although the newly cut road was still crude and stump-ridden.

But such expeditions were a rare treat for the boy. Most of his days were spent more routinely, with chores to do around the farm or the mill. With the mechanical genius he showed in later years, it is likely that he was adept at making repairs to keep the mill in running order. That may be where he first learned how a series of gears turning and enmeshing resulted in specific mechanical actions, information he most certainly possessed later when he was working out technical improvements on steamboats. He attended the area school and was an apt student.

When he was free from such duties, Henry often went down the millstream, Washington Run, to its mouth. There he saw the emigrants and the boatbuilders who constructed flatboats for them. Near the water, there were sawpits for cutting planks from the stock of white oak logs piled up nearby. The beams and planks used for the boat construction were assembled by means of holes drilled with hand-turned augers, into which wooden pegs were pounded. The area boys whittled these oaken pegs, an inch across at the thick end and five inches long. Henry perhaps carried a bucket of these down to the boatbuilders, the result of work in his evenings at home, for he was an industrious person.

When he was a little older, Henry probably participated in "boat-turnin's." These were a middle step in flatboat construction. The boat was built by first constructing the bottom frame of timbers, two for the length of the boat (up to fifty feet) and four or more for the beam, usually from seven to twelve feet. When the rectangular frame was pegged together, it was floored over with boards up to two inches thick, ripped with a whip-saw over the sawing pit. These rough planks were pegged onto the frame and the cracks sealed with oakum and pitch. With this boat bottom made watertight, it was time for the turning, which necessitated calling in a few extra hands, such as young Henry, and was an event looked forward to by the neighborhood boys. The heavy boat floor had to be turned over and set afloat for the construction to continue. It was rolled on logs to the water, and by an ingenious method involving loads of rock dumped along one side of it for weighting, and employing agile young men with poles, the heavy structure was flipped over, aided by the push of the river current. With the "boat-turnin'" accomplished, the regular builders could then complete the structure, building up the sides about four feet and roofing over a large part of the deck.[3]

The work of the boatbuilders and conversations with those who traveled the rivers fascinated the boy. His growing-up years, 1790 to 1800, were at the peak of the emigration by river through the Fayette County, Pennsylvania, region. It is not surprising that he acquired a feeling for the rivers that lasted throughout his life. The Pittsburgh *Gazette* of November 24, 1787, tells of what Henry could have observed about him. "Upwards of one hundred and twenty boats have [recently] passed by this town on their way to Kentucky, which at an average of fifteen persons each, will add eighteen hundred inhabitants to that young settlement,"

3. J. E. Phillips, "Flatboating on the Great Thoroughfare," *Bulletin of the Historical and Philosophical Society of Ohio,* V (June, 1947), 11–32.

the reporter wrote. In late winter, the road leading to Brownsville was lined on both sides with wagons and families camping, waiting for the ice to break so that they might be on their way by flatboat.

The year 1799 was a turning point in Henry Shreve's life. It was a very difficult year for his father, who was in poor health and also in financial straits. His payments to George Washington had fallen in arrears. Washington himself was also ill and having financial troubles, and he became quite disturbed when Colonel Shreve failed to make his full payments on time. The general decided to take legal steps, instructing the sheriff of Fayette County to serve foreclosure papers against Colonel Shreve.

As soon as he sent off the order to Sheriff Thomas Collins, former president Washington had second thoughts. He immediately wrote a letter to his old comrade from the days of the Battles of Trenton and Monmouth. Its tone was quite severe in regard to the delinquency, but at its close Washington softened a bit. He wrote, "Notwithstanding what has been done, and in consideration of our ancient friendship, I give you further indulgence. Take this letter to Col. Thomas Collins, sheriff of Fayette County, and it will operate as a stay of execution."[4]

The letter was delivered immediately to the sheriff and Colonel Shreve managed to hold onto the property. But on December 14 of that year both George Washington and Israel Shreve died. Family legend has it that "the last words of Colonel Shreve were, 'Washington! O, Washington!'—their spirits passing to the great beyond at the same hour." The land transaction had not been completed, but the legal problems were finally cleared in June, 1802, and the property conveyed to the heirs of Israel Shreve.[5]

Those heirs were many in number, and young Henry, just turned fourteen when his father died, was far down the line. He had to consider his assets as being other than financial. Physically, he was not very tall, but was slender and wiry. He was known as the fastest runner in his home area and also as a crack rifle shot, a skill acquired by many frontier boys as they aided their families in getting supplies of meat. It is also highly likely that Henry had a basic education and that he had mechanical skills. From his father he had inherited (or learned) a shrewdness in business dealings and in planning his future steps. He was already known as a person who

4. Ellis, *History of Fayette County*, 711.
5. L. P. Allen, *The Genealogy and History of the Shreve Family from 1641* (Greenfield, Ill., 1901), 345.

did what he set out to do, a reputation that stayed with him all his life. He also had acquired from his father a hero worship of George Washington and a strong spirit of patriotism.

As the new year and a new century began, Henry and his family had to evaluate the situation. The boy knew what he wanted to do. The rivers called him, and soon he was learning the ways of the riverboatmen. There is no record of exactly when he took to the rivers, but it is probable that it was very soon after his father's death. He may have hired on first with a flatboat crew, going down the river with a load of freight. If he went by flatboat to New Orleans, he walked back, following the Natchez Trace up through Tennessee in the company of other boatmen. In his youth, he would have been physically unready to start out working on a keelboat, for a keelboatman's work demanded a strength beyond that of a slender youth, no matter how well muscled.

As Henry matured, he reached a height of five feet eleven inches, above average for his generation. He was still slender, but he was not slight, for he had well developed shoulder muscles from years of poling and rowing and laboring to move heavy boats. He had not lost his litheness or his reputation for agility and speed in running. His hair was brown and somewhat wavy, worn in the style of the day, no longer long enough to tie back in a club but still at a below-the-ears length. People noticed his intense gray eyes.[6]

In 1807, before he was twenty-two, Henry had saved enough money to invest in a keelboat and become a merchant-navigator. His first boat was rather small, said to have been of thirty-five tons burden. On such a boat, he could not carry enough cargo to make the long voyage from Pittsburgh to New Orleans pay off, but he quickly found another way that a boat of that size might serve to make money for him. The reasoning behind the plans he made was related to trends in national development at that time.

In 1807 Lewis and Clark's reports of their exploratory expedition up the Missouri River were having a major effect. One of Lewis and Clark's assignments was to observe the wildlife of the parts of the Louisiana Purchase through which they traveled, and their notations and the specimens they brought back made those engaged in the fur trade wildly enthusiastic. The reports were the news of the day just before Henry

6. Florence L. Dorsey, *Master of the Mississippi* (Boston, 1941), 10–11.

Shreve bought his first keelboat, for the explorers' return was in 1806, with their arrival in the little fur-trading village of St. Louis taking place on September 23.

Especially in that town, there was immediate reaction to the new knowledge of the vast, almost uninhabited West. Lewis and Clark spoke of countless streams feeding into the Missouri River, some large and some small. The tributaries they had taken time to investigate were fed in turn by swift little mountain creeks that in the meadows broadened into quiet waters. Each stream had "beaver sign"—the telltale dams and chewed sapling stumps that bespoke a colony of beavers. No doubt there were many similar streams beyond the scope of their exploration, and rich fur-trapping areas off the major branch rivers, such as the Yellowstone.

At this time, the demand for beaver pelts was approaching an all-time high. Tall beaver hats were very fashionable in eastern seaboard cities and in the cities of Europe. Immediately after the Lewis and Clark reports came in, expansion plans were made by owners of fur-trading companies, principally in St. Louis. They would contact the Indians in the upper Missouri River and Yellowstone River regions. Representatives of the fur companies would try to induce the Indians to trade beaver pelts, which they could easily obtain, for lengths of European or American-made blanket cloth, bolts of yellow or red cotton fabrics, beads, trinkets of many kinds, iron pots, and of course the most desired items the white man had—guns, ammunition, and whiskey. The first to start upriver to contact the untapped sources was St. Louis' Spanish fur trader, Manuel Lisa. Lisa had an expedition ready to leave St. Louis in the spring of 1807.

Just as the Lewis and Clark reports shaped Lisa's and other fur traders' plans, they also shaped those of Shreve, who had his twenty-first birthday on October 21, 1806, and went into business for himself immediately. He read the newspaper reports of the Lewis and Clark expedition with great interest, perceiving the great stimulus this would provide to the fur trade. He would use this new development as an opportunity to make his own success as a merchant keelboatman.

Other keelboats routinely took merchandise from the upper Ohio area down the Ohio River to the Mississippi, where they continued downriver to New Orleans, there to sell their goods and reload with bulky cargo— sugar from the West Indies, cotton, hemp, tobacco, tea, and coffee. Shreve's keelboat was not large enough to carry many tons of such goods, and if he made any profit after paying off his crew, it would be slight. He reasoned that in terms of dollar value per hundredweight, the most valuable cargo he could bring back to Pittsburgh would be furs. He learned that middlemen in Pittsburgh would be able to transfer his pelts to the big Conestoga wagons that plied the transmontane road to Philadelphia.

At the time he was making his plans, all the furs handled in St. Louis went downriver to New Orleans, there to be loaded on board sailing ships and taken to the coastal or foreign market cities. Shreve foresaw a good supply of furs on hand in St. Louis as the rush to beaver waters began; he also foresaw such growth in the fur-trading village that the goods he could bring to St. Louis from Pittsburgh would probably sell at a better price than in New Orleans, where the competition was greater. Few keelboats made their way upriver to St. Louis.

When his boat was ready, he decided, he and his crew of ten men would go down the Ohio to the Mississippi and then turn upriver. On board the keelboat would be hardware and glass from Pittsburgh and some Brownsville millstones, certain to be wanted in Missouri, where the frontier was in rapid development. The fact that no one had tested the feasibility of this idea did not deter Shreve.

In the years ahead, he would be known for many firsts on the inland rivers. It was characteristic that his career as Captain Shreve, merchant keelboatman, should start with one of them.

2 / **Keelboat down the Ohio**

In that spring of 1807, anyone looking for Henry Shreve knew where to look first. He was usually at the mouth of Dunlap Creek in Brownsville, at the boatyard operated by Neal Gillespie and Robert Clark. Shreve no doubt checked carefully on the selection of each piece of lumber to be used in his keelboat, for the hazards of river travel were great; poor lumber could be ripped all too easily by a snag, resulting in the loss of a valuable cargo.

The boat's hull was designed for maximum freight space with minimum draft, fashioned to be as flat-bottomed as was practical without increasing the hull's resistance to the flow of the river currents. Usually a loaded keelboat the size of Shreve's could float in two feet of water. As in the building of a ship, the construction began with the laying of a keel, usually of straight white oak, in a cradle set up near the water's edge. The keel was four to six inches thick and ten or twelve inches high, hewn from a suitable tree trunk from the nearby woods. At the prow, this sturdy beam extended to take the brunt of collision with obstacles under the water's surface.[1]

To the keel were attached the ribs and framework to make the hull,

1. Leland D. Baldwin, *The Keelboat Age on Western Waters* (Pittsburgh, 1941), 42–47.

19

which came to a point at both the bow and the stern. The keelboat may be described as cigar-shaped, with a length-to-width ratio of four to one or even narrower. When the framework of the hull was completed, the whole was planked, caulked, and launched, to be completed while afloat.

A covered cargo area occupied the entire hull with the exception of ten to fifteen feet of open deck at each end and about fifteen inches of space along each side. This side space, between the cargo box and the "gunnels," was planked and had cleats pegged in crosswise at intervals. On a freight boat such as Shreve's, very little roofed-over space was allowed for living quarters; the crew would sleep on the deck area or sometimes ashore.

The cargo box roof was often slightly rounded to provide better drainage. From the roof's center rose a mast, about twenty-five to thirty feet tall, to be fitted with a square sail that was occasionally useful when the wind was right. A Y-shaped rest for the long rudder sweep was provided at the stern; the sweep was often long enough so that the man who controlled it could stand on the roof for better visibility. With a cordelle attached to the mast, a few oars and setting poles on board, and a crew of robust men, the keelboat was ready for action.

The cleated walkway along each side, left open to the sky, was called a "passé avant" by the French boatmen and a "running board" by Americans.[2] It was needed in poling, one of the means of propelling the keelboat used when the depth of water permitted. The setting poles, preferably of white ash, were about twenty feet long, iron-shod at one end and with a leather covered "button" at the other end, so that a boatman could put his full weight against it at his shoulder. Three or four boatmen on a boat the size of Shreve's, and more on a larger keelboat, would take positions along each running board, facing the stern of the boat. The boat's captain or mate, often called the patroon or patron, would call out commands.

"Stand to your poles!" Then, "Set poles!" and "Down on her!" With this, the men leaned into their work, walking toward the boat's stern, with the pole's end in position on the river bottom. As they reached the limit of the pole's extension, they bent forward, ending in a crawling position. At the instant the first man reached the end of his walk, the patroon

2. *Ibid.*, 63.

called out, "Lift poles!" Instantly the men turned about, lifting their poles as they did so. They ran back to their starting places, ready for the command "Set poles!" before the boat could lose its forward momentum.[3]

The keelboat also had a few oars. But the main reliance for propulsion was upon the cordelle, a name adopted from the early French boatmen. The cordelle was a stout rope, up to a thousand feet long, fastened to the top of the mast. The rope ran through a loop of a short rope fastened by means of a metal ring at the bow of the boat. This short rope, known as the "bridle," was to prevent uncontrolled swinging about of the boat as it was towed. When the water was too deep for poling and the wind inadequate to move the boat against the current, the crew cordelled the boat upstream.

One of the men swam ashore with the end of the cordelle grasped firmly, usually with his teeth. Others of the crew followed, swimming toward the riverbank. They moved ahead of the bow of the boat some distance, and then each grasped the cordelle and with it over his shoulder struggled forward as best he could. Tree trunks and boulders, brambly vines and bushes, slippery mud and sheer rock faces, all had to be crossed or gotten around in order to make progress. It was the meanest, hardest kind of toil.

When the cordelling reached a point where progress halted because of insurmountable difficulties (such as crosscurrents, snags of tree limbs, or rapids), the crew might have to resort to warping. Sometimes a second rope was used to facilitate this. In warping, the skiff that was often towed by the keelboat was useful, with a couple of crew members manning it to carry the rope upstream as far as the rope would reach. They moved close to the shore, and one of the men wrapped the rope around the trunk of a stout tree. The other end of the rope was held on board the keelboat and, if the boat was equipped with a capstan, attached to it. As the rope was wound about the capstan or pulled shorter by brute strength, the keelboat moved upstream. The same principle could be used with greater difficulty on a boat lacking a skiff. The crewmen expected to plunge into the river frequently, as they had to when cordelling or in warping without a skiff.

Occasionally the boat could be moved upstream by "bushwhacking"

3. *Ibid.*, 62–63.

from within the boat. When the water was deep enough close to shore and the brush grew close to the water, the crew, standing at intervals along the running board and working in cooperation, could pull the boat forward by grasping bushes just at the limit of a man's reach.

Whatever the method chosen, progress upriver was always slow, and it demanded day after weary day of hard work by the crew to ascend a river, mile upon torturous, tortuous mile, from dawn to dusk, rain or shine. The Ohio was less difficult to ascend than the Mississippi in most of the thousand miles of its length. An old history of St. Louis, written by John Thomas Scharf, recalled the time intervals involved in keelboat transportation: "A voyage from St. Louis to New Orleans and return occupied from four to six months; consequently only two round trips could be made in a year. Even with the assistance of sails, a keelboat could not make the ascent in less than seventy or eighty days."[4] This was a distance of about 1,250 river miles. The two-thousand-mile journey from Pittsburgh to New Orleans was usually made but once a year, for ice became a hazard in the winter months at the upper end of the voyage.

The human toil the upriver length of each voyage demanded of a man was greater than that of almost any other employment. Yet, hundreds of men were working as keelboatmen on the rivers when Shreve hired his crew of ten men in 1807. They were a hard-muscled, profane, hard-drinking lot. Often a boatman bore a permanent mark of his occupation in the form of an ear partially bitten off or cauliflowered or a nose with its fleshy portion sacrificed in a no-holds-barred fight. The man who backed off from a challenge had a hard time winning the respect of his fellows.

Shreve had spent enough time on the rivers to be well acquainted with these "half-horse, half-alligator" fellows. His years from the age of fourteen to twenty-one had taught him to depart from his Quaker upbringing sufficiently to hold his own among men such as these. Now as the master of a keelboat, his strength would be severely tested. He was shrewd enough to realize that it was essential to hold his crew's respect in order to keep the upper hand.

His men wore the standard "uniform" of the Ohio River boatman—a red flannel shirt worn above pants of deerhide or linsey-woolsey, usually shrunken skintight from the many river dunkings each man had to take.

4. John T. Scharf, *History of St. Louis City and County* (2 vols.; Philadelphia, 1883), II, 1089.

The pants were tucked into boots, sometimes of tanned leather but more likely to be of the soft type of high-cut deerhide moccasins. The boatman wore a belt by necessity, not to hold up his pants but to hold his knife, various pouches, and anything else he wanted at hand. In cold weather the belt was worn over a short, dark-blue woolen coat. His hair was usually shoulder length and topped with a knitted cap into which a feather might be jauntily stuck. In most cases one man on the boat and one man only could wear a red feather in his cap. He wore it proudly, for it was the symbol of his undisputed—for a time, anyway—championship in man-to-man fighting.

Shreve stocked his boat with only a few staple items of food, for meat would be available along the way through a short hunting session when the boat tied up for the night. A small space was left in the weather-protected cargo box for a supply of dried beans, cornmeal, and bacon. One of his men set up a makeshift cooking stove of stones set in sand in a shallow box. This would serve for cooking in rainy weather or when a campfire could not be built on the shore. They would do a full day's cooking at a time at day's end.

Each man's meager personal baggage was stored under the roof, but the valuable cargo space was not sacrificed to make a sleeping area, except for a small space for the blanket roll of a man who might have the misfortune to fall sick. "There were no medicines, no physician, no nurses or attendants, and nothing but the coarsest food," writes Hiram Chittenden. "The prospect was enough to frighten everyone into keeping well."[5]

As master of the boat, young Shreve automatically acquired the title of captain, and it is easy to imagine how proudly he stood atop the cargo box of his trim little keelboat and for the first time raised his new brass horn to blow a long, mellow blast announcing the boat's readiness for embarkation. His place on this voyage and on all those in the future was the position of honor, from which he would be in charge of the long rudder sweep set into the boat's forked branch near the stern. From the cargo box roof, he commanded a view of the river and of his crew. Up near the bow his bosun took a position, pole in hand, to aid in the steering. This man was chosen for his strength and reliability, for it was his responsibility not only to push the boat clear of hazards but also to observe the water ahead

5. Hiram M. Chittenden, *Early Steamboat Navigation on the Missouri* (2 vols.; Minneapolis, 1903), II, 108.

closely. He warned the captain of danger in time for him to push the rudder sweep into position to avoid the snag, rock, or sandbar the boat was approaching.

As he started his first voyage as a captain, Shreve is sure to have had on his person a copy of a slim little handbook, *The Navigator*, prepared by Zadok Cramer, a Pittsburgh printer.[6] As the boat moved out into the river, Shreve is likely to have pulled the book from his pocket for a quick glance to see if he remembered the channel correctly and to remind himself of any precautions Cramer might have to offer.

This Pittsburgh printer had never gone down the rivers himself, but he made it his business to learn from his scouts and all returning voyagers who tied up at Pittsburgh all the details of the Monongahela, Youghiogheny, Allegheny, Ohio, and Mississippi rivers. Cramer was a New Jersey Quaker, like Israel Shreve, and had come to Pittsburgh to open a print shop, which was distinguished by a painting of Benjamin Franklin on its signboard and referred to as being "at the sign of the Franklin Head."[7] In 1801 he brought out the first edition of *The Navigator*, designed to make boatmen heading down the Ohio aware of the landmarks and hazards of the river, and of the distances between marked points. He always indicated the location of the main channel in the riverbed, a great help to the boatmen when the water was low.

Captain Shreve's keelboat moved smoothly down the Monongahela, already weighted down with a partial cargo of millstones and glass for St. Louis and some local farm produce for sale at Pittsburgh. There he would fill his cargo space to the limit of his boat's burden. He looked forward to his stop at the city, even though he had long since fulfilled his boyhood dream of seeing Pittsburgh.

There were now about four thousand people living there, on the small triangular area bounded on the northwest by the Allegheny River, on the southwest by the Monongahela, and on the east by a series of hills. Fort Duquesne, constructed by the French at the extreme of the point, was now gone, leveled in 1758 by its builders when they had to abandon it to British-American attackers. Its replacement, Fort Pitt, was much larger,

6. Baldwin, *The Keelboat Age on Western Waters*, 57–61.
7. *Ibid.*, 57.

partially built of brick, and located near the Monongahela. But it, too, was already showing the inevitable signs of decay from lack of occupation.[8]

In 1807 there were clear indications that Pittsburgh would soon expand beyond the small triangle west of the hills. There were already some commercial establishments and a few homes on the left bank of the Monongahela. They were lined up close to the river, for there was only a narrow strip of ground between the river and a steep bluff known as Coal Hill. An enterprising person named O'Hara had begun a glassworks there, making use of one of the available resources, sand. Out in the river was a large sandbar that was an island except at times of high water, a convenient source for the glassmakers. There was another glassworks in the main part of Pittsburgh.

The region was also making use of its other natural resources. Already there was a gray pall over the city much of the time from the burning of the soft coal, abundant in many of the hills besides Coal Hill. Some of it was used to fire an iron foundry, Beelen's, which was a busy place, using another of the local resources. There were several small manufacturing shops that made hardware items from bar iron.

The first business establishment the keelboat passed on the approach to Pittsburgh was a boatyard, with its cradles and sawpits standing alongside a creek known as Suke's Run. Farther on, facing the river, were taverns and warehouses along with a few shops and residential buildings. Most of the structures were still of log, but brick was beginning to be used in many of the newer buildings and in replacing old log houses.

Shreve went on to the boat landing at the foot of Market Street, arriving there at the day's end. Except for two men left on board to guard the cargo, the crew were free to spend one last evening at liberty before the downriver voyage began in earnest. The captain would attend to his buying and selling of cargo in the morning. For the time being, he could sit with other rivermen at the Sign of the Green Tree and learn what was happening in Pittsburgh.

Much of the talk was of steam power. For many years there had been experiments with steamboat building in the East, and it was widely ex-

8. Zadok Cramer, *The Navigator: Containing Directions for Navigating the Monongahela, Allegheny, Ohio, and Mississippi Rivers* (1814; rpr. New York, 1966), 49–72.

pected that steamboats would soon replace keelboats to a large extent on the Ohio and Mississippi rivers. This was despite the fact that no one had yet established regular steamboat service even in the much more densely populated northeastern states. John Fitch had demonstrated a good, working steamboat and operated it for many miles successfully in the 1790s, but he failed to get the financial backing he needed to continue its development. But in 1807 the prospects were strong for progress. Robert Fulton was building a steamboat on the Hudson River, and he had plenty of financial backing. His partner was Robert R. Livingston, now back from a mission in Paris in which he had assisted in the diplomatic work leading to the Louisiana Purchase. He and Fulton had met in Paris and built an experimental steamboat there. The first American Fulton-Livingston boat would be tested before this summer of 1807 was over.

There was more news of the growing use of steam power, of vital interest to Shreve. Right there in Pittsburgh there was to be a new flour mill, not operated by water or horse power, but by the power of a steam engine of a type quite different from the English Boulton-Watt engine that was going into the Fulton steamboat. It was not so much the automated design of the flour mill or the fact that it was the first steam-powered flour mill to be built anywhere in America that was of such interest to Shreve. It was the steam engine itself. Fulton's engine was of a low-pressure type invented for use in pumping water from flooded mines. The flour mill's engine was a high-pressure engine invented by Oliver Evans of Philadelphia.

The term *high-pressure* convinced some that danger was involved in the use of Evans' engines, that explosions were likely to occur. Others repeated Evans' explanations of how the boilers used were constructed to be safe at even higher pressures than those developed by the engines. Evans had used one in a steam-powered river dredge he had been operating in the Delaware River at Philadelphia for two years without accident.

Evans was convinced that steam power from engines like his was the key to practical steamboat operation. He also believed it could be used on "horseless carriages." Before he launched his dredge, he put wheels on it and drove it through the streets of Philadelphia. But people only laughed at his clumsy contraption, called the *Orukter Amphibolus*, and Evans had given up on the idea of a steam-powered land vehicle for the time being.

He still had hopes of seeing his engines used in steamboats but lacked the funds to build a boat himself. He had been successful in promoting a flour mill for Pittsburgh that would combine his system of mill automation, which made it possible for two men to handle the grain flow that had taken the work of five or six, with his high-pressure steam engine to move the belts and turn the wheels and millstones. The people of Pittsburgh were to be the first to see such a mill in operation, in 1809, when it would begin turning out sixty thousand bushels annually from three pairs of millstones powered by one steam engine.[9]

In all this, Shreve was intensely interested. He planned a long career on the rivers and was astute enough to realize that he must be in the vanguard with the most efficient vessel possible if he was to achieve the success he desired. He would follow avidly the news of developments in steamboat power and especially the reports of Fulton's steamboat trial in the East. For the time being, however, while his keelboat was docked at the foot of Market Street, his primary responsibility was to get merchandise on board his vessel that would bring the greatest dollar return per hundredweight in the St. Louis market. Kegs of nails and other hardware items would be a good choice. Glassware, some green and some clear, would also be wanted in St. Louis, he was sure.[10]

With his keelboat loaded with such goods, Shreve started down the Ohio the following morning. At the start, Cramer instructed him:

> On shoving off at Pittsburgh, if the water should be high, your boat will require but little attention, otherwise than keeping her bow foremost and giving her headway by the application of the oars. But in low water, for which these directions are intended, it requires more circumspection, in the first place, to prevent the boat grounding on a large flat bar at the mouth of the Allegheny, nearly meeting the foot of the Monongahela bar. There is, however, a good passage between these two bars, in a direction a little above the Point or junction of the two rivers, towards O'Hara's glassworks. Before you get quite opposite the Point, incline to the left, and you will get into the chute, keeping the foot of the Monongahela bar on the left hand, and the head of that of the Allegheny on your right. From thence you will find the best water near the left shore, until you begin to approach Hamilton's Island, No. 1.[11]

9. *Niles' Weekly Register*, April 29, 1815.
10. Cramer, *The Navigator*, 54–55. Cramer lists in detail the "manufactures" of Pittsburgh in 1807.
11. *Ibid.*, 73.

Shreve followed Cramer's instructions scrupulously, with additional guidance from his mate on duty at the bow and alert for the shifting hazards, such as driftwood and sandbars. Many vessels, especially the flatboats handled by inexperienced steersmen, had a corner hung up on the sandbars and found themselves swung broadside to the bar despite Cramer's advice to "keep her bow foremost."

Besides the valuable aids to navigation, Cramer also provided interesting sidelights on the passing vistas, which Captain Shreve could read when the sailing was relatively clear. For example, right after *The Navigator*'s instructions on how to avoid hanging up on underwater snags in the approach to Logstown, an old Indian settlement about eighteen miles upriver from Pittsburgh, the book gave the following information about the next town:

> Legionville is just below Loggstown [sic], on the right side of the river. General Wayne made an encampment here in the year 1792, preparatory to his campaign against the northern Indians, which terminated in the total defeat of the latter, on the 20th August, 1794.—Some of the old chimnies of the cabins, built by general Wayne are still standing on the ground, which is an extensive flat, high and timberless, except a thick growth of young scrub oaks. On this flat there are considerable appearances of bog iron ore, as also in the banks of the small stream above the encampment, which you cross on the road from Pittsburgh to Beaver.[12]

Soon after watching for the "chimnies," Shreve would see Big Beaver Creek, "60 or 70 yards wide at its mouth," and the town of Beaver, thirty miles from Pittsburgh, "on a high stony plain, where the old fort M'Intosh stood, about 200 feet above the level of the river."[13] There the Ohio changed course, after having followed a generally northwesterly direction from the start of the voyage, and turned to the southwest for the overall direction of its flow. With this major turn accomplished, the young captain felt that he was indeed on his way to the West.

When the keelboat had journeyed ninety-six miles by river (fifty-six miles by land, according to Cramer) from Pittsburgh, it approached Wheeling, on the left bank and at that time in the state of Virginia. This town, which would become important to Shreve a few years later, was the oldest white settlement on the upper river below Pittsburgh. Ebenezer

12. *Ibid.*, 76.
13. *Ibid.*, 78.

Zane and his brothers settled there in the winter of 1769–1770. They were joined by others from Virginia and soon found themselves subject to Indian attacks. They built a log blockhouse and fort, named Fort Fincastle and renamed Fort Henry in 1776 in honor of Patrick Henry. When Indian attacks ended, a settlement grew, principally on the bluffs that rose above the riverfront.

Fort Henry was on lower ground, however, on a bench above the Ohio, which sloped toward nearby Wheeling Creek. As Shreve and his crew made a brief stop, they found the fort in tumbledown condition. But between the old log structure and the creek were a public inn, a warehouse, a rope walk, a few general merchandise stores, and of most interest to Shreve, a busy boatyard alongside Wheeling Creek. The main part of the town was on a high bluff between the creek and the river, on one street a mile long. This street ended the extension of the Cumberland Road from Brownsville, reached via ferry across the Monongahela. Soon to become a segment of the National Road, it ended on "Wheeling Creek hill, which is steep and lofty, and so narrow at the top, that in some places there is scarcely room for a wagon to pass along, and nearly a perpendicular precipice to the bottom of the creek," according to *The Navigator*.[14]

Despite its difficult approach by land, many emigrants came to Wheeling to embark upon a flatboat because sometimes the Monongahela at Brownsville dropped to such a low level that it was difficult to navigate safely on an awkward flatboat. The Ohio at Wheeling was always navigable except when an unusually cold winter brought ice to the river's surface.

Cramer warned steersmen to be wary as they approached Wheeling Island, which was about a mile long, "a fine large island, well farmed and owned by col. Zanes [sic], a very respectable old gentleman, and among the first adventurers to the country." His instruction to the steersman was to keep to the left side of the island "until you see the town, then bear towards the island to avoid some logs near the left shore. After passing the town, keep near the middle of the river. Across the river, on the right side of this island, there is a rope fixed from bank to bank to facilitate the passage of ferry flats, but which prevents the descent of boats."[15] Without this warning from Zadok Cramer, the boatmen would indeed have been in deep trouble.

14. *Ibid.*, 85.
15. *Ibid.*, 84.

The logs of which he often warned the voyagers were not simply floating sections of cut tree trunks. More often they were great limbs or even
whole trees fallen into the water after a severe storm or carried down a
side stream into the Ohio at times of fast-running water or floods. The
logs were the accumulations of many years of storm, wind, and river action upon the woodlands. Sometimes a large tree with many branches
would be concealed entirely or in most part by the water. Avoiding contact with such "snags," as they were called, was almost impossible in
those days before navigational engineering of the rivers. A boat striking a
snag unexpectedly could be punctured even if its timbers were sound,
and rotted wood was likely to mean the loss of a valuable cargo or even of
lives as water poured into the craft. Hence the necessity for choosing timbers carefully in the construction of a keelboat.

A particularly dangerous type of snag was known as the "sawyer," more
common in the Mississippi than in the Ohio. This was an old tree that
had, in effect or actually, taken root in the river bottom. The flow of the
water might conceal it entirely from view at times, as the current pushed
against it, giving it an up-and-down sawing motion. "Planters" were similar, but so firmly rooted in the river bottom that the largest boat running
against them could not budge them.

Navigators had to be alert also for rocks that could be especially treacherous at times of low water and for the sandbars that were likely to have
shifted from the positions ascribed to them in *The Navigator*. Shreve's
first trip in his own keelboat is not recorded in detail, but there must have
been some moments when the whole crew fought to avoid wreckage due
to such hazards.

Below Wheeling there were quite a few settlements by 1807. One was
Marietta, Ohio, 183 river miles from Pittsburgh, the first permanent settlement on the north bank of the Ohio River, founded by a company of
New Englanders led there in 1788 by revolutionary war general Rufus
Putnam. The location at the mouth of the Muskingum River was chosen
because of the presence of a company of soldiers at Fort Harmar on the
opposite (upriver) side of the Muskingum. When Shreve passed Marietta,
the old fort was gone, and the settlement had expanded to both sides of
the Muskingum. There was the usual busy boatyard and the accompany-
ing rope walk, a brand new bank, a flour mill, and an assortment of business houses and churches, plus an academy, of which Marietta was quite
proud. Where New Englanders went, education was never neglected.

Sixteen miles farther down the Ohio, the keelboat approached an island about which the men were very curious, for it was much in the news in 1807. This was Blennerhassett's Island, the location from which Aaron Burr had made his escape late in 1806. In February of 1807 the former United States vice-president had been apprehended in the Territory of Mississippi, and as Shreve and his crew were making their way downriver, his pretrial hearings were taking place in Richmond, Virginia.

Shreve had noticed the beautiful house on the island, so unusual for this part of the United States, on previous trips down the river. It was a spacious house of frame structure, two stories high with two wings connected to its main part by semicircular porticoes. Its grounds were beautifully landscaped. Shreve had learned that the interior had some unusual features for a frontier home, including a handsome staircase, a library, and even a chemical laboratory.[16] It was built around 1800 by Harman Blennerhassett, a cultured gentleman who had emigrated from Ireland for political and personal reasons. Wanting an ideal retreat for himself, his wife, and their two small sons, Blennerhassett found and purchased in 1798 an uncultivated island two or three miles long. In that day of log structures of the crudest sort on the frontier, the beautiful house on a remote island was truly remarkable.

As the keelboat approached the island, the Blennerhassetts were no longer there, having been forced to flee late in 1806. Blennerhassett, charmed by the compelling personality of Aaron Burr, had agreed to invest his funds and his reputation in the construction of a fleet of boats for Burr's use in a planned expedition to the west and south. Federal troops arrived at Blennerhassett's Island just as the flotilla was preparing to embark. Burr escaped. So did Harman Blennerhassett; Mrs. Blennerhassett and the children fled soon afterward. The desecration of the beautiful grounds began the night the troops arrived, and neglect was evident to the keelboat crew as they passed by, even though the estate was under the supervision of the caretaker. The fine house burned to the ground in 1811.[17]

Forty-six miles below the island, they reached Letart's Rapids, calling for expert navigation for safe passage. There were turns in the river and many small islands, and then, following an abrupt turn to the right, they

16. "Cuming's Tour to the West," in Reuben G. Thwaites (ed.), *Early Western Travels* (32 vols.; Cleveland, 1904–1907), IV, 128–30.
17. *Ibid.*, 129n.

came upon what appeared to be a smooth sheet of water, rippling on either side and coming to a point below. Shreve followed Cramer's advice and stayed as near the middle of the fast-moving water as possible in entering the rapids. The entire crew was kept busy avoiding rocks and sandbars. With this accomplished, they were soon in easier water, passing the mouth of the Great Kanawha River and then the town of Point Pleasant, Kentucky. Soon afterward, on the right, they reached the settlement of Gallipolis, Ohio.

Gallipolis had been, in earlier years, the subject of the first great American real estate swindle. Promoters went to France to induce potential emigrants from that revolution-torn nation to pay for new homes in what was described as a veritable Eden in America. When about five hundred French colonists came down the Ohio in 1790, they found a few rough log cabins hastily constructed in a small clearing between the river on the south and deep woods on the other three sides, far removed from the amenities of civilization to which the newcomers were accustomed. A few hardy souls remained; others returned to France. Some American pioneers joined the uprooted Frenchmen, and Gallipolis, in 1807, appeared to have a chance of survival and even growth.

Below Gallipolis, the crew worked through many twists and turns in the river, with entrapped snags at the turns adding to the difficulties. There were a few more tiny riverbank settlements and then "The Queen City of the West"—Cincinnati. The reason for its less glamorous epithet, Porkopolis, was quite evident as Shreve docked his keelboat. A large herd of hogs was being driven aboard a flatboat already stocked with barrels of hams and bacon. Pork was the chief export of Cincinnati, for a frontier family could raise hogs in the wild before there had been time to clear land for planted crops. The loaded flatboats usually headed down to New Orleans, a five-week voyage.

This frontier "city" flourished after the 1795 Treaty of Greenville and by 1807 had acquired a population of about 1,600—making it the largest settlement on the Ohio below Pittsburgh. For a long time, the residents had needed the protection of soldiers stationed at Fort Washington, in the center of the village. The fort, as Shreve's craft arrived, was no longer staffed and was about to be torn down so that its land could be laid out in city lots.

Just beyond Cincinnati was North Bend, the home of William Henry Harrison, governor of the Indiana Teritory. Indiana was on the right as

the keelboat proceeded downriver, and the crew was wary of Indian attack, for few areas were open to white settlement. The town of Jeffersonville, about seventy miles below North Bend and across the river from
Louisville, Kentucky, was the principal settlement open by purchase from
the Indians.

The Ohio River just above Jeffersonville and Louisville took on a different character. This was the location of the Falls of the Ohio, the only
major blockage to open navigation of the river. The falls had no large,
sudden drop of water, but consisted of a series of small falls and rapids
over rock ledges for a distance of about two miles, with a sea-level drop
totalling 22½ feet. The effect was to create a rapid current that could
swing a boat about and wreck it upon the rocks. After many boats had
been overturned, wrecked, or hung up in this passage, the governments
of the Indiana Territory and the state of Kentucky had ruled that an official pilot was to board each boat for passage of the Falls of the Ohio.

On the upper end, the falls began after a series of islands, commencing
where Bear Creek entered the Ohio from the Kentucky side. One of the
farthest downriver of the larger islands was Corn Island, which had served
as the campground and headquarters for George Rogers Clark as he assembled and trained his motley army in revolutionary war days. There
Clark prepared for his successful surprise attacks upon Kaskaskia and Vin-
cennes, manned by British troops.

Louisville, directly across a span of river from Corn Island, began about
the time of Clark's activity. The location seemed excellent, because though
it provided access to the river, the riverbank sloped upward steeply
enough for probable freedom from flooding except in times of unusually
high water. The people expected a city to grow there because rivercraft
had to stop there or at Jeffersonville for passage of the falls. Most of the
boatmen chose to stop at Louisville.

When the water was unusually low, the larger boats had either to wait
at Louisville for a rise in the river or to transfer their downriver cargo to a
boat embarking from below the falls. Thus, Louisville took on a middle-
man function. The cargo to be transferred was hauled by wagon two miles
to a settlement at the foot of the falls, Shippingport. Very little cargo arrived at Shippingport for the reverse procedure in those days before the
steamboat, and in 1807 there was little more at Shippingport than a landing, a warehouse, a mill, and a general store.

But even then people were planning for the day when there could be a canal cut from Shippingport to Louisville, bypassing the falls. In 1804 Aaron Burr used an investigation of canal-building possibilities there as a pretext for his much more ambitious interest in the West.[18] Burr may have been responsible for kindling a lasting interest in this project, for he talked of it to many people, including Benjamin H. Latrobe, the architect and engineer. Latrobe, who was also involved in working on the Philadelphia steam-powered water system at the time, was invited to submit a construction proposal to Burr and even made arrangements for workers (whom he called "my Irishmen") to go to Louisville to work on the project. He wrote, late in 1805, "I am in a bad scrape with my Irishmen, for Col. B. has never once noticed the subject of the Canal since I made conditional arrangements with them."[19] The project seemed to have died then, but it was soon to be revived, although it was many years before the canal was actually built. In the meantime, the falls played an important role in the opening of the steamboat era, soon to come.

Shreve paid a Louisville pilot the fee of two dollars to guide his keelboat through the "middle chute." The fee seemed high, but the penalty for an unauthorized person taking a boat through the falls was ten dollars; even this was less expensive than the loss of cargo that could follow an error in navigation. Over near Jeffersonville (where the federal government had purchased 150,000 acres from the Indians to be awarded to George Rogers Clark and his men) the passage was easy only in times of high water. This was also true of the passage between Louisville and Corn Island. Cramer said in his guidebook, "The course between Rock and Goose Islands, called the *Middle Schute*, is a safe and easy passage in all situations of the water above the middling stage."[20]

After dropping off the pilot at Shippingport, Shreve and his crew were on their way again, leaving most signs of civilization behind them for the remainder of the length of the Ohio River. The stretch of water ahead was quite dangerous in the years between 1800 and 1810 for reasons beyond the natural hazards of the river. There were two other sources of danger, serious enough to cause slow-moving flatboats to form convoys when possible in traveling along the Indiana and Illinois shores.

18. John Dos Passos, "The Conspiracy and Trial of Aaron Burr," *American Heritage*, XVII (February, 1966), 70.
19. Talbot Hamlin, *Benjamin Henry Latrobe* (New York, 1955), 221.
20. Cramer, *The Navigator*, 18.

One danger was that Indians were likely to attack the boatmen. This was the period of greatest activity by Tecumseh and his brother the Prophet, as they strove to unite tribes of the entire Mississippi River system. The attacks were made in a desperate effort to stop the persistent encroachments of white settlers upon Indian lands, encroachments that were often in disregard of Indian rights guaranteed in treaties with the United States government. In northern Indiana, near Tippecanoe Creek, a central encampment was growing, as Indians gathered for a planned concerted attack upon American settlements. As Shreve made his 1807 voyage, the danger was great as tribesmen moved toward Tippecanoe. It continued until 1811, when William Henry Harrison led an attack on the encampments, in the Battle of Tippecanoe, which resulted in the defeat of Tecumseh's forces.

The second source of danger was from outlaws, river pirates who would stop at nothing. There was one area where this menace was so great that many river travelers lost their property and sometimes even their lives. On the right bank of the Ohio, about thirty miles below the mouth of the Wabash, was a natural formation known as Cave-in-Rock. Zadok Cramer described it in some detail.

> For half a mile on your right, before you reach the cave, you have a front view of a beautiful, perpendicular, smooth limestone wall, a solid mass of rock, with regular horizontal strata, of about 100 or 120 feet in height above the low water mark, and whose summit is handsomely clothed with a growth of small red cedars, the roots of which springing through the close fissures, and apparently receiving their nourishment from the rocks. The cedars on the top of these rocks appear to be peculiarly the haunt of birds of prey, for what reason I know not.
>
> This Cave or House of Nature, opens to view fronting the river a little above high water mark, its mouth is about 60 feet across at the base, narrowing from both sides as it ascends, forming an arch of about 25 feet in its highest part, and running back to a point of about 120 feet deep. The top and sides of the cave bear the names of thousands who have visited it from time to time, and the dates of the year, & c. . . . Families have been known to reside here tolerably comfortable from the northern blasts of winter. The mouth of this cave was formerly sheltered and nearly hid by some trees growing in front of it.[21]

This "House of Nature" that had been so welcoming to travelers earlier had become, by 1807, a place to be passed quickly and with caution.

21. *Ibid.*, 134–35.

Here, about 1800, flourished a number of outlaw bands. So inviting a stopping place served as a trap for the unwary. Even for those who knew of the river pirates in waiting, there was no guarantee against disaster.

Boat crews were often attacked, and many men were murdered. The outlaws would then sell the valuable cargo, often manning the pirated boat to take it down to New Orleans. They were also on the alert for boatmen returning from the port city; these were especially ripe plums, for they had their cash profits on their persons or in their gear. The pirates were a thriving group until law and order finally prevailed in the area. This happened following accelerated settlement of Indiana and Illinois lands after the War of 1812.

There is no report that Shreve had an encounter with the outlaws, but he is sure to have been on guard in passing through this segment of the Ohio River. Because of the sandbar that blocked the channel on the left side, it was necessary to use the channel running on the right side of Cave-in-Rock Island, close to the cave entrance. For the boatmen, there was no way to avoid giving the outlaws an opportunity to attack if they were so inclined.

From Cave-in-Rock onward, the rest of the downriver course to the mouth of the Ohio was about one hundred miles of winding river without settlements anywhere in view. As Shreve reached the mouth of the Ohio, less than three weeks had passed since he pushed off from the dock at the foot of Market Street in Pittsburgh. He had come 1,132 river miles of his planned voyage of 1,300 miles to St. Louis. With only about 170 miles to go, it would seem that he would soon be at journey's end. But not so. Nearly three weeks more would be needed for the remaining miles.

3 / **Merchant Navigator**

The keelboat was untied at dawn from its overnight mooring just above a point of land overgrown with willows—the point where the Ohio and Mississippi shores met. The bank on the north side of the Ohio appeared to be washing away and apt to flood at the slightest rise of water level. When Shreve's crew shoved off, the Ohio seemed reluctant to part with the keelboat as its currents met those of the Mississippi. The Mississippi, in its turn, worked to force the keelboat downstream instead of up.

There began the most twisting, winding, difficult span of river that Shreve had yet experienced. As soon as the little vessel found its way into the Mississippi channel and faced the force of the current, the hard labor began—the cordelling and the warping, the poling and pushing and striving to make headway and at the same time avoid the hazardous sandbars and snags. They encountered vicious sawyers and deceptive planters; for not one moment could the men relax. Before the day was over, the keelboat had gone in every direction of the compass, including southeasterly, the opposite of the general course they were to follow.

The obstacles to navigation were far more numerous in the Mississippi than in the Ohio. Besides the planters, sawyers, and other forms of snags, there were also "rafts," or "wooden islands" as they were sometimes called, formed by the clinging together of floating driftwood. Many of these eventually became soil-covered and took on the appearance of true islands, with willow and cottonwood sprouts and grasses growing upon them as years added to their substance. Another problem, especially when a boat tied up for the night, as was customary in that part of the river, was the caving in of the riverbanks. Cramer describes this danger.

> The instability of the banks proceed from their being composed of a loose sandy soil, and impetuosity of the current against their prominent parts (points), which, by undermining them unceasingly, causes them to tumble into the river taking with them everything that may be above. And if, when the event happens, boats should be moored there, they must necessarily be buried in the common ruin, which unfortunately has sometimes been the case. For which reason navigators have made it an invariable rule never to land at or near a point, but always in the sinuosity or cove below it.[1]

It took much time to get the keelboat into the proper channel of the Mississippi, near the west bank. The change was startling to the men, for the Ohio River was placid by comparison to the Mississippi. Now they were constantly having to pull hard just to make progress, avoiding islands and sandbars and fighting against crosscurrents and whirlpools in the water. In some places it took a great effort by the entire crew to prevent the boat from being swept downstream at the whim of the currents, and their full strength to make some progress upstream. The current was estimated to be about four miles an hour.

At the end of the first ten miles of struggle, consuming a whole day from dawn until dusk, the keelboat crew came to a horseshoe bend in the river known as the Grand Turn. There followed another day and then another of the same strenuous labor. When they had gone forty miles above the Ohio River they at last saw signs of human habitation, on the west bank. All were more than happy to pull for shore and go into the village for a few hours of relaxation.

They had reached Cape Girardeau, Missouri, predominantly American in population despite its French name. In the first years of the 1800s, many Americans had been attracted to the region after learning of generous land grants by the Spanish government. The flow of settlers increased after the Louisiana Purchase. At Cape Girardeau, Americans built a settlement around the nucleus of an old French trading post on a high, rocky

1. Cramer, *The Navigator*, 164–65.

bluff that was safe from flooding. The year before Shreve's visit, a town had been platted. Among the most-used buildings was a jail, according to a female visitor in 1807: "Cape Girardeau is a very beautiful place but it is very wicked. There is no chance to hear the Gospel preached without going 10 miles over a wretched road to a small Chapel. The main way the men spend their Sundays is in drinking and gambling, horse racing and chicken fighting."[2]

In contrast, the next village on the west bank was markedly French in appearance and custom. It was the oldest permanent settlement in Missouri, Ste. Genevieve, reached after seventy-six more miles of dragging the keelboat up the Mississippi. Shreve soon learned to distinguish early French settlements by the architecture of the homes and by the large shared fields and pastures adjacent to the village, where all the farmers resided. Unlike the Americans, the French chose to live in communities rather than in isolation on land claims. French building methods also differed from the American custom in that the Frenchman usually set his logs vertically and constructed a hip-roofed house with a large chimney rising in the center. French sociability was likewise evident in the large verandas across the front and often also around the ends of the house.

Of interest to Shreve was the fact that Ste. Genevieve was a shipping point for lead from mines located about thirty miles inland. As early as 1723, the French had come to this area seeking silver deposits; finding none of the more precious metal, they built smelting furnaces and soon were producing bars of lead. About five hundred slaves, taken from the Caribbean islands to New Orleans, were brought up the Mississippi to work the mines. The problem of transporting the lead bars to Ste. Genevieve, founded in 1735, was solved by shaping them to fit over the backs of packhorses, collar fashion. Lead became an important export, along with fine animal pelts, from New Orleans. Ste. Genevieve added to its cargoes for downriver shipment with its agricultural products and with its salt, which was "made" by the evaporation of the waters of saline springs nearby.

Ste. Genevieve, by then moved to a high bluff from its original lowland site because of severe flooding, was thriving when Shreve's boat reached its waterfront landings in 1807. The crew from Pennsylvania found the

2. Works Projects Adminstration Writers' Program, *Missouri: A Guide to the "Show Me" State* (New York, 1941), 201.

French village quite charming. It was noted for the gaiety of its people, still French in their customs despite years under the Spanish goverment. Zadok Cramer, writing of it, was more impressed with the industry of the inhabitants than with their social life. He gave the population as around 1,400 and described the common field they shared as being about 7,000 acres, "its products apportioned to the inhabitants according to the property held by them in the town."[3] Cramer believed this field to be the largest in the United States and observed that though corn was the main crop, almost any grain could be grown there. He also mentioned the lead production in the area.

The men embarked from Ste. Genevieve revived for the remainder of the voyage, taking heart, for the end was not far ahead. Old French forts on the Illinois side spoke of the day long gone when European nations competed for possession of this great river and its valley. The last landmark before St. Louis was a shot tower at Herculaneum, on the Missouri side, where some of the lead was used in the manufacture of ammunition. Finally the fur-trading village of St. Louis came into view. With the possible exception of little St. Charles, a very short distance up the Missouri River, St. Louis was the westernmost city of the United States in 1807 and rapidly becoming the principal riverport on the Mississippi above New Orleans.

It was probably with a feeling of great joy that Shreve directed the tying of the keelboat at the foot of Rue Bonhomme, which he learned the Americans were already renaming Market Street. It had been a long and arduous voyage from Market Street in Pittsburgh to Market Street in St. Louis.

St. Louis was not much larger than Ste. Genevieve, but it had a much more commercial atmosphere because of the settlement's origins. Actually a stepchild of New Orleans, it was founded as a shipping center for the fur trade, where enterprising fur dealers saw the possibility of expansion through having a collecting point close to the source of the pelts. The firm of Maxent, Laclede, and Company began in New Orleans in 1762 and wasted no time in getting the French government to grant its members exclusive rights to the Indian trade in the country west of the Mississippi River. A junior partner in the firm, Pierre Laclede Liguest, thereafter

3. Cramer, *The Navigator*, 170–71.

known as Pierre Laclede for reasons unexplained, set out the following spring to find the right location for the "branch office," voyaging by keelboat up to Fort Chartres on the Illinois side of the river. With him were several company employees and a boy of fourteen, Auguste Chouteau, soon to become Laclede's stepson.

A few miles upriver, they found an ideal site just below the mouth of the Missouri River, convenient for the voyageurs who would travel by way of the Missouri to find Indians willing to trade fur pelts for European trading goods. Laclede, unaware that France had recently surrendered this land west of the Mississippi to Spain, chose this location for construction of a new settlement to be known as St. Louis. He had other business to attend to and delegated supervision of the construction of the first buildings to young Auguste Chouteau. Work began in mid-February, 1764. The future city was laid out in a fashion similar to New Orleans, even to the point of having a square near the river to be named the Place d'Armes. Five north-south streets, roughly paralleling the river, were marked and named, as were cross streets running to the river. Work began immediately on Laclede's large stone house on Rue Royale, the first of the five longer streets.

When Shreve arrived there for the first time, St. Louis reached seven blocks back from the river and was nine blocks from north to south. The Laclede house still stood but was overshadowed by an even larger home in the next block to the south, also facing Rue Royale. This was the home of Auguste Chouteau, now fifty-eight years old. He and his brother Pierre were now the most important business and civic leaders of St. Louis. The brothers were engaged in the fur trade, as might be expected, and this was still the town's leading commercial activity. There were around one thousand free residents and several hundred slaves. Over the years, agriculture had developed, and St. Louis, like Ste. Genevieve, had its large common fields and pastures. There was a mill near Chouteau's Pond at the edge of the parklike estate of the Chouteau family, producing flour for the town that had once been nicknamed Paincourt (short of bread) but was now able to feed its residents.

The St. Louis that Shreve viewed from the landing was still a village. Yet it had the air of a cosmopolitan settlement on the verge of great happenings. Shreve had some difficulty finding a clear space for the docking of his fifty-foot keelboat. There were only one or two other keelboats at the riverfront, but the log canoes called pirogues were many in number. Some were made into cargo-carrying rafts with a platform set between a pair of canoes. Shreve learned that these were the craft used by the voyageurs, most of whom had recently returned from a fur-trading expedition up the Missouri River. A pair of voyageurs—lithe, muscular, bearded fellows in stained buckskins and long blue shirtlike garments held in with a belt—were unloading square bales of pelts from one of the pirogues, apparently just arrived from upriver. Others lounged about the sloping, hard-packed bank.

There were several flatboats at the landing. One was just arriving from upriver. Shreve's crew, curious about what was in the barrels that were being rolled off the decks and up the landing area, learned that this was a load of salt, brought down from a salt spring near the Missouri River but 220 miles distant from St. Louis. The old pioneer Daniel Boone and two of his sons, Nathan and Daniel Morgan Boone, had discovered the salt springs while on one of their hunting and exploring expeditions by following the trail of deer and other wild animals to the licks where they went to supply the demands of their bodies for salt. Old Daniel, still alive in 1807 and residing just west of St. Charles, Missouri, was not as active as he had been, but his sons had returned to the salt springs. The route they followed near the north bank of the Missouri River was also being used by a few pioneers heading west with their wagons. The developing wagon road was known as Boon's Lick Trail.

In 1806, Nathan and Daniel Morgan Boone with some partners from St. Charles had loaded a dozen huge, twenty-gallon black iron kettles into a wagon and had taken them to the salt springs. This flatboat being unloaded was one of the first shipments of salt they had made at the springs, boiling away the salty water and collecting the residue. Salt was a valuable product in those days before refrigeration, for it was used to preserve meat and other foods. Some would be reshipped on another of the flatboats waiting to be loaded with cargo for New Orleans.

Shreve set up a schedule for his men to guard his cargo before going up the slope toward the settlement. He saw a variety of people as he made his way up Rue Bonhomme. There were French farmers coming into town from the fields with their two-wheeled *charrettes* filled with garden produce, and French housewives inspecting the vegetables for purchase. Other people on the street hailed each other in Spanish, and the Americans, it seemed, were everywhere. Most of them resembled the Kentuckians whom Shreve knew so well, but a few were dressed more in keeping with life in an eastern city.

The number of Americans in St. Louis had increased, Shreve learned, since the United States government had made its presence felt in this old French-Spanish settlement. The Territory of Upper Louisiana (to be reorganized in 1812 as the Territory of Missouri) had been separated from the Territory of Orleans, which was roughly equivalent to the present state of Louisiana. St. Louis was named as capital of the huge Territory of Upper Louisiana. Bureaucracy was already bringing a new class of citizens to the frontier town. For an example, there was Silas Bent, father of the future western traders and builders of Bent's Fort, Charles and William Bent. Silas Bent, who had come to St. Louis via Ohio and West Virginia, was the new deputy surveyor in charge of Upper Louisiana Territory. His was a monumental responsibility and task, involving the work of many crews to carry out the actual survey and mapping of the newly acquired American lands.[4]

At the head of the new bureaucracy was the hero of the day, Captain Meriwether Lewis, now Governor Lewis; his partner in leading the Louisiana expedition, William Clark, was superintendent of Indian affairs and would succeed Lewis as governor in 1813. The American influence in St. Louis was growing rapidly, and among the subjects under discussion was the establishment of English-language schools to hasten the Americanization of old St. Louis.

Shreve made his way up the street to the building for which the voyageurs with their bales of pelts were also headed. It was Auguste Chouteau's warehouse, a stone building fifty-four feet by thirty feet, facing on Rue Bonhomme, just past Rue Royale, at the north end of the square in which the big Chouteau family home was located. Shreve had no doubt of the identity of the warehouse as he approached it, for its redolence was unmistakable.

Inside were stacked the bales brought from the regions where the Osage Indians hunted, an area mostly in the present state of Missouri. Soon there would be a company warehouse near the great bend of the Missouri River, where Kansas City is today, for the United States govern-

4. David Lavender, *Bent's Fort* (New York, 1954), 17–27.

ment was about to build Fort Osage high above the river just below the bend. The fur trade was far from its peak in 1807, for the day of the trapping rush to the eastern slopes of the Rockies had not yet come, and the period of the annual rendezvous in western Wyoming was still twenty-five years away. In the meantime, Missouri's own rivers were still rich sources of beaver pelts, and bears, otters, and buffalo were still plentiful. The evidence was all about Shreve in the stuffy, malodorous warehouse, bales stacked upon bales and each holding a hundredweight of pelts. A standard pack held eighty prime beaver pelts, bundled face to face to protect them. Otter were sixty to a bale, and buffalo robes only ten. A bale of silky, small muskrat pelts numbered about six hundred.[5]

Young Captain Shreve introduced himself to Auguste Chouteau, a man of whom he stood somewhat in awe. Chouteau's name was known far and wide, and it was synonymous with success. The astute fur trader, meeting this quiet-spoken young man in the garb of the riverboatman, thought Shreve looked more a boy than a merchant navigator. Chouteau's step-father, Pierre Laclede, had said on that long-ago day when he and young Auguste stood together and chose the site for St. Louis that it would someday be one of the finest cities in America. Auguste Chouteau, before his death in 1829, would see Laclede's prediction begin to come true largely because of the work of the man he was now meeting.

The two took each other's measure as the bargaining began. Each apparently was satisfied with the deal he made, Chouteau in purchasing or trading for Shreve's Pittsburgh cargo and Shreve in obtaining the bales of pelts he was soon taking on board his keelboat for the return trip down the Mississippi and up the Ohio River to Pittsburgh. He was already making plans to return to St. Louis in 1808.

He and his crew made their way back to Pittsburgh without unusual incident. Dealers there were delighted to handle the cargo of pelts, which they shipped on to furriers in Philadelphia via Conestoga freight wagons. Freight rates were high on the wagon line, but the value of the cargo per hundredweight was also very high. As other keelboat owners learned of Shreve's success, they too began to make the voyage to St.

5. Walter Williams and Floyd C. Shoemaker, *Missouri Mother of the West* (5 vols; New York, 1930), I, 146.

Louis. The St. Louis-to-Pittsburgh fur trade continued to be profitable for Shreve for three seasons, but the profit margin was narrowing by 1809.[6]

Even though he was doing well, the young captain was still a bachelor. He had chosen the young lady he wanted for a bride—pretty, auburn-haired Mary Blair, who was six years younger than he. Her father was Adam Blair, a successful merchant and leading citizen of Brownsville. But Shreve knew better than to ask her father for his daughter's hand in marriage until he could convince him that he was on the way to equal financial success. He realized he must find a way to increase his income before another young man impressed Mary and her father.

He had time to think and to discuss possibilities, for in the summer of 1809, while he was in St. Louis, he was chosen a member of the jury for a murder trial—at a time before residency requirements were tightened. The case resulted in the judgment of guilty. The defendant was named John Long, Jr., and his hanging went on record as the first capital punishment in the courts of the Territory.[7] During the hearings, Shreve had opportunities to discuss business prospects with fellow jury members Silas Bent, Auguste Chouteau, and John B. C. Lucas, all of whom remained his friends for years to come.

By summer's end, he had another trail-blazing idea. He observed that the market for bar lead, which was molded into shot and bullets as well as used commercially, was wide open. The supply never equaled the demand in the early 1800s. One reason was the rapid development of the fur trade, for each expedition needed to be well stocked with bar lead as it left St. Louis for the trapping and hunting areas. The nature of the fur trade was changing as Indian hostility increased. Each year traders depended less upon inducing Indians to trap and hunt to obtain pelts and more upon non-Indian hunters and trappers. Each trapper, as he loaded his pirogue for the trip up the Missouri River—and their number was growing rapidly—needed plenty of bar lead with which to mold bullets. The demand for lead was also increasing as pioneers, depending largely upon hunting for sustenance, joined the westward movement in ever-

6. [Samuel Treat (?)], "Henry Miller Shreve," *U.S. Magazine and Democratic Review,* XXII (1848), 164.
7. Frederic L. Billon, *Annals of St. Louis in Its Territorial Days from 1804 to 1821* (St. Louis, 1888), 15.

growing numbers. Additionally, the United States government was seeking lead supplies because it was intent upon building up its defense forces. These were the years when the tensions were developing that culminated in the War of 1812.

When Shreve left St. Louis at the close of his business there in 1809, he had made up his mind what his next move would be. He would not attempt to become involved in the transport of lead from the mines of southeastern Missouri down to New Orleans, for it was already in competent hands. But in his conversations, he had learned of another source of lead as yet untapped by American merchants. It was a source that the British, coming down the waterways from Canada, were not overlooking, however. To cut in on the British source of lead for ammunition, Shreve thought, would be a patriotic act in those days when Great Britain was an adversary accused of encouraging Indian attacks on the American frontiers, cooperating with Tecumseh, and supplying guns and bullets to the Indians. It seemed that Shreve was in a position to be able to add to American lead supplies and at the same time turn a neat profit for himself.

The source of lead that he had learned of was the Fever River region of northern Illinois, Indian country in 1810, when he planned to go there. Fever River is an early name given the Galena, a tributary of the Mississippi that rises in southern Wisconsin and flows through the northwestern corner of Illinois before entering the Father of Waters about fifteen miles south of the Wisconsin-Illinois line. The French, when they explored this region in the early 1600s, were constantly alert for evidence of mineral deposits. While they hoped to find silver or gold, they did not turn away from a good lead deposit. Wherever they went, they asked the Indians about the presence of minerals and their questions led them to the veins of silverlike ore near the Fever River.

At that time the Indians were learning about the white man's firearms, and they soon discovered the value of lead as a necessary adjunct to their use. The French were receiving pelts from the Indians of the unsettled northern regions, and they gave a few firearms to the Indians in trade. The Indians quickly learned how to mine and smelt lead for their own use in munitions manufacture and as a valuable commodity to trade to the whites.

The lead of this region was known to the French as early as 1659, if not sooner. Nicolet visited the Wisconsin and Illinois Indians in 1643 and was the first to instruct the Indians in the use of firearms. Other French explorers followed—Radisson and Groseilliers in 1658–1659, and Joliet and Marquette on their journey on the Mississippi that ended in 1673. Hennepin showed a lead mine at the future site of Galena, Illinois, on a map he drew in 1687. Almost every report by a French explorer mentioned the lead deposits along the Fever River, often referred to as Rivière à la Mine. Some stopped there long enough to smelt lead to meet their own needs before journeying onward.

But the French could no longer claim the mines on the east bank after the treaties that gave the land to the British at the close of the French and Indian War. Nevertheless, although the city that bears his name today is on the west bank of the Mississippi, it was a Frenchman who became most involved in the development of the Galena lead mines. The man was Julien Dubuque. Dubuque was a trader who was skilled in establishing good relationships with the Sauk and Fox Indians, dominant tribes of the region. They sat with him in council at Prairie du Chien, Wisconsin, in 1788 and granted Dubuque the right to work the mines without disturbance. He had already discovered that the lead deposits extended to the west bank of the Mississippi as well as being quite widespread on the Illinois side. Dubuque soon had Indians working for him on both sides of the river.[8]

In his St. Louis conversations, Shreve learned that, although the Frenchman had been working in the mines for many years, he was probably still alive. Someone reported firsthand information that Dubuque had still been at the Fever River mines in 1805 and in apparent good health. Shreve reasoned that considering the enmity between France and England, a Frenchman might well be willing to divert lead from the hands of English buyers to those of Americans. It was certainly worth risking.

On the return voyage to Brownsville in 1809, Shreve observed that his keelboat was showing the wear and tear of three years of battling the snags of the rivers. Although it would add to his costs, he decided to invest in a new boat for the venture he was planning. A boat the same size as his first one would be adequate, for a hundredweight of lead took up little space, and the smaller the craft, the easier it would be to take so far

8. Reuben G. Thwaites, *How George Rogers Clark Won the Northwest and Other Essays in Western History* (Chicago, 1904), 299–332.

upriver. Once again he spent his winter days with Gillespie and Clark at the boatyards at Dunlap Creek—and his evenings, when she was agreeable to it, with Mary Blair.

His new boat was ready early in March, 1810. It was loaded with all it could possibly carry of eastern goods—hardware, glass, pottery, cloth, and food items—and off he went with a crew of twelve. He had, while in St. Louis in the last season, made an arrangement with a man named Fergus Moorhead to market his goods for maximum profit. On April 23, 1810, this advertisement appeared in the *Missouri Gazette*: "H. M. Shreve & Co. (Fergus Moorhead) have brought from Philadelphia and opened next door to the house of the late Joseph Robidoux, a complete assortment of Dry Goods, Groceries, Hardware, China and Queensware, Iron, Steel, Castings and Stationery, to be disposed of low for Cash."

Leaving his stock of goods in Moorhead's hands, Shreve restocked his keelboat with the type of Indian goods so readily available in St. Louis and on May 2 was on his way upriver. His was the first American keelboat crew to attempt the voyage so far up the Mississippi River, and for most of the way, the young captain would be without a book like Cramer's *Navigator* to guide him.

They took little food with them, depending almost entirely upon hunting and fishing for their meals. The distance between St. Louis and the lead mines was estimated to be five hundred river miles. Shreve expected most of the route to be through snag-infested waters with treacherous currents such as those between St. Louis and the mouth of the Ohio River. But to his surprise and pleasure, above the mouth of the Missouri River navigation was fairly easy. The land on either side of the river leveled off into low bluffs and gently rolling low hills; often there were open vistas of prairie. Although there were still hazardous sandbars, much of the distance could be accomplished without the use of the cordelle. They made the voyage from St. Louis to Galena in just fourteen days.[9]

But when they arrived at the mining region, they found that the Indians were not following their usual routines and that no work was going on at the mines. The tribesmen were mourning their longtime friend Julien Dubuque, who had died recently. The Indians had given him a chieftain's funeral and felt they had lost a leader who truly cared for them.

9. [Treat (?)], "Henry Miller Shreve," 164.

Shreve had to be careful not to say or do anything to antagonize them. He waited, and when the right time came, he was able to deal with the chiefs. The keelboat stayed at the mines about six weeks. Family tradition has it that in this time, Shreve won the respect of the Indians in many ways, not the least of which was his ability to outrun any of them in a footrace.

In that six weeks, the Americans from western Pennsylvania learned much about the Indians' ways of living, especially about how they mined the lead. In earlier days, the Indians had used primitive diggers fashioned of buckhorns, but by 1810 they were supplied with the white man's hoes, shovels, and crowbars. The ore was loaded into rough deerskins in the bottom of the shaft and then dragged up by the use of long thongs of hide to the smelting site. The old men and squaws did much of this part of the labor, whereas the younger men did the smelting. They had also progressed from more primitive smelting methods, which were simply to build a fire and, when white heat was reached, drop buckets of ore on it and then, when the ashes cooled, retrieve the lumps of lead. They had learned to dig a pit and lay a crisscrossed, boxlike structure of sticks over it. At day's end, this was lighted and the ore dumped upon it. At the conclusion of the process, the bottom of the pit held a sizable lump of lead, which was then remelted and cast into the shape of bars or into the horse-collar shape, each of about seventy pounds weight. The Indians had further refined this process with the use of trenches properly sloped and lined with stones for better heat conduction and separation of molten lead.

Shreve contracted to buy about sixty tons of lead with the goods he had brought. Now he had a new problem—his thirty-five-ton boat was inadequate for transporting this amount to market. But the Indians had a mackinaw boat, similar to a flatboat but pointed at the ends, that he could buy, perhaps left by Dubuque. Part of the lead could be carried on it. The men built a small flatboat, for Shreve did not want to overload any craft so that it rode so deeply in the water that it was likely to hang up on sandbars. He placed a crew of four on each of his vessels, and the little flotilla set off from Fever River on July 1. Less than two weeks later they tied up at Laclede's landing in St. Louis. Soon the three boats were en route again to the best market, New Orleans. From there, the lead would be shipped to Philadelphia on coastal sailing ships.

Selling his other two vessels for lumber, Shreve and his crew returned to St. Louis with his keelboat, no doubt with sugar or other bulky goods from the South for sale in St. Louis. On August 11, 1810, a notice appeared in the *Missouri Gazette*: "The Firm of H. M. Shreve & Co. is this day dissolved. Fergus Moorhead will continue alone at the old stand." The "old stand" was in the first block up from the river, on Elm Street, according to an old map of St. Louis that shows the location of the Robidoux house, next door. His partnership with Moorhead at an end, Shreve headed for home having realized eleven thousand dollars on his summer's work and in all likelihood taking with him another cargo of furs from St. Louis.

Word of his great success spread like wildfire back in Pittsburgh and Brownsville, inspiring other boat owners to try the lead trade. In fact, his flotilla had scarcely shoved off from St. Louis before enterprising merchants in that town, too, were en route to the mines with six keelboats. Seeing so many others copying his idea, Shreve decided he had taken the cream off the top and would leave further voyages to the lead mines to others. The American trade that he pioneered thrived for many years afterward and was reported in 1848 to amount to three million dollars annually.[10]

Henry Shreve, just turning twenty-five years old, was considered the boy wonder of Brownsville. He had no trouble convincing Adam Blair that he could support Mary, who was now nineteen years old and still waiting for him. A wedding was planned for February 28, 1811, one week after Mary's twentieth birthday.

While awaiting the great event, Shreve supervised the building of a splendid new keelboat, one as fine as any on the rivers. It would carry ninety-five tons, and with it he could profitably enter the Pittsburgh–New Orleans trade. By the day of the wedding, the new boat was almost ready.

Shreve also acquired a home, purchased from Adam Blair, to which he would bring his bride. It was located on Front Street in Brownsville, the street that had at one time been the end of the ride from his boyhood home to Brownsville. It had been a street of log and frame buildings that mostly housed business establishments. The new Shreve home was located at 301 Front Street, at the corner of Front and Grog House Alley, a

10. *Ibid.*

name that hints at the type of house the new one may have succeeded.[11] At that time, respectable brick houses were replacing the old, more primitive buildings, since many of the businesses were moving two blocks away to Market Street, paralleling Front Street. Market Street had been chosen by the National Road directors as the proper route through Brownsville.

It was undoubtedly a busy winter for Shreve, one that included a trip to Pittsburgh, perhaps to purchase fittings for his new keelboat. As he approached the city, he saw a boat—a ship, actually, from its appearance—being framed in a cradle alongside Suke's Run, sheltered from the north winds by Boyd's Bluff. It was to be a steamboat, he was told. Robert Fulton's launching of the *Clermont* in the Hudson River in 1807 had been the opening of a new era of steamboat transportation on the eastern rivers. Fulton and his backer and partner, Robert R. Livingston, confidently announced they would soon have steamboats plying the inland rivers also. This boat now under construction at Pittsburgh was to be the first one employed in regular freight and passenger service both up and down the rivers between Pittsburgh and New Orleans.

Shreve knew immediately that his next boat would be steam-powered. Steam power would be the means to achieve the speed and ease in transportation vitally needed for the people of inland America. He visited the boatyard at Suke's Run to see for himself the framing of this boat, which was to be named the *New Orleans*.

11. Fayette County Land Records, Book K, 346–47, Fayette County Courthouse, Uniontown, Pa.

4 / **The Coming of the Steamboat**

Even before Shreve was born, there was talk that the steamboat would be the solution to the problems of the inland rivers. The idea of the steamboat reached far back in time. A steamboat had been tested for the first time—and succesfully—one hundred years before Robert Fulton's demonstration of the *Clermont* in 1807. That first demonstration of giving mechanical power to boats by means of steam was made by a Frenchman residing in Germany in 1707, an inventor named Denis Papin. Local boatmen, convinced the invention of a steamboat would eliminate their jobs, destroyed the steamboat and attacked the inventor. Papin found this treatment too discouraging to repeat his experiment.[1]

Even in America, Fulton's demonstration was by no means the first. No patents had been issued prior to 1802 because the Patent Office did not open until then. But by that time at least sixteen steamboats had been built and launched. Patents had been issued in England and in France to steamboaters after Papin's disastrous experiment. In 1785, the year of Shreve's birth, John Fitch of Pennsylvania was ready with a working

1. Seymour Dunbar, *A History of Travel in America* (New York, 1937), 348–49.

model of a steamboat. His invention was in the form of a skiff equipped with an endless chain set over a pair of rollers, supporting rectangular floats and paddleboards, powered to move through the water by a small steam engine of the vertical type. That same year on August 29, Fitch wrote a letter to the Congress of the United States.

> The subscriber begs leave to lay at the feet of Congress, an attempt he has made to facilitate the internal navigation of the United States, adapted especially to the Waters of the Mississippi. The machine he has invented for the purpose, has been examined by several Gentlemen of Learning and Ingenuity, who have given their approbation. Being thus encouraged, he is desirous to solicit the attention of Congress, to a rough model of it now with him, that, after examination into the principles upon which it operates, they may be enabled to judge whether it deserves encouragement.[2]

The letter was referred to a committee of three members, but the committee placed no report on file, and minutes of congressional sessions made no reference to Fitch's invention. Fitch left New York, then the seat of federal government, in anger and dismay. He had, while in New York, approached the Spanish minister, who was greatly intrigued. But he wanted Fitch to grant exclusive rights to the king of Spain in exchange for funds to develop the steamboat, and to this Fitch would not agree.

Poor John Fitch met with one frustration after another in his efforts to develop his invention, so badly needed in a land blessed with many rivers and too vast for rapid highway development. Had he been more personable perhaps he could have succeeded, but he was not a man to inspire confidence on the part of would-be investors. At times he seemed a babbling madman—almost incoherent in his enthusiasm and his earnestness to impress his listeners. Physically he was tall and gaunt, shabbily dressed and often unkempt. Even Benjamin Franklin, a prolific inventor himself, underestimated Fitch and the potential value of his invention.[3]

Fitch demonstrated his first version of the steamboat in 1786 on the Delaware River at Philadelphia, despite his failure to get financial backing. This was the first successful steamboat demonstration on American waters. By selling a few shares of stock in his steamboat endeavors, he was able to build a second boat with a system of upright paddles at the sides, which he demonstrated in 1787. That it operated successfully was attested

2. *Ibid.*, 234.
3. *Ibid.*, 239.

to by several members of the Constitutional Convention then meeting in Philadelphia. They took time off from their task to witness the demonstration on August 27, 1787.[4] There was agreement that the invention was badly needed, but few came forth with offers of financial assistance.

The inventor went from state to state seeking funds after he had built a third successful steamboat in 1790. He operated that boat more than a thousand miles at a speed of four miles per hour or better against the current, occasionally achieving three or four times that speed. The states of Pennsylvania, New York, and New Jersey even offered him exclusive rights to steam transport on their rivers if he could build enough boats to fill the needs adequately. He met with eminent individuals, including George Washington, and at times seemed on the brink of success. But his appearance and personality were against him. He also seemed plagued by ill fortune, such as in the timing of a trip to France to meet a potential backer, only to arrive there at the outbreak of the French Revolution. Early in 1798 Fitch went to Bardstown, Kentucky, embittered and in utter poverty. He traded his claim on a tract of land for a supply of whiskey, with which he attempted to drink himself to death. Before the year was out, he succeeded.[5]

Others were experimenting with steamboats after Fitch's demonstrations to the extent that building a steamboat became almost a fad. There was a New Jersey man named William Longstreet who, while living in Georgia, ran a boat against the current in the Savannah River at the rate of five miles per hour, but did not go on with the boat's development. James Rumsey of Virginia was a rival of Fitch's for claims to invention of the steamboat. His idea for propulsion was a form of jet stream, pumping water from ahead of the boat by steam engine and ejecting it forcefully at the stern. Rumsey was still trying to perfect his model when he died of a heart attack in December, 1792.

Among others working in the United States was Rhode Island's Elija Ormsbee, who built a boat with side paddles that moved back and forth. His boat was similar to one conceived by Fitch, and Ormsbee demonstrated it successfully in 1792 but could find no backers. Discouraged, he did not persist, but took the engine out and gave it to the man who had

4. E. W. Gould, *Fifty Years on the Mississippi; or, Gould's History of River Navigation* (St. Louis, 1889), 5.

5. James Thomas Flexner, *Steamboats Come True* (New York, 1944), 242–43.

made his castings, to pay the bill. Samuel Morey demonstrated a stern paddle-wheel steamboat in the Connecticut River in 1794 and also tried side paddle wheels.

Concurrently, there were reports of successful demonstrations in the British Isles, seat of invention as the Industrial Revolution began. Engineers there were no doubt capable of designing a practical steamboat, but in the island nation there was not the great felt need that kept American inventors working on steamboat invention in a land where river transportation was so vital. In the field of textile manufacture and in making mining profitable, Great Britain pioneered in steam-power application. Steam engines for pump operation were built to keep open the mines upon which British industry was so dependent, but there was not a comparable dependence upon improved water transportation within the islands. In the United States, transportation needs rivaled or exceeded those of industry. Hence, in America experimentation with steamboats was bound to persist.

By 1798, the year of Fitch's death, the need for a steamboat was a matter of great public interest, and among the experimenters was a well-known public personage. Robert R. Livingston, scion of a wealthy New York state family, descended from the Dutch patroons of early colonial days, prominent in colonial political life, had a side interest that was almost a consuming passion—the designing and building of a steamboat. This member of the Livingston family was for many years the presiding judge of the New York court of chancery, a position that gave him the title of chancellor, which was used to distinguish him from other eminent Livingstons. He was the inheritor of the family estate, located on the Hudson River about 110 miles above New York City and known as Clermont. This was officially his residence, although he was frequently in Philadelphia or New York.

Livingston knew that Fitch had been granted an exclusive right to the operation of steamboats on New York waters by the state legislature. With Fitch gone to Kentucky in obvious abandonment of this privilege, Livingston decided early in 1798 to have the exclusive rights transferred to himself. He had confidence in his own conceptions of how a steamboat should be built. If he worked fast, he could turn a great profit, he theorized.

He got in touch with the one American engaged in steam-engine manufacturing at that time. This was Nicholas J. Roosevelt (great-granduncle of President Theodore Roosevelt), a member of another old New York family. The Livingstons, however, considered themselves to be higher on the social scale than the Roosevelts of those days, for some of the Roosevelts were middle-class artisans. Nicholas' father was a goldsmith and not as wealthy as most of the Livingstons.

Roosevelt was flattered to hear from the eminent man and to be asked to work with him on a steamboat. He was thirty-one years old in 1798, twenty years younger than Livingston. About all they had in common was an interest in steamboats. When Nicholas Roosevelt was fifteen, in 1782, he had designed a model boat intended for steam power if built to full scale. The model moved by means of spring-powered paddle wheels hung over the sides. He felt this idea was original with himself, a belief he later pursued to the point of having a patent for it granted in his name. In his adult years, he had been busy involving himself in one project after another and, at the time Livingston communicated with him, had not yet had time to build his full-scale steamboat.

Roosevelt's major interests were his steam-engine factory and a copper mine, both near the Passaic River in northeastern New Jersey, close to New York City. The copper mine was workable only because water was pumped from it by means of one of Roosevelt's steam engines. His steam-engine manufacturing was successful largely because he employed two men, J. Smallman and Charles Staudinger, who had worked in the famed British steam-engine plant of Boulton and Watt before coming to America.

Livingston wrote to Roosevelt in December, 1797, saying that he had learned of Roosevelt's "desire to apply a steam machine to a boat. Every attempt of this kind having failed, I have contrived a boat on perfectly new principles which both in the model and one on a large scale have exceeded my expectations."[6] Livingston went on to hint that he could send to England for an engine, but offered to sell his design to Roosevelt if Roosevelt would build the boat and furnish the engine. Roosevelt, having his own ideas, was not buying. They finally settled on a partnership, however, because Roosevelt felt it would be an advantage to work with a man so famous and politically powerful. He agreed to use Livingston's plans.

But when Roosevelt and his engineer, Staudinger, studied the plans, they both shook their heads in dismay. Livingston's boat hull would be too

6. *Ibid.*, 263.

Fig. 1 Mount Pleasant, the Shreve family homestead and Henry Miller
Shreve's birthplace, in Burlington County, New Jersey, as it appeared in 1980
Photograph by the author

Fig. 2 Reconstruction of Shreve's boyhood home on the Washington
lands in Fayette County, Pennsylvania. The Shreve farm was platted in
1814 as the town of Perryopolis, and the house is now within the town limits.
Photograph by the author

Fig. 3 The old Washington mill, built about 1774, purchased by Israel Shreve in 1795, and operated by the family during Henry Shreve's boyhood. Repaired in 1859, it continued in use until the early 1900s, the date of the old postcard on which this sketch is based.

COMMERCE OF THE OHIO.

—

*We have been obligingly favoured with a transcript from
the books of Messrs. Nelson, Wade, and Greatsinger,
for two months, viz. Nov. 24, 1810, to Jan. 24, 1811,
197 flat, and 14 keel boats, descended the falls of Ohio.*

18,611 bls. flour	59 do. soap
520 do. pork	300 do. feathers
2,373 do. whiskey	400 do. hemp
3,759 do. apples	1,484 do. thread
1,085 do. cider	154,000 do. rope yarn
721 do. do. royal	681,900 do. pork in bulk
43 do. do. wine	20,784 do. bale rope
323 do. peach brandy	27,700 yds. bagging
46 do. cherry bounce	4,619 do. tow cloth
17 do. vinegar	479 coils tarred rope
143 do. porter	500 bushels oats
62 do. beans	1,700 do. corn
67 do. onions	216 do. potatoes
20 do. ginseng	817 hams venison
200 gross bottled porter	4,609 do. bacon
260 galls. Seneca oil	14,390 tame fowls
15,216 lbs. butter	155 horses
180 do. tallow	286 slaves
64,750 do. lard	18,000 feet cherry plank
6,300 do. beef	279,300 do. pine do.
4,433 do. cheese	

ALSO,

A large quantity of potter's ware, ironmongery, cabinet
work, shoes, boots, and saddlery—The amount of which
could not be correctly ascertained.

☞ Taken from the Pilot's books, at Louisville, Ken.
this 8th Feb. 1811. By JAS. M'CRUM.

Fig. 4   Typical list of products shipped down the Ohio in days
before the steamboat

Reprinted from Zadok Cramer, *The Navigator* (Pittsburgh, 1814).

Fig. 5   Mary Blair Shreve

Courtesy Shreve Memorial Library
Collection, Shreveport

Fig. 6   The house that currently stands at 301 Front Street, Brownsville,
Pennsylvania, the first address of Mr. and Mrs. Henry M. Shreve. Although extensively remodeled, this house was probably the Shreve home.

Photograph by the author

Fig. 7   Robert R. Livingston

Courtesy National Portrait Gallery,
Smithsonian Institution, Washington, D.C.

Fig. 8   Robert Fulton

Courtesy National Portrait Gallery,
Smithsonian Institution, Washington, D.C.

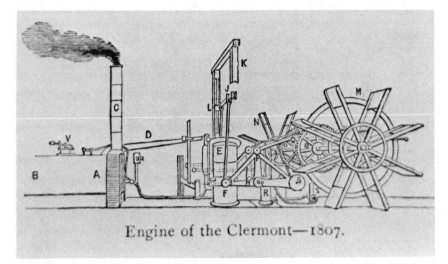

Engine of the Clermont—1807.

Fig. 9   The engine of the *Clermont*, typical of low-pressure steamboat
engines such as the one in the *Vesuvius*. The drawing's scale is not accu-
rate. The cylinder was two feet in diameter, the paddle wheels fifteen feet.

Reprinted from Thomas W. Knox, *The Life of Robert Fulton* (New York, 1890), 101.

Fig. 10   The *Vesuvius*, built in 1814, the second Fulton-Livingston boat on the Mississippi River

Reprinted from Thomas W. Knox, *The Life of Robert Fulton* (New York, 1890), 139.

Fig. 11   Shreve's *Enterprise*, the first steamboat to make the voyage from Pittsburgh to New Orleans and back. The mast was discarded before the return voyage.

Reprinted from Frederick Brent Read, *Up the Heights of Fame and Fortune and Routes Taken by the Climbers to Become Men of Mark* (Cincinnati, 1873), facing p. 78.

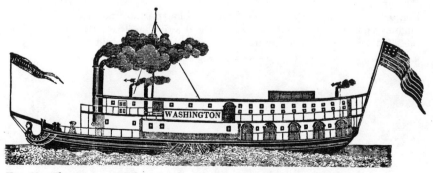

Fig. 12   The *George Washington*, built in 1824, Shreve's steamboat that was the prototype of the "floating palace" of the Mississippi River

Courtesy Frederick Way, Jr.

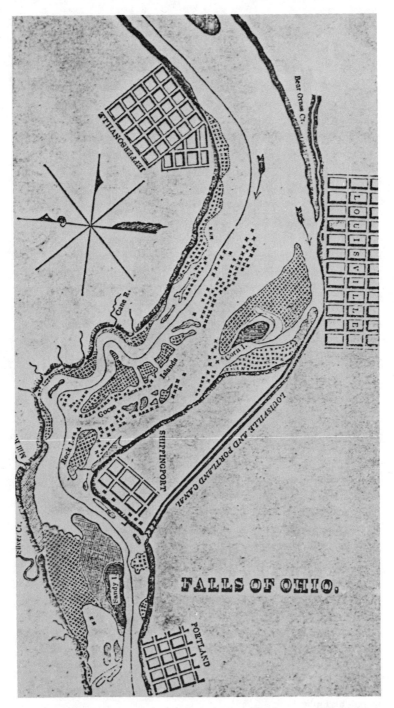

Fig. 13   The Falls of the Ohio after completion of the Louisville and Portland Canal. The x's indicate hazardous rocks of the falls. From 1816 to
1838, Shreve's home and business headquarters were at Portland, now a
part of Louisville.

Reprinted from Samuel Cumings; *The Western Pilot: Containing Charts of the Ohio River and the Mississippi*
. . . (Cincinnati, 1837).

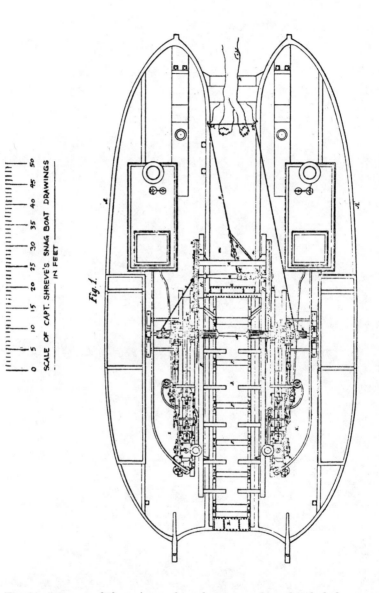

Fig. 14 Diagram of Shreve's snag boat drawn to scale and included in his patent application

From Henry M. Shreve, "Specifications Forming Part of Letters Patent No. 913, September 12, 1838," U.S. Patent Office, Washington, D.C. (scale added by Lloyd Hawthorne).

Fig. 15   Shreve's snag boat the *H. M. Shreve*, built in 1837. From a litho-
graph drawn for Shreve. The somewhat portly gentleman on the boiler-
house roof is a representation of Shreve himself.

Reprinted from Henry M. Shreve, *A Memorial: Official Evidence in Support of the Claim of Capt. Henry M. Shreve* . . . (St. Louis, 1847).

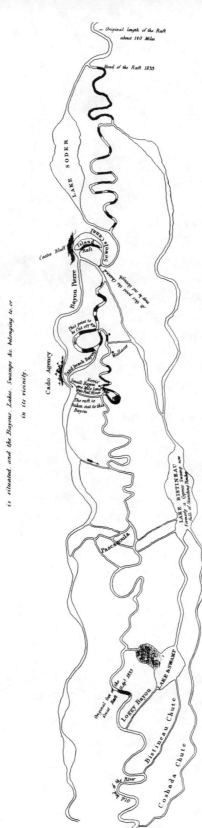

Fig. 16 Shreve's rough sketch of a segment of the Great Raft, submitted as part of his annual report on work done in the year ending September 30, 1833

Reprinted from *Executive Documents*, 23rd Cong., 1st Sess., No. 98.

Fig. 17 "Captain Henry M. Shreve Clearing the Great Raft from Red River, 1833–38," oil painting by Lloyd Hawthorne

Fig. 18   Monument to Captain Shreve erected near the riverfront in
Shreveport, 1967

Photograph courtesy of The Shreveport *Times*

Fig. 19 Side-wheelers at New Orleans, part of the fleet that plied the Red River regularly to Shreveport and beyond after the removal of the Great Raft. This photograph is probably from 1867.

Courtesy the Joseph Merrick Jones Steamboat Collection, Howard-Tilton Memorial Library, Tulane University, and Special Collections, Murphy Library, University of Wisconsin–LaCrosse

Fig. 20   The Shreve monument in Bellefontaine Cemetery, St. Louis, in
the center of a family circle. Shreve's grave faces east. The small monument to the left, inscribed "Our Little Florie," marks the grave of Shreve's
last child. The larger monument with the ship's prow statue, to the left of
Shreve's, is that of Walker R. Carter, husband of Rebecca Shreve Carter.
The imposing monument behind Shreve's is in the circle of the family of
John O'Fallon, Shreve's eminent St. Louis contemporary. The two families
were joined through the marriage of Shreve's granddaughter Sallie Carter
to Benjamin O'Fallon in 1854.

Photograph courtesy of Kathleen Van Buskirk

flimsy to stand up under the vibration of machinery. Of even more importance, both Roosevelt and Staudinger were convinced that Livingston's
plan for propulsion would not work. The plans called for a wheel placed
horizontally in a box at the stern of the boat, with each paddle blade fully
submerged and all expected to push constantly against a river's current.
The steam engines of that day were not powerful enough to keep such a
wheel turning.

The Roosevelt engines were almost identical to those being manufactured in England at the Boulton and Watt factory. This British engine had
been developed from the "fountain engine," an early type of steam engine
designed to pump water. The principle, simplified, was to fill a large cylinder with steam, forcing out the air. As the steam was cooled, it con-
densed, becoming liquid that occupied much less space than the steam;
thus a vacuum was produced. The vacuum drew up water, as for example
from a mine, through a pipe into the cylinder. A valve closed under the
column of water. Steam forced into the cylinder then pushed out the water, and the process—a slow one—began again. James Watt had made a
major improvement, the addition of a separate condensing chamber. This
improved condenser-type Boulton and Watt engine was the kind Smallman and Staudinger had worked on and had copied in design for Roosevelt. It worked effectively in Roosevelt's copper mine, and he was sure it
could be modified to be practical in a steamboat as well.

He had in mind to build a steamboat with side paddle wheels such as he
had experimented with as a boy. The paddles would strike the water one
at a time, calling for far less power than would be needed in Livingston's
plan. Staudinger agreed that Roosevelt's idea was workable, and he tried
to convince Livingston that the plans should incorporate the side paddle
wheels. Livingston was adamant; his plans were not to be altered. Staudinger wrote to Roosevelt: "That the Chancellor cannot be convinced that
his plan is not the best I told you before. Everyone has a certain proportion of philauty [self-love] and rich people particularly. They are not used
to hear the truth, and their idea is exalted by flatterers." Later the engineer wrote to Roosevelt that he and Smallman would make the drawings
"according to his [Livingston's] description, but if it should not succeed
and have not the expected effect, do not blame us for it."[7]

7. *Ibid.*, 263–64.

Nicholas Roosevelt soon regretted going into the partnership. Livingston hinted frequently that Roosevelt's hesitation to follow the plans was due to his secret knowledge that his engines were inferior and that perhaps a Boulton and Watt engine should be ordered. When Livingston insisted that the weight of the engine could be offset by using lightweight timbers for the hull, Roosevelt scribbled on the back of the letter, "How can an engine be kept in order when every part of the boat gives?"[8]

It came as no surprise to Roosevelt that when the boat was completed in August, 1798, the engine would not turn the paddle wheel. Livingston was incensed, insisting the fault lay in the engine. An outside expert was called in; he found the engine exceeded specifications called for. The only concession Livingston would make was to let Roosevelt raise the horizontal wheel somewhat. He allowed this because he had already induced the New York legislature to transfer Fitch's exclusive rights to him and had a time limit on demonstrating a practical steamboat.

The legislature required that the steamboat must move at least four miles per hour against the current in the Hudson River.[9] In October, Roosevelt had a steamboat ready with the modified paddle wheel. It could move, traveling in quiet water, at three miles per hour. Time was growing short. Roosevelt tinkered some more and thought he might as well bring an end to this operation he knew to be doomed to failure. While Livingston awaited the arrival of the boat at Clermont, Roosevelt took it a short distance up the Hudson, where it met currents too strong for further progress. Livingston awaited its arrival in vain.

Since Livingston refused to allow him to try the side paddle wheels, Roosevelt gladly turned his full attention to other matters. He had a new project, the building of two large steam engines to power a pumping system to supply water for the city of Philadelphia. But Livingston wrote to him once again, claiming he had designed a new and more powerful steam engine. Would Roosevelt built it for him? A wiser man by then, Roosevelt refused to test Livingston's engine, "which he wishes tried at my expense."[10]

The Philadelphia water system assignment brought Roosevelt a new friendship, one that was to be of major importance in his life. In 1796,

8. *Ibid.*, 264.
9. Dunbar, *A History of Travel in America*, 353.
10. Flexner, *Steamboats Come True*, 266.

Benjamin Henry Latrobe, a talented and handsome young man, came from England to live in Virginia. He had had a promising career in England as an architect, artist, and engineer until political changes and some personal matters brought him into disfavor. A widower with two children, he had come to America to rebuild his life. Soon he was involved in architectural planning, portending his future fame as the architect of many buildings in Washington, D.C., including important parts of the Capitol. He met Roosevelt in Philadelphia in his dual capacity as designer of the Bank of Pennsylvania and as engineer for the new city waterworks, for which Roosevelt was supplying the engines.

Roosevelt was thirty-two and Latrobe thirty-five when they met. The two were similar in nature—mercurial, emotional, and always optimistic and heavily involved in a variety of activities. The friendship was almost severed, however, when Latrobe's daughter·Lydia, at age thirteen, announced she was in love with Roosevelt, who confirmed that it was a mutual attraction. In 1808, when Lydia was seventeen, the two were married, and soon afterward, as we shall see, they were plunged into the chronicle of steamboat development.

In the meantime Livingston, Roosevelt's former partner in steamboat building, had formed a new alliance to promote his own involvement. He was still in the grip of his steamboat obsession when he was appointed minister to France by President Thomas Jefferson at a time of great concern by the United States over control of the mouth of the Mississippi River and the seaport city of New Orleans. Livingston sailed for Paris late in 1801, and perhaps he whiled away the hours on board the sailing vessel by mulling over his experiences thus far in steamboat building. He may even have admitted (to himself only) that his theories could have been faulty and that perhaps he should have allowed Roosevelt to try the boat with his side paddle wheels.

When Livingston arrived in Paris, he was introduced to another American residing there, a young man about the same age as Roosevelt and Latrobe, thirty-six-year-old Robert Fulton. Fulton had come to Europe from Philadelphia, where he had his own shop as a miniature painter, in pursuit of further training as an artist. After some study in London he moved to Paris in 1797. There, as in London, he found his portrait commissions too few and far between to meet his financial needs and began to develop ideas in the field of invention and engineering.

Before he left the United States, Fulton had some contacts with those who were experimenting in steamboat designs. He was present in Philadelphia at the time of Fitch's steamboat demonstration in 1786, and since his shop was only a block from the Delaware River, it is likely that he joined the crowds who watched Fitch's steamboat move under the power of its engine. Somewhat later he was in communication with James Rumsey, Fitch's polished, versatile rival in steamboat building. He again met Rumsey in 1788 while both were in London; Rumsey had come there to make a deal with Boulton and Watt to supply him with steam engines for his boats. Rumsey was nearing a point at which he could justify his claim to be the inventor of a practical steamboat, and the conversation naturally turned to his plans and the great need for improved water transportation in the United States.

Fulton's attention appears to have turned principally to the field of engineering and invention from this time on. He designed a system of inclined planes to be used in the development of England's canal network. Soon after he learned of Rumsey's death late in 1792, Fulton publicly criticized Rumsey's jet-propulsion design and put forth his own ideas. He proposed the building of a steamboat propelled by a paddle that worked like the tail of a fish. The engine would wind up a cord on a large, bowlike contraption to build up tension and then unwind to let the stern paddle move with its fishlike motion. He made a model of this boat in 1793, found that his idea was impractical, and then began to experiment with paddle wheels on his model.[11]

He was soon diverted to a project that remained his primary interest throughout the rest of his life. He drew up plans for a submarine. His thinking was stimulated by a study of the details of a little submarine built by David Bushnell of Connecticut and planned as an aid to American victory in the revolutionary war. Bushnell's submarine was contrived like two turtle shells put together vertically, with a conning-tower extension. Water in a box under the "turtle" weighted it to keep it underwater, and foot pedals pushed water out to raise the submarine on demand. A screw propeller and a rudder were also operated by foot pedals. The little submarine would make its way unseen to the hull of a ship and through the conning tower force a spike into the wooden hull. A rope tied to the spike

11. *Ibid.*, 219–20.

was also attached to a bomb. The bomb was pulled close to the ship and set to explode when the submarine had moved a safe distance away.[12]

Fulton drew up a design similar in principle but large enough to permit several men to be inside the submarine to turn the screw propeller and handle the other work, a cigar-shaped arrangement. The screw propeller had been demonstrated by John Fitch on one of his steamboats, but Fulton did not plan steam power for his submarine. He was living in Paris by the time his work on the submarine began, and he tried to sell the design to the French government. However, the postrevolutionary government was unstable, and Fulton had to find private financial backing. He supplemented his funds by inventing a projector to show pictures on the inside of a dome for entertainment-starved patrons.

Livingston met Fulton in 1802, when the young inventor had made several frustrating, unsuccessful attempts to prove the worth of his submarine to the French government. Livingston was ready to finance the building of a steamboat, even though it would have to be done in Paris. Should the boat built in Paris be successful, he and Fulton would return to the United States and try to build a boat before Livingston's exclusive rights were withdrawn.

With a backer ready to pay the costs, Fulton turned from his submarine experiments for the time being and gave full attention to the designing of a steamboat. Benefiting from his own mechanical experience and from his observations of what others had done in steamboat tests, Fulton could draw up a plan incorporating the latest scientific knowledge. Before putting together the machinery, he attempted to determine exactly how much power would be needed for propulsion and what the Boulton and Watt engine could produce. He had at hand the most complete studies of water resistance available in that day.

Fulton's preliminary tests were made with a model boat four feet long and two feet wide, driven by clockwork springs. With this he tested the speed made by the little boat on a pond with various types of paddles and wheels. He decided that the most effective was a plan similar to Fitch's first steamboat—flat, boardlike paddles attached to a chain that ran over pulleys at bow and stern. However, he discovered that this plan was already patented in France, even though not used in practical application.

12. Robert M. Speck, "200 Years Under the Sea: The Connecticut Water Machine Versus the Royal Navy," *American Heritage*, XXXII (December, 1980), 33–39.

He then changed to the use of side paddle wheels, which tested second best on his model.[13]

This time, Livingston knew better than to dictate the details of the design himself. He did limit the size of the boat, fearful that Fulton might be too free with his patron's money. It was not to be more than 120 feet long, 18 feet wide, and 15 feet deep and was required to produce a speed of eight miles per hour in still water and four against a current, carrying sixty passengers. The patent, Livingston agreed, would be in Fulton's name and "for a new mechanical combination of a boat."[14] Profits would be divided evenly, since Livingston considered his capital and political clout as important as Fulton's work.

He used that influence immediately in writing to the New York legislature. His monopoly had expired for a second time, but he assured the legislators that he was now about to produce a successful steamboat and wanted a renewal. A new agreement was reached, specifying that within two years a boat of twenty tons was to be run at four miles per hour upon the Hudson. By that time, the legislature was apparently skeptical that a practical steamboat would become a reality. In a letter to the *National Intelligencer* of Washington, D.C., an unidentified person later wrote, "When the late Chancellor Livingston applied for his grant for the exclusive navigation by steam on the North River [another name for the Hudson] to the Legislature of the State of New York, for thirty years, on condition that he should actually accomplish it, a very sensible member of the Legislature told me he could very easily have had a grant of any further extent, as the navigation by steam was thought to be much on a footing, as a practicability, with the navigation of the *reindeer* in the Chancellor's park."[15]

In 1803, the boat was under construction in Paris. It had the side paddle wheels Livingston had so summarily rejected when they were proposed by Roosevelt. The hull, seventy feet long and eighteen feet wide (plus the projecting paddle wheels), was launched and then fitted with its machinery. But one stormy night preceding the planned demonstration before invited guests, disaster struck. Fulton was awakened at dawn by someone pounding on his door to tell him that the boat had sunk. Fulton

13. Flexner, *Steamboats Come True*, 282–83.
14. *Ibid.*, 285.
15. Reprinted in Gould, *Fifty Years on the Mississippi*, 92.

raised the boat and determined that the weight of the engine had been too great for the hull's resistance to the agitation of the water during the storm. The craft had split in two.

The steamboat was rebuilt with a sturdier hull and on August 9 was ready for a trial. It performed fairly well, making four runs up the river a short distance and back in an hour and a half. But its speed was a great disappointment to Fulton. In his calculations, he had determined that it should achieve an upriver speed of sixteen miles per hour. Even John Fitch had built a steamboat that traveled eight miles per hour more than ten years earlier. Fulton's boat would go only three miles per hour upriver and would definitely not meet the requirements set by the New York legislature.

The inventor assured Livingston that certain defects in the engine could be corrected to produce greater power; with the right engine, the requirements for exclusive rights on the Hudson could most certainly be met. They placed an order with Boulton and Watt of Birmingham, England, to build the new engine and ship it to the United States. Delivery was promised for 1805 in New York.

Meanwhile Fulton turned again to his principal love, the submarine, trying to sell his ideas to Napoleon, who was at the time considering an invasion of Britain. When Napoleon rejected Fulton's offer, the inventor was approached by a secret agent of the British prime minister.

Later Fulton was widely criticized for conspiring with the agent and eventually agreeing to sell his ideas to England for use against France, host to his steamboat experiments. After asking for a total of £100,000, Fulton prepared to demonstrate his submarine by an underwater attack against French ships in Boulogne harbor. His torpedoes exploded harmlessly, leaving the ships intact, though a subsequent torpedo-attack demonstration with an old brig succeeded. But events, including Nelson's victory at Trafalgar, terminated the British interest in Fulton's submarine and torpedoes. Fulton left for America unable to collect the full £100,000 but with the rights to his inventions returned to him. He arrived in the United States in December, 1806, and soon afterward got in touch with the United States government to spark an interest in his torpedoes.

But now it was time to build the steamboat. While the hull was under construction, Fulton was building a submarine for the United States government to use as a threat against the British in the growing conflicts that eventually led to the War of 1812. Supervising the building of the steamboat was Charles Staudinger, formerly Roosevelt's steam-engine expert and assistant in building the Roosevelt-Livingston steamboat.

While the steamboat was being completed, Fulton had his opportunity to prove the worth of his submarine. After the British fired upon the *Chesapeake* in June, 1807, the United States government agreed to allow Fulton to blow up a brig in New York harbor as a demonstration. This successfully accomplished, he turned to checking the final steps in his steamboat's completion. Livingston kept the monopoly from expiring by getting an extension from the New York legislature for two more years.

He and Fulton were already making plans to extend the monopoly to other states and territories, expecting to acquire exclusive rights to the use of steam-powered vessels on all American rivers. The prime goal was a monopoly on the Mississippi-Ohio-Missouri system, where they envisioned a line of steamboats in action as soon as the first one was demonstrated on the Hudson and the boats for a fleet constructed.[16] Fulton was sure his steamboat would revolutionize transportation for all of the United States.

He registered the steamboat as *The North River Steamboat of Clermont*. The *Clermont* appendage came from the fact that it was taken to Livingston's Hudson River estate on its maiden voyage, and though Fulton himself continued to refer to it as the *North River*, others called it the *Clermont*, which is the name that has come down to posterity.

The *Clermont*, 150 feet long and 13 feet wide, pointed at stern and bow and with unshielded side paddle wheels, was in the Hudson River for its first test on August 9, 1807. It went only three miles an hour, and Fulton wrote to Livingston that there was still some work to be done on it but that it would make the required four miles per hour. To help it along when winds were favorable, the *Clermont* was supplied with two masts and sets of sails. In his letter to Livingston, Fulton showed his intention to use such boats on inland rivers when he wrote, "Whatever may be the fate of steamboats on the Hudson, everything is completely proved for the Mississippi, and the object is immense."[17]

As it turned out, he was overoptimistic about the potential of his own boats but correct in his estimate of the overall impact of steamboats on the

16. Flexner, *Steamboats Come True*, 320.
17. *Ibid.*, 318.

Mississippi River. Henry Miller Shreve, young and eager and learning the ways of the inland rivers as these events were taking place, would be ready for the role he would play in fulfilling Fulton's vision of a transformation on the inland rivers. He no doubt was following the progress toward steam-powered boats closely and was probably cheered to learn that a steamboat was operating on the Hudson River late in 1807. It was only a matter of time.

5 / The *Clermont* and the *New Orleans*

In the crowd of people who gathered for the departure of the *Clermont* on Monday, August 17, 1807, on its initial run upriver to the estate where Livingston awaited it, was Nicholas J. Roosevelt, erstwhile steamboat builder. He fairly fumed as he saw what was taking place. There before him was a steamboat of almost identical design to that he had proposed to Livingston years ago, the design with the side paddle wheels that he had known would bring success to their joint venture. And there was Robert Fulton, taking credit as the inventor. As if to rub salt into Roosevelt's wounds, Livingston and Fulton had lured Staudinger away from Roosevelt's steam-engine plant to oversee the boat's construction.

Roosevelt watched as seventeen passengers, dressed as if for a lawn party, boarded the steamboat. Some of them were members of the Livingston clan; most of these looked a bit skeptical, having seen the results of Chancellor Livingston's earlier mechanical projects. They considered the steamboat as likely to be another extravagant failure. But smiling admiringly at the tall, handsome Fulton, now forty-two years old, was the chancellor's niece Miss Harriet Livingston, who was reported to be on the verge of engagement to Fulton. The announcement hinged upon his success on this day.

80

Roosevelt felt a bit smug when the *Clermont*, after a noisy start about one o'clock, moved only a few feet before her engines stopped. He saw a shirt-sleeved Fulton, visibly perspiring with more than the heat of the August day, working frantically to get the paddle wheels turning once more. He succeeded after a few minutes. This time the steamboat moved slowly but steadily up the Hudson, black smoke pouring from the sheet iron stack, naked paddle wheels splashing. The young ladies on board screamed as sparks and splashes touched their clothing, but their screams were nearly lost amidst the clatter, rumble, and screech of the mechanism.

The boat made almost five miles an hour, to Fulton's intense gratification, completing the voyage up to Clermont, somewhat more than a hundred miles, in approximately twenty-four hours. All along the way it was hailed by curious people who hurried to the riverbank to see the cause of the strange sounds. When night came, many were terrified at the boat's sight and sounds.

The passengers tried to sleep in makeshift beds, since the bunks and other furnishings had not been installed for the initial voyage. But between noisy rumbles and vibrations from the engines, the shuddering of the craft with every stroke of the piston and turn of the wheels, and trepidation lest the unproven monster blow up or strike something in the darkness, sleep must have been nearly impossible.

Livingston was jubilant when he heard and saw the approach of the steamboat at Clermont early the next afternoon. Soon after the boat was tied at his landing, he came on board and announced the engagement of Harriet Livingston to Robert Fulton. The guests no doubt appreciated the opportunity to rest at Clermont overnight before the boat continued its maiden voyage to Albany. This city was forty miles farther upriver, a distance traveled in one day's time. Nonmechanical boats usually took four days for the voyage from New York to Albany.

The *Clermont*'s later voyages did not equal this first one in terms of speed, for Fulton had left the craft almost stripped of all but the engine and the most necessary equipment for the test run. Fully furnished, the steamboat began passenger service, managing to make three round trips in two weeks except when necessary repairs delayed the schedule, which happened frequently. Fitch had done little to accommodate passengers on his steamboat, but Fulton had people clamoring for passage, serving meals on board and providing bunks in cabins, with ladies and gentlemen separated. For six weeks, the *Clermont* ran a busy schedule before being laid up for the winter months, and it showed a small profit.[1]

Fulton was lionized. His connections with the Livingston family paved the way for him to become a social success. He and Harriet were married in January, 1808; one of her father's mansions, overlooking the Hudson, became the Fultons' summer home. They went to Washington to visit, and there they met the Latrobes.

Nicholas Roosevelt, engaged to young Lydia Latrobe, was present during one of Fulton's visits. The two men were civil, but they were mutually guarded and distrustful. Roosevelt did not keep quiet about his feelings concerning Fulton's use of side paddle wheels, which he was sure Livingston had suggested because of Roosevelt's advocacy of this propulsion device. With the knowledge of hindsight, he wished he had gone ahead and built a steamboat based on his own design, for he was most capable of doing it on his own.

But when Livingston had left for Paris, Roosevelt had been deep in his project with Latrobe on the Philadelphia water system and also trying to meet a navy contract for rolled copper. The years had slipped by. Latrobe had moved to Washington when the Philadelphia contracts were completed, for he had been appointed surveyor of the public buildings of the United States by President Jefferson. He was also Engineer of the United States Navy. But Roosevelt continued to be a frequent visitor in the Latrobe home. He and Lydia were married in November, 1808. After the wedding, they returned to the Roosevelt home, Laurel Hill, near Newark.

Benjamin Latrobe had met with Livingston just prior to Livingston's departure for Paris. At that time, Livingston urged Latrobe to help Roosevelt and John Stevens, Livingston's brother-in-law, continue with their steamboat work, a request he appears to have forgotten as soon as he met Fulton in Paris.[2] Latrobe later agreed with Roosevelt that Livingston had in all probability suggested Roosevelt's side paddle wheel to Fulton when they were planning the Paris steamboat. Roosevelt felt so strongly about this that he threatened to sue Fulton and Livingston and began efforts to have the patent for this steamboat feature granted to himself. (He eventually obtained the patent on December 1, 1814.)

1. Flexner, *Steamboats Come True*, 317–30.
2. Hamlin, *Benjamin Henry Latrobe*, 371.

But Latrobe tried to bring about a reconciliation. He talked with Livingston and Fulton and helped negotiate an agreement that would placate Roosevelt. Fulton and Livingston were building more steamboats for the eastern rivers and were also ready to begin construction of one for the Mississippi as well. Why not let Roosevelt, temporarily looking for more projects, supervise the building of a Mississippi boat for a share in the profits? This would forestall his suit against Fulton and Livingston.

Latrobe wrote to Fulton on February 7, 1809, suggesting that the three—Fulton, Livingston, and Roosevelt—would all profit from a "union of all three interests and abilities."[3] Subsequently, the three men formed the Mississippi Steamboat Navigation Company. Roosevelt would immediately go to work paving the way for a Mississippi River steamboat. Fulton would design the boat when the time came, but he was currently designing a warship he hoped to sell to the United States government. Livingston was by this time in his sixties and semiretired to Clermont. He would continue as a financial backer, but all three were to attempt to sell shares of stock in the new company. They were to split the profits from the Mississippi venture three ways.

Soon after the formation of the company, Roosevelt went to Pittsburgh to oversee the construction of an elaborate flatboat. In it, he and his eighteen-year-old bride, Lydia, with a crew of four, plus a male cook and a maid, were to go down the rivers to New Orleans for the purpose of determining the feasibility of steamboat transportation over the route. They would have in tow a large rowboat for frequent use by Roosevelt and one or two of his crew to take measurements of river depths and strength of currents that would be encountered on an upriver voyage.

Lydia Roosevelt wrote to her father that she intended going along on what she anticipated as a great adventure. He replied on May 11, 1809, "As to Fulton's scheme of sending your husband to the Ohio I highly approve of it so far. It will give you a charming jaunt."[4] Obviously, Latrobe had no experience in flatboat travel down the Ohio and Mississippi rivers.

The first part of the voyage was indeed a rather "charming jaunt," with overnight stops at villages or cities. Roosevelt played host at all the major stops, telling people his next voyage would be in a steamboat. But beyond Louisville there were no cities and scarcely a village for more than a thou-

3. *Ibid.*
4. *Ibid.*, 372.

sand miles. The occupants of the flatboat were subject to all the hardships and hazards that riverboat crews encountered, and any desire for adventure Lydia harbored must have been more than fulfilled. Before they reached Natchez, illness incapacitated all but Lydia, who served as nurse, cook, boathand, and maid, although she herself was pregnant. Because of illness, Roosevelt had to forgo measurement trips in that part of the Mississippi, a segment known for its strong and treacherous currents.

In those difficult waters near Natchez, the flatboat was so badly damaged that it had to be abandoned. The remainder of the voyage to New Orleans was made in the rowboat. Often the open boat had to serve as sleeping quarters, for there had been so many crimes committed by travelers who had preceded the Roosevelts in seeking lodging that people were afraid to take in strangers. No doubt by that time the travel-worn couple presented an appearance unlikely to inspire confidence. And they found that crude inns, such as the one in Baton Rouge where they sought shelter on a rainy night, were a poor alternative to spending the night in the rowboat. They were relieved to arrive in New Orleans about December 1 and soon left on the return voyage to New York by coastal sailing vessel.

Even before the test voyage began, Roosevelt had his mind made up that steamboat travel on the inland rivers was feasible. He was so certain of this that, seeing coal on the banks of the Ohio, he could not resist another investment. According to J. H. B. Latrobe, Lydia's half brother, Roosevelt purchased some of this land and "opened mines of the mineral, and so confident was he of the success of his project that he caused piles of fresh fuel to be heaped up on the shore in anticipation of the wants of steamboats whose keels had not yet been laid."[5] Roosevelt's reports to Fulton and Livingston, upon his return to the East, were enthusiastic. He was convinced he could built a steamboat, equipped with one of his own engines, that could move against any of the currents in the Ohio or Mississippi rivers.

Not long after their return and the birth of their first child, a daughter, the Roosevelts took up residence in Pittsburgh, where the construction of the steamboat was to take place. Soon Roosevelt was busily organizing the various shops and yards, getting timbers cut in the woods just up the Mo-

5. Gould, *Fifty Years on the Mississippi*, 83.

nongahela, opening a machine shop, and getting parts from the East. He also engaged boatbuilders from the New York yards. Captain Shreve, coming through Pittsburgh in the fall of 1810, saw the activity and found it highly interesting. Perhaps, he considered, when this first Mississippi steamboat was completed and tested, he would contract to purchase one for himself. His reckoning was made while he was still in ignorance of the monopoly held by the Fulton-Livingston group and the policy they would follow of licensing other steamboat operators only if they were willing to settle for so small a share of the profits as to make their efforts almost worthless.

When spring came in 1811, Shreve had to leave his bride, knowing that she was pregnant and that he could not see her again for six months. It was time for him to assume the captaincy of his new keelboat, which was as fine a boat as any on the rivers, capable of carrying ninety-five tons of merchandise and with accommodations for several passengers. With this boat, it could be profitable to make the long Pittsburgh-to-New Orleans run. He planned to take time in Pittsburgh to make careful purchases of cargo. While in the city he also wanted time for a closeup view of the new steamboat, already off the ways and floating near the mouth of Suke's Run. He saw the *New Orleans* as his keelboat approached the docking at the foot of Market Street. The hull, painted a slate blue, looked huge, completely dwarfing his keelboat that he had thought so large and splendid.

His first order of business was to purchase cargo, seeking bargains and dickering until he knew he had a purchase price on which he could show a profit when the goods were sold at New Orleans. While his crew loaded the merchandise and stowed it away in the depths of the cargo box, Shreve had time to satisfy his curiosity about the steamboat. He learned that it had nearly been accidentally launched before the hull was caulked and painted, for an unexpected rise in the waters of Suke's Run and the Monongahela had flooded the boatyard, almost taking the boat from its cradle and setting all the materials afloat. But when he saw the boat in early March, the hull had just been launched; finishing work would be done with the *New Orleans* afloat. The paddle wheels were being assembled, and in the shop most of the work of assembling the steam engine was finished. There was still much carpentry work to be done, for the steamboat was to be provided with excellent passenger accommodations.

Shreve was struck by the resemblance between the hull of this boat, intended for rivers with many shallows, and that of an oceangoing sailing ship. Fulton had altered his design and made this boat deeper-running than the *Clermont*. The *New Orleans* reminded Shreve of the oceangoing ships he had seen under construction in the Pittsburgh yards in his days as a river greenhorn. Six or seven brigs and schooners had been built; several had been damaged in attempts to get them down to New Orleans, and all had met with great difficulty in getting over the Falls of the Ohio. The attempt to build ocean ships at Pittsburgh had been abandoned in 1805 because of this difficulty.[6] It appeared to Shreve that this steamboat would be able to get through the chutes only in most favorable high-water conditions.

He was much interested in a visit to the shop where the pipe fittings and other metal parts needed were being made ready for the installation of the steam engine in the boat. He learned that the engine, built at Roosevelt's New Jersey factory, had been shipped by freight wagon over the Pennsylvania Turnpike from Philadelphia after having been brought there by boat from Newark. The engine, including the boiler, was to be placed deep in the hold of the steamboat. A large cylinder measuring thirty-four inches in diameter—the principal part of this steeple engine—would be in a vertical position. The engine was rated at slightly higher horsepower than the one on the *Clermont* and would operate under a pressure of between ten and twenty pounds per square inch. The machinery, which was quite bulky, with connecting gears and beams, would be placed aft of the paddle wheels, which were about sixteen feet in diameter. Between the cylinder and the wheel axle, the men were fitting an assemblage of arms that would connect with the piston. There was also a condensing chamber, an essential part of the Boulton and Watt–type engine.

Shreve examined it all, hesitating to interrupt Roosevelt, who was busy going about his task of supervision. But after a while he got Roosevelt's attention for a few minutes. Roosevelt was immediately defensive when Shreve questioned him about his engine. Was Roosevelt aware of river conditions on the Mississippi? Was he sure that this engine could produce the needed power for the difficult stretches of river?

Roosevelt was indignant. His engine was the most powerful of any ever

6. Ibid., 162–63.

used on a steamboat, he said. Of course it would be a success—he himself had personally checked the currents it would encounter in ascending the Mississippi River. He excused himself then to get back to his work. Shreve spent a little more time examining the boat before leaving. There was a small cabin being built between the engine area and the stern of the ship. This was the ladies' cabin. The forward space was taken up by a much larger cabin for male passengers and for a dining area, the galley, and other purposes. It was all to be furnished in the finest style, he was told. Freight would be carried in the remainder of the hold space. Two masts for supplementary power lay ready for installation. Shreve estimated the length of the *New Orleans* to be about one and a half times the length of his keelboat, in proportion to the length, and the width of Roosevelt's steamboat was also greater. The *New Orleans* did not follow the long, narrow lines that rivermen had found most practical on the Ohio and Mississippi rivers. He also learned that the *New Orleans* was only the first of a planned fleet of steamboats with which the Mississippi Steamboat Navigation Company intended to capture the river traffic from Pittsburgh to New Orleans.

He left the boat with mixed feelings. He was certain that he would not have the Mississippi Steamboat Navigation Company build a steamboat for him. For one thing, he had found out about the company's monopoly and its licensing policy.[7] Furthermore, he did not feel that the company was building a steamboat that could be successful on the inland rivers.

Apparently, the *New Orleans*' engine would be of little more than twenty-four horsepower. Horsepower was defined by James Watt in terms of the early uses of the steam engine. One horsepower was the force needed to raise "32,000 pounds [of water] . . . one foot high in one minute. . . . This horsepower is sufficient to grind and bolt a bushel of wheat per hour. It will drive 100 cotton spindles with the cards and other preparation machinery."[8]

Shreve went from the boatyard to the brand-new steam-engine manufacturing plant in Pittsburgh, the Pittsburgh Steam Engine Company, owned by the Evans family. Evans engines, he had been told, operated on a different principle from those of the Boulton and Watt type, developing much higher pressure and producing greater horsepower. He was al-

7. Dunbar, *A History of Travel in America*, 387–88.
8. *Niles' Weekly Register*, September 30, 1815.

ready convinced that Roosevelt's engine would not have adequate horse-power for the task it had to perform, despite Roosevelt's confidence in it.

The Evans shop was run by George Evans, son of Oliver Evans, the man who drove the *Orukter Amphibolus* through the streets of Phila-delphia in 1805. Oliver Evans was the first man to compete with Roose-velt in American-built engines, having opened a shop in Philadelphia in the early 1800s. His automated, steam-powered flour mill that Shreve had seen as he came through Pittsburgh in 1807 was a great success, and his engines were being installed in other Pittsburgh factories as well. This had created the need for a steam-engine plant in that city.

It was only through a freak weather event that Oliver Evans had not shared credit for the invention of the steamboat and beaten Fulton in the race for a successful demonstration. He would definitely have been first to build the engine for a steamboat for the inland rivers. In 1803, when all America was keyed up over the acquisition of the mouth of the Mis-sissippi River and the possibilities thus opened for inland development, two riverboatmen of New Orleans got in touch with Oliver Evans. They wanted him to supply them with one of his high-pressure engines to power a boat they were building at the port city. The engine was built at Evans' shop in Philadelphia and sent via sailing ship to New Orleans.

The hull was completed and launched, but the spring brought heavy rains and sudden flooding to the New Orleans area. Before the engine was installed in the boat, the hull was carried away on floodwaters and deposi-ted high and dry at some distance from the river when the waters re-ceded. The two men had no means of getting it afloat until the river's whim should again bring water lapping about it. Creditors were pushing them for payment of bills, and the only person who would help them pay their debts insisted they drop the nonsensical idea of a steamboat and put the Evans engine to work in a sawmill. Discouraged, the two agreed to do it, but their troubles were not over.

As Oliver Evans wrote in 1810, they had the mill sawing "2,000 feet of boards in twelve hours, when incendiaries set fire to the mill and reduced it to ashes. They have both written to me frequently, that they were con-fident that the power of the engine was quite sufficient to have insured success in propelling the boat. The engine for this boat was only nine inches in diameter, the stroke of the piston three feet. I believe my prin-ciple is the only one suitable for propelling boats up the Mississippi. The engine is ten times more powerful than the best English engine of equal dimensions."[9]

Shreve's thoughts were turning to the possibility of doing what the two New Orleans rivermen had planned to do. An engine similar to the Evans engines would certainly be lighter in weight and produce more horsepower than the one in the *New Orleans*. Some people were fearful that the higher pressure they developed would bring explosions, but Oliver Evans was convinced of the engine's safety. His mill in Pittsburgh certainly functioned well. Its engine turned three pairs of millstones, grinding about sixty thousand bushels of wheat, corn, and rye annually. Shreve examined the nearly finished engine that George Evans was working on in the shop. It was much smaller than Roosevelt's, yet Evans claimed it would be more powerful. Shreve questioned him about its operation.

As he left the shop, Shreve was already thinking of the kind of boat he would have next, and he had not yet completed a single voyage in his new keelboat. Back at the boat, the men had finished loading the freight, and Shreve set about checking details in preparation for embarkation for New Orleans. Early in the morning his crew of twelve was poling down the Ohio as he stood atop the cargo box manning the sweep.

The voyage went well. In New Orleans he sold his cargo at a good price and began to bargain for a return cargo of cotton, sugar, indigo, and some coffee and tea. As he went about the town, he learned that people were looking forward to the arrival of the *New Orleans* later in the season.

Livingston had been busy, making sure that his investment would pay off by requesting the same monopolistic rights in the operation of steam-powered vessels on the inland rivers that he had been granted in the East. His involvement in the Louisiana Purchase had brought to his attention the tremendous potential for development offered by the inland rivers, including anticipated growth in the port city of New Orleans. His enthusiasm was contagious and soon his younger brother, Edward Livingston, decided that opportunity lay in that city. He went there in 1804, as soon as American governmental control was established, to open a law office. He had already become well known in New Orleans when his brother sought exclusive rights on the waters of the Territory of Orleans for the Mississippi Steamboat Navigation Company's vessels. The gover-

9. *Louisiana Gazette*, October 20, 1810, quoted in Gould, *Fifty Years on the Mississippi*, 150.

nor of the Territory of Orleans, William C. C. Claiborne (who later, in 1812, became the state of Louisiana's first governor), on a visit to New York in the autumn of 1810, met with Fulton and Livingston to discuss the matter. Livingston stated that he would not go on with the building of steamboats unless the legislature saw fit to grant the exclusive privileges. Since the people of New Orleans saw the steamboat as the key to great progress, the legislators granted the Fulton-Livingston interests the rights on April 19, 1811. Any steam vessel licensed by the company would have free use of New Orleans port facilities and of any other ports and all waterways that were within the territorial boundaries (which were roughly the same as the state of Louisiana).

The Territory of Upper Louisiana was separated from the Territory of Orleans in 1804, with the seat of government at St. Louis. Livingston attempted to get the monopolistic grants there and also from the other territories and states that lay along the Ohio and Mississippi rivers. Although the granting of exclusive rights by the government was a fairly common practice in the East, many westerners were fiercely protective of the people's rights and saw the granting of special privileges as undemocratic. Neither Robert Livingston nor his brother Edward could make headway in getting any of the legislatures north of Louisiana to grant them a monopoly in steamboat operation. Had it been someone from west of the Appalachians making the request, it is possible the attitude would have been different among these people who had at one time considered their "right of deposit" at New Orleans of sufficient importance to threaten secession from the Union over the problem. They were indignant at the presumption of any easterner, especially one as politically powerful and as wealthy as Robert Livingston, to expect any special privileges on their rivers.

When Shreve arrived in New Orleans, the Fulton-Livingston group had already been granted their privileges by the legislature of the Territory of Orleans. He undoubtedly heard much discussion of the matter in the waterfront taverns where the boatmen gathered. Shreve's convictions were as strong as anyone's. Western Pennsylvanians sided with the frontier states in their politics, for they shared the Ohio-Mississippi system as their economic lifeline. Westerners, including Shreve, felt that in a democracy there was no place for the granting of special privileges of any kind. There was also the question of whether the exclusive rights granted to the Fulton-Livingston group were constitutional. Most of the boatmen felt they were not. Shreve declared he would not pay anyone for the right to use the rivers in any kind of boat he chose to operate. The rivers belonged to all the people, not just to a select few.

But how would an ordinary riverboat operator, one without a wealthy backer, be able to fight the powerful Livingston-Fulton group, especially with Edward Livingston so influential in New Orleans legal circles? The exclusive rights held by the steamboat company granted it the right to seize any steam-powered vessel that had not paid the license fee.

Shreve began the return trip to Pittsburgh with his cargo on board and a few extra hands to help in the long, foot-by-foot struggle to drag the keelboat upstream. Summer arrived as the voyage began, and perspiration made the men nearly as wet when they worked on the deck as the river did when they plunged into it to cordelle the boat upstream. There was seldom a breeze to make it worthwhile to open the square sail on the keelboat's mast.

Summer on the lower Mississippi was a suffocating experience in any year, but in that summer of 1811 it was more oppressive than usual. There was a feeling in the air different from any the boatmen had experienced before. Rumors were rife of impending disaster, for a great comet appeared nightly in the skies—a sign of trouble to come, many said, and even those not inclined to superstition felt a little uneasy.

Another member of the Latrobe family, Charles Joseph Latrobe, nephew of Benjamin, wrote in his book *Rambler in North America* of the unusual occurrences of that summer.

> During the earlier months, the waters of many of the great rivers overflowed their banks to a vast extent, and the whole country was in many parts covered from bluff to bluff. Unprecedented sickness followed. A spirit of change and recklessness seemed to pervade the very inhabitants of the forest. A countless multitude of squirrels, obeying some great and universal impulse, which none can know but the Spirit that gave them being, left their reckless and gamboling life, and their ancient places of retreat in the North, and were seen pressing forward by tens of thousands in a deep and solid phalanx to the South. No obstacles seemed to check their extraordinary and concerted movement. The word had been given them to go forth, and they obeyed it, though multitudes perished in the broad Ohio which lay in their path. The splendid comet of that year long continued to shed its twilight over the forests.[10]

10. Gould, *Fifty Years on the Mississippi*, 89.

Others spoke of the air being still and the sun veiled, obscured by mists. Through this strange, oppressive atmosphere, Shreve's crew labored on and on. He himself was anxious to bring the voyage to a successful end, for this was the first time he had brought so large a boat, with ninety-five tons of valued merchandise aboard, up the river all the way from New Orleans. The strange feeling to both the days and nights, plus the worry that all might not be well with his wife, Mary, at home, made the voyage even more wearisome. Autumn was changing the sumac leaves to red, and some of the poplars and sycamores were tinged with yellow by the time they approached Shippingport, Kentucky, early in October.

Shreve docked at the little town below the Falls of the Ohio to await a pilot's assistance in making the difficult passage. After the unusually rainy spring, the fall rains were late in coming, and the water was still low. He hoped his wait would be brief, for each day brought a little nearer the time for the baby to make its appearance, and he wanted to be at home should the infant come early. He used the waiting time to go up to Louisville on foot to see the *New Orleans*, for he was told as soon as he stepped foot ashore that the steamboat was there, awaiting a rise in the rivers so that it could be piloted over the falls.

The *New Orleans* and the people aboard it were the talk of Louisville. The steamboat had been launched at Pittsburgh in early September for its first experimental run up the Monongahela. It was then pronounced ready for embarkation upon the voyage to New Orleans. Nicholas and Lydia Roosevelt would not listen to friends who thought that, since she was about seven months pregnant, she should not go along on this voyage. In that day, a woman did not usually even set foot outside her home in such condition. The tongues wagged furiously in Pittsburgh, and Roosevelt's friends did their best to convince him that he was wrong in allowing his wife to accompany him. But even Lydia's father could not dissuade her.

So she was on board on the day the *New Orleans* started down the Ohio, with most of the people of Pittsburgh on hand to see the beginning of the voyage. The crew consisted of engineer and captain Nicholas Baker, pilot Andrew Jack, and six hands. There were also a waiter, a cook, and two female servants. Roosevelt had tried in vain to get some paying passengers. He was, as usual, in need of money, for the cost of the steamboat had run over the estimated $20,000 to $25,000 and Fulton was holding back on payments. The *New Orleans* is said to have cost $38,000.

The boat had proceeded down the Ohio, making occasional stops along the way. At Cincinnati it had created a great deal of excitement, but not so much as at Louisville. Shreve heard the story over and over. It seemed that everyone in Louisville had been awakened in the small hours of the night by the sounds of clanking and banging and then a loud hissing. Some looked out the window and were sure that the comet was landing in the Ohio River, for to go with the hissing there were sparks and flames out in the darkness. The hissing proved to be the sound of steam escaping through the valves as the engines were stopped for the docking.

There was much discussion also of an event that had taken place an evening or two later. Roosevelt, ever the host, had invited the leading citizens of Louisville to a dinner aboard the *New Orleans* in its main cabin. Someone had just commented, after the drinking of toasts, that Roosevelt had kept his word given when he stopped at Louisville on the flatboat voyage that he would return in a steamboat.

But the guest added that he found the idea of the boat's going *up* the river under steam power to be absurd. Immediately there was a loud rumbling, and the glasses and dishes rattled on the table. The frightened guests, convinced they were adrift and about to be dashed to pieces on the Falls of the Ohio, rushed to the deck. They were amazed to see that the steamboat was moving upriver, away from the falls. Their doubts of the boat's ability to move against the current were dispelled. Nevertheless, no one volunteered to be a passenger when the voyage was resumed.

The big blue boat stood at anchor as Shreve's keelboat was piloted over the falls a few days later. Seeing it there, he was more convinced than ever that its deep hull, twelve feet in depth and riding low in the water, was wrong for the rivers. At the same time, he knew that steam power must be developed to end the slow, backbreaking drudgery he and his crew endured to come up the rivers. He would look into possibilities as soon as he could.

The following spring Shreve learned the details of the *New Orleans'* voyage from Louisville to New Orleans, among the most perilous ever made upon the Ohio and Mississippi rivers. There was one advantage to the delay at Louisville, for Mrs. Roosevelt's baby was born there, where help was available. The new member of the family was a boy, to his parents' joy. When the rains finally came and the river began to rise, Roosevelt decided to start, even though the water was deeper than the draft of the boat by only five inches in some passages. With a falls pilot on board, they decided full steam ahead was the best procedure to insure getting through. The black rocks were dangerously close, but the steamboat made it through this first ordeal unscathed.

In calm water at Shippingport, they dropped anchor to let the pilot off the boat. Before they could start again, the *New Orleans* shuddered and creaked as if she were running aground. This was the first hint of what was to come. The tremors of the New Madrid earthquakes had begun, among the most severe ever reported in the United States. They centered at New Madrid, Missouri, just a short distance down the Mississippi River from the mouth of the Ohio.

Into this violence the *New Orleans* proceeded. Cramer's *Navigator* became almost useless in the havoc that came to the rivers that December of 1811 and early January of 1812. Banks caved in and great trees crashed into the river. In some places river currents reversed, exposing the bottom of the channel before a great wall of water washed over all again. One night they tied the boat to a tree on an island. The next morning the island was no longer there. The earthquakes brought dramatic changes to rivers and land alike. The river channels shifted and were never the same again; Reelfoot Lake appeared in Tennessee, east of New Madrid, where dry land had been. The cracks and upheavals in the earth made the formerly productive farmlands untillable, and the village of New Madrid collapsed.

If Lydia Roosevelt wanted adventure, she must have had enough to satisfy her for the rest of her life on this voyage. Alarmed at nature's strange behavior and at the apparition of a boat breathing smoke and flames and making unearthly noises, some Indians shot at the steamboat. Others once gave chase in canoes, but the *New Orleans*, full steam ahead, outran them. Lydia had another fright one night when she awoke to screams and was sure Indians had attacked. Instead, there was a fire in the forward cabin, but the crew managed to extinguish the blaze before it burned through the stout Pennsylvania timbers. Near New Madrid, homeless people called to them from the riverbanks for help. The journey was a living nightmare, and the fact that no lives were lost is testimony to the skill of the captain and the pilot.

The steamboat's experiences just before arrival at Natchez reveal the reason for Roosevelt's decision to put the *New Orleans* into service only in the lower Mississippi, below Natchez, where the currents were less strong and the river more stable. In its approach to the city the steamboat rounded a bend to a position opposite the Natchez landing but too far downstream. The attempt to get back to the landing against the current was nearly a failure. People watched from the bluffs and from Natchez-Under-the-Hill as the *New Orleans* seemed about to be washed on down the river, out of control. At first no progress upstream could be made. The engine was stopped to build up full power of steam and fresh fuel was loaded into the firebox. It was only by lifting the safety valve and allowing the pressure to build up that the boat could be put into motion to go back up the river. All the people cheered and clapped as finally the landing was made.[11] Arrival at New Orleans was on January 12, 1812.

The information that the *New Orleans* could not return upriver farther than Natchez reached Shreve in due time. He was more than ever convinced that the Livingston-Fulton steamboats were not going to meet the pressing need for improved transportation on the Mississippi and Ohio rivers. So he began to make plans.

11. *Ibid.*, 86–87.

6 / **Plans and Progress**

Captain Henry Shreve was back home in Brownsville in mid-October, 1811. A few weeks later, on November 28, his wife, Mary, gave birth to their first child, a daughter whom they named Harriet Louise. Soon both mother and baby were doing well, and Shreve could turn his attention to exploring possibilities in steamboat building, a matter given added impetus when he stopped at Pittsburgh en route home.

He had had a day or two to wait while his cargo was being moved to the warehouses of Bosler and Company, middlemen who handled the imported goods. The city was buzzing with the talk of how steam engines were bringing new prosperity as they turned the wheels in the textile plants, in the Evans flour mill, and in metal and woodworking shops newly opened. A paper mill and a wiredrawing mill were under construction, planned for steam power. Over at Beelen's foundry, not far from the

Suke's Run boatyards, much of the work now consisted of boring cylinders and making air pumps and pipes for steam engines.

Somewhere in the city, probably at Beelen's, Shreve met a newcomer to the city of Pittsburgh named Daniel French. French had recently come to the West from New York. There he had been among the several mechanics and inventors who were challenging Fulton's rights to his patents and to the exclusive use of steam power on the rivers. French built a steamboat before he left New York, designing his own engine for it. Fulton's first patent was dated February 11, 1809; French was granted one on October 12 the same year for the steamboat with an "oscillating engine."

The use of side paddle wheels was a part of Fulton's patent applicaton, a claim that had immediately brought about the clash with Roosevelt. Patent battles were making it so difficult for those with original ideas in steamboat and engine design in the New York area that French left for Pittsburgh in 1811. Apparently he decided he could do better by building a steamboat for use on the Ohio River. Earlier that year, Fulton and Livingston had succeeded in getting the New York legislature to strengthen their monopolistic rights, enabling them to seize legally any steamboat they claimed to be in violation of their privileges without waiting for court orders. This step further convinced French that he should move his steamboat operations to the inland rivers.

When Shreve met him, he was preparing to build a boat and had found a partner named Samuel Smith to assist in the financing of the construction. His would not be the only steamboat under construction in Pittsburgh in 1812, for the Fulton-Livingston cradles were about to be occupied again. Excluding Roosevelt in a company reorganization, Fulton and Livingston began operation as the Ohio Steamboat Navigation Company. John Livingston, Mrs. Fulton's brother, was to be in charge of building a second steamboat, the *Vesuvius*. Although they looked for ways to stop the construction of any competitor's steamboat, the Fulton-Livingston group found no grounds for a suit against Daniel French. His boat and engine designs were different from Fulton's and covered by his own patent. His boat, the *Comet*, would not even conflict with Roosevelt's patent claim on paddle wheels, for French worked with a stern paddle wheel, not "over-the-sides."

Even though the Fulton-Livingston group could not sue him for his current activities, French resented the fact that exclusive rights had been granted to the company in the East and in Louisiana. In this, he and Shreve found grounds for agreement. They both believed that granting exclusive rights to any individual or group was undemocratic and that it tended to stifle progress through free enterprise. The two men also agreed that a steamboat engine needed to be more powerful than the standard low-pressure engine, copied from the English Boulton and Watt design, that was being used in the Fulton boats, including the one under construction. French had patented a steam engine of a different design, one that, though it was not truly a high-pressure engine as the Evans engine was, nevertheless developed more pressure than the Fulton engines.

Shreve was very interested in seeing the steamboat that French was building in Pittsburgh. He knew immediately upon seeing the *Comet* that it would not suit him, however, as a replacement for his keelboat. It was to have a capacity of only twenty-five tons, too small to make a profit on the Pittsburgh-to-New Orleans run. Of greater interest to Shreve was French's engine design. It was built to develop forty pounds of pressure to the square inch as compared to twenty to twenty-four for the Fulton engines.

In the old records, French's engine is not fully described. It is called an "oscillating engine," and the term "vibrating cylinder" was used to differentiate it from the Boulton and Watt type. Shreve's interest was aroused chiefly by its capacity to build up higher pressure and hence more drive to its piston. It dispensed with the heavy beam of the low-pressure engines and had fewer moving parts in its connections to turn the stern paddle wheel than the Fulton boats used in their machinery.[1] These differences were enough to impress Shreve with the possibility that French might be able to build a boat that he could use to replace his keelboat. Whether through Shreve's influence or not is unknown, but about the time the construction of the hull for the *Comet* began in Pittsburgh, French moved to Brownsville to open his own engine shop, where he would build the boat's machinery. Another influence on French could have been complaints from George Evans about French's use of the high-pressure principle, patented by Evans, and perhaps French felt he would be freer to develop his own ideas at some distance from any other steam-engine builder.

1. Louis C. Hunter, *Steamboats on the Western Rivers* (Cambridge, Mass., 1949), 136–39.

That winter and early spring were interesting times for Shreve. It was a novelty, after his years of bachelorhood, to return to a wife and to a home of his own, and there was the fascination of watching his daughter in her first months of life. In addition, he soon settled into a pattern of going each morning to the machine shop that French opened in Bridgeport, just across Dunlap Creek from Brownsville. He also had more routine tasks to perform, such as planning the next season's keelboat voyage and repairing his boat.

There were other concerns as well—problems that faced all Americans, especially those who lived in what was then called the West. The tensions between the United States and Great Britain were building toward the War of 1812. Americans were incensed at evidence that the British were enlisting the aid of Indians and encouraging them in frontier attacks. After William Henry Harrison brought an end to Tecumseh's attempt at a large-scale organized resistance movement by defeating the Indians at the Battle of Tippecanoe, the Indian chief and his men formed an alliance with British military leaders stationed near Detroit. Meanwhile, on the open seas and in seaports, Great Britain was using impressment as a means to increase the manpower of its navy for the ongoing sea battles against Napoleon's navy. The British navy was stopping American ships on the high seas and going aboard to seize any sailors suspected of being British deserters. In some cases American citizens were being taken, both from their ships and in port. Among the war hawks in Congress, with widespread popular support, a feeling was rising in favor of retaliation against Great Britain for these offenses.

Shreve heard much of the war talk, for there were many proponents of a declaration of war in the western states. Both Henry Clay and Andrew Jackson favored war. Clay had just finished a term as United States senator from Kentucky. In 1812, acknowledged leader of the war hawks, he was in the House of Representatives trying to convince Congress that war should be declared against Great Britain. Highly approving of Clay's speeches was Jackson, as yet not nationally prominent but a major general in the Tennessee militia with ten years' experience and great local renown.

Most western citizens, including Shreve, supported the war hawks, primarily because of the frontier problems. President Jefferson's Embargo Act had been a failure, and westerners had been angered at the way it had affected the import and export trade at New Orleans. All merchant navigators of the Mississippi were keenly aware of the need to assert American rights on the high seas, even though they confined their own work to the rivers. Shreve's patriotic drives were further strengthened by attitudes he inherited from his father, Colonel Israel Shreve.

Shreve joined in the discussions of the problems with Great Britain at the stops he made en route to New Orleans in that spring of 1812. As a topic of conversation, impending war rivaled the earthquake and the voyage of the *New Orleans*. On the subject of the earthquake, people were still uneasy. Although there had been no major tremors since February, minor ones were still occurring even as summer began. Navigating the rivers demanded constant vigilance and all the skill at Shreve's command. Old trees that had stood as landmarks to guide him in avoiding bars and other hazards had been torn away and swept down the rivers in their turmoil. He could not assume that the river channels were where they had been on his 1811 voyage; old islands had disappeared and new ones had come into being. At the settlement of New Madrid, the people were in despair. Many had moved on to other locations, but those who remained were finding that they could not plant their fields this spring.

No doubt Shreve and his crew were thankful to complete this voyage without encountering any major problems. While he was in New Orleans attending to the selling of his cargo and purchase of return freight, he made it his business to learn how the *New Orleans* was faring.

The arrival of the first steamboat in the Crescent City had created widespread excitement. The greeting had been tremendous, and there was so much curiosity about the boat that Roosevelt arranged an excursion on it just three days after the steamboat's arrival in New Orleans. An announcement was placed in the newspapers to draw customers, since, unlike the one in Louisville, this was not a free demonstration. Roosevelt was not in a financial position to continue to be as generous. The notice in the *Louisiana Gazette and Advertiser* on January 16 read: "For the *English Turn*—The steamboat New Orleans will run from this place to the English Turn and back on Friday next, to start precisely at 10 a.m. Tickets of admission may be procured at the two coffee houses at three dollars each. It is expected the boat will return at three o'clock. All persons who desire to dine before that hour it is expected will carry their provisions with them."

Apparently the excursion went almost as planned, for the newspaper reported on January 18: "Yesterday the citizens were gratified with the power of steam in this vessel. She left this place at 11 o'clock, went five leagues down, and returned at 4 o'clock. A number of gentlemen were on board. The day was fine and general satisfaction was given."

After the excursion, the *New Orleans* made repeated runs to Natchez and back, carrying passengers and cargo. Ads appeared regularly, such as this one from the *Louisiana Gazette* of January 21, 1812: "For Natchez. THE STEAM-BOAT New-Orleans. Will leave this on Thursday next, the 23rd inst. For freight or passage apply on board, or to Talcott & Bowers." The ad was illustrated with a cut of a sailing vessel. Apparently the printer did not yet have one of a steamboat, though it was not long before he did.

Never again did the *New Orleans* attempt to move against the currents above Natchez, but the trips between New Orleans and Natchez proved profitable. Soon the Livingston-Fulton organization had decided to build the *Vesuvius*, the steamboat that Shreve saw on the ways at the Pittsburgh boatyards as he headed downriver. The plan was to divide the Pittsburgh-to-New Orleans route into three parts. The lower-river run would be handled by the *New Orleans*. The *Vesuvius* would pick up freight and passengers at Natchez and take them as far as Shippingport. To avoid the problem of passage of the Falls of the Ohio, a third steamboat would make the run between Louisville and Pittsburgh. As soon as possible, additional boats would be built for the three divisions.

The newspapers continued to report on the *New Orleans* and the problems she encountered in the journey upriver. The *Gazette* of February 8 carried this item: "The steamboat was at Fort Andrews, 50 miles below Natchez on her way up, on Saturday last. She was detained by breaking one of her wheels." The issue of February 12 reported, "The steamboat left Natchez on Thursday afternoon and arrived here on Monday evening last, and will start again we are informed on Saturday next."

Nicholas and Lydia Roosevelt stayed in Louisiana long enough to see that the steamboat was established in its new role. Before they left, Roosevelt attempted to sell shares in the steamboat company, for he was still in arrears in his accounts and in dire need of the funds that Fulton was resisting paying to him. Fulton resented the fact that the enthusiastic reports in the newspapers ignored his part in the success of the *New Orleans*, speaking of "Mr. Roosevelt's steamboat" and of Roosevelt's heroism in making the voyage despite the unusual hazards brought by the earthquakes. Furthermore, Roosevelt's accounts were carelessly kept, and reports he claimed to have mailed en route to New Orleans were lost.[2] Fulton and Livingston decided not to pay part of what Roosevelt claimed.

Roosevelt was still trying to raise money in New Orleans two months after his arrival there. This ad, signed by Roosevelt, appeared in the *Monitor* of March 5, 1812: "STEAMBOAT.—The persons who desire to take an interest in the steamboat held under the patent of Messrs. Livingston & Fulton, destined to navigate upon the Mississippi and Ohio and Cumberland, and to the Falls of the Ohio, will please address the undersigned at the house of Messrs. Talcot & Bowers, from eleven o'clock until two. The subscription books are open every day until they are filled."

Quoting a "gentleman passenger," the *Gazette* reported that the steamboat "can stem the current at the rate of upwards of three miles an hour." The general opinion in the region was that the *New Orleans* was a success. Nicholas and Lydia Roosevelt returned home to New York via sailing vessel as they had done before. Talcott and Bowers acted as agents in New Orleans, while supervision of the entire operation was the responsibility of Edward Livingston. This was the situation in the summer of 1812 when Shreve prepared for his return voyage to Pittsburgh and Brownsville. He was fully convinced that he must take steps toward acquisition of a steamboat for himself as quickly as possible, before the Fulton-Livingston group had a firm grip on shipping contracts and passenger service. The exclusive rights they held to steam-powered vessels in Louisiana were a problem he would have to face.

At Pittsburgh, he saw that the *Vesuvius*, the new Fulton-Livingston steamboat, was much like the *New Orleans* in appearance, judging from the hull, which was almost completed in its cradle near Suke's Run. The talk around the city was that the engine was to be somewhat larger than the one for the *New Orleans*, with some improvements but still basically the same as the one that had proved to be too weak. Fulton, it seemed, had little time to change the plans for the steamboats, for he was back working at his old love, the building of naval war machinery. Congress had declared war against Great Britain during Shreve's absence. President Madison requested war on June 1, and after two weeks of heated

2. Hamlin, *Benjamin Henry Latrobe*, 373.

debate, the official declaration came on June 18. Fulton was building a warship for the United States government.

To his surprise, Shreve also saw preparation under way for the laying of the keel of another steamboat. It appeared to be the twin of the *Vesuvius*, and he learned that it, too, was to be named for a volcano. The *Aetna* would carry fewer passengers and more freight, however. Roosevelt's former engine partner, Charles Staudinger, was supervising the construction of this, the third of the Fulton-Livingston boats.

Before he left Pittsburgh, Shreve went to see the *Comet*. It looked small indeed after his recent view of the Fulton boats. He withheld judgment, pending a test against the current. If this small boat operated well, perhaps French could begin work on a larger one that could carry enough to make the voyages pay.

The *Comet* was still not completed when spring came again. Shreve was uneasy as he prepared for his usual keelboat voyage that spring of 1813. He was fairly certain that before he returned, his wife would give birth to their second child. He was also uneasy about the war. The Americans' plans had not worked out well thus far. Many Americans thought Canada would join in the conflict against Great Britain, but the Canadians seemed to have no such intentions. The United States had only a small standing army and navy, and had Great Britain not been involved in the Napoleonic Wars, events would most likely have gone even worse for the young United States than they did.

That summer, foreign trade for the United States almost ended as the British succeeded in blockading the harbors. It semed to Shreve upon his arrival in New Orleans that a curtain of gloom hung over the city. Many people feared that the cities on the east coast would soon fall and that their city would be next under attack. General Andrew Jackson had been sent to help protect New Orleans, but when he reached Natchez with his 2,500 Tennessee militiamen, the order had been canceled by the secretary of war. Jackson was told to disband his army, to demobilize the companies at Natchez without even returning them to their home area. The general was furious and refused to do this. He led his men home through the five hundred miles of wilderness, earning the nickname Old Hickory because he showed himself to be "as tough as hickory wood." His name was well known to the people around New Orleans. They were keenly disappointed that the Tennessee troops were not allowed to remain to support the United States troops—too few in number—stationed at Fort St. Philip, on the Mississippi a few miles below the city.

Had the Mississippi River been the only possible invasion route, the people of New Orleans might not have been so concerned. The river could be fortified well enough to stop an approach by boat. But, though it was evident that ships and boats would be used in the invasion, the English soldiers could arrive near the city by land, by the bayous and lesser rivers, or even by way of Lake Pontchartrain. The Spanish claimed both East and West Florida, but they were cooperating with the British in allowing them to use the region as a base of operations. The people of New Orleans had good reason to worry.

Shreve also continued to follow news of the *New Orleans*. It appeared to be doing well, with an estimated profit of around $20,000 (not considering cost of the steamboat or depreciation) for its first year of operation. He studied the posted figures for passenger and freight rates, set by the state of Louisiana in 1812.[3] From New Orleans to Louisville, the rate for heavy goods, which took up less space than lighter cargo items, was to be 4½¢ per pound. Lighter goods, such as cotton, were shipped at 6¢ per pound. The average charge per ton of cargo was $112. There were also set rates for passenger fares. Passage to Louisville from New Orleans was $125 per person, with half price for passage downriver, because the boat could travel at a greater rate of speed. Intermediate landings were listed and also had set rates posted. In his calculations, Shreve decided that it would definitely pay to provide good passenger accommodations. As for the little *Comet*, Daniel French would have to begin to think bigger—a twenty-five-ton vessel was far too small for profitable operation. The *New Orleans* was making money by carrying large amounts of freight and many passengers. Often there were as many as eighty people making the trip up to Natchez, at $25 per person.

With the hold of his keelboat filled with cotton and other domestic products since the usual cargo of imported sugar and other goods was unavailable, Shreve began the tedious voyage to Pittsburgh. There was just one event of interest as he ascended the rivers. He saw the *Comet* chugging along, making good speed going downriver toward Louisville. It was

3. Cramer, *The Navigator*, 31.

her second voyage. He did not linger in Pittsburgh any longer than necessary because of his concern about his wife, but he did see that the *Vesuvius* was nearly completed and that the *Aetna*'s hull was ready for painting. Measuring 160 feet, these steamboats were even larger than the *New
Orleans*, and they were designed to bear a burden of 480 tons.[4] Fulton
and his partners in the Ohio Steamboat Navigation Company must have
been very confident that the improvements made in the engines would
move these boats successfully up the rivers, for it was much publicized
that the *Vesuvius* was to specialize in the voyage between Natchez and
Louisville (or rather Shippingport, to avoid the Falls of the Ohio). The
Aetna, at least until another boat was in operation, was to run between
Pittsburgh and Louisville. There were rumors that a fourth boat was
about to be built, this time under the supervision of none other than Benjamin Henry Latrobe. Fulton was in a hurry to get the boats in operation
to corner the market above Natchez by getting there first, even though he
did not have exclusive privileges above Louisiana.

Shreve had hardly arrived in Brownsville when his new daughter, Rebecca Ann, was born in early October, 1813. He was also cheered at the
news of the victory on Lake Erie on September 10, 1813, by a small fleet
of warships under the command of Oliver Hazard Perry. This enabled
American ships to blockade the Detroit harbor, preventing the occupants
of the fort from receiving supplies. Fort Detroit was still held by General
William Hull and his British troops, assisted by the surviving members of
Tecumseh's warrior army. Commodore Perry was the hero of the West
that winter of 1813–1814, and the words on the banner of his flagship, the
Lawrence, DON'T GIVE UP THE SHIP! were repeated over and over. Perry
chose that motto in deference to the American hero of the Battle of the
Chesapeake three months before, James Lawrence, whose dying words
these were. Perry's victory seemed sweet revenge to western Americans.

Shreve could also be pleased about his own economic progress. On December 15, he paid off his debt to Adam and Rebecca Blair for his home.[5]
Then he met with Daniel French for a serious discussion about a steamboat to replace his keelboat, which was showing the effects of several difficult voyages. French did his best to sell Shreve on the idea of using the

4. Gould, *Fifty Years on the Mississippi*, 90.
5. Fayette County Land Records, Book K, 346–47, Fayette County Courthouse, Uniontown, Pa.

Comet, for its trial runs to and from Louisiville had demonstrated its ability to combat the currents, in French's opinion. But Shreve, with his first-hand knowledge of the Mississippi River currents and of the economic factors involved in the New Orleans trade, was adamant. So small a steamboat was not acceptable.

They began to discuss the construction of a larger boat. French did not want to attempt a boat as large as the Fulton steamboats, which both men were convinced would not be capable of the upriver Mississippi voyage, despite Fulton's expectations to the contrary. They settled on a design for another stern-wheeler, eighty feet long and with a burden of seventy-five tons.[6] This was smaller than Shreve's keelboat and would carry a lesser payload, but he felt he would be able to make at least two voyages per season with steam power as against one with the keelboat. French assured him that with a boat of that size there was no doubt of his engine's capabilities against the Mississippi currents. With three other investors, including another riverboat navigator, Israel Gregg of Bridgeport, they drew up plans. The boat would be built at the boatyards near the mouth of Dunlap Creek, in Bridgeport, just south of the creek. It would be named the *Enterprise,* and it was agreed that Shreve would be its first master on a New Orleans voyage.

Shreve had much on his mind in that winter of 1813–1814. There were moments when he questioned his business judgment in investing in the *Enterprise.* While French's engines seemed much better in terms of power potential than the Fulton steamboat engines, he was inclined to believe the high-pressure engines George Evans was building in Pittsburgh might be even better. Shreve had a family to care for now and could not afford to make bad investments at this point in his life. But in the past his judgment had always been sound, and for better or worse he had committed his money and his time to the *Enterprise.* He spent many days that winter at the boatyards, making sure that only good timbers went into the boat. It was being constructed more along the lines of a keelboat than a ship, in the way that western boatbuilders had learned to build rivercraft. Even so, he was concerned about how deep into the water the boat would ride, for the machinery was very heavy, adding to the expected freight load.

6. Hunter, *Steamboats on the Western Rivers,* 13.

He was also preoccupied with the war and, as a riverboatman, especially with the fate of New Orleans, which he hoped was being adequately defended. It was good to hear late in the winter that Detroit was back in American hands. The people of the West were once again grateful to Oliver Hazard Perry, who had made possible the blockade of Detroit.

All winter, Shreve worked on the *Enterprise*, hoping it would be ready for the New Orleans voyage in the spring. He learned that Robert Livingston had died in 1813, but the Fulton-Livingston concern, which by this time involved many members of the Livingston family, was more determined than ever to fight for its monopoly. There was no doubt that when Shreve did get to New Orleans with the *Enterprise*, his right to do business there and start back up the river with a load of freight would be challenged. What could he, a frontier man with no wealthy backers, do if the courts allowed the seizure of the *Enterprise*? What would he do if he arrived in New Orleans and found that the city had been captured by the British?

But his worries about arriving in New Orleans by steamboat could be postponed. By February it was evident that the *Enterprise* would not be ready for a spring departure, and Shreve would not change his mind about the *Comet*. He prepared once more for a voyage in his keelboat.

The *Comet* duly embarked for New Orleans from Pittsburgh, and it became the second steamboat to make the two-thousand-mile voyage. When Shreve arrived in Pittsburgh, he saw that the *Vesuvius* was preparing for departure. The *Aetna* was well begun but would obviously not be coming down the rivers this season. To his surprise, he saw that Fulton's fourth boat for the inland rivers was also taking shape. This one, the *Buffalo*, was on a new cradle near the older boatyards but a short distance down the Monongahela where new machine shops were being constructed behind the cradle. When he had docked his keelboat, Shreve had confirmation of the rumors he had heard last fall that the man in charge of this fourth Fulton boat was Benjamin Henry Latrobe. Latrobe had reversed his thinking, apparently, since making an antisteamboat speech in 1803 before the American Philosophical Society of Philadelphia. In his address to the learned members he had set forth six objections to the use of the steam engine in boat propulsion.[7] Perhaps his close association with Roo-

7. Thomas Knox, *The Life of Robert Fulton and a History of Steam Navigation* (New York, 1890), 89.

sevelt and Fulton had changed his thinking in the ten subsequent years. Latrobe's steamboat was intended for the Louisville-to-Pittsburgh segment of the river, and it was somewhat smaller than the *Vesuvius* and the *Aetna* but designed by Fulton on lines similar to the other boats.

Shreve left Pittsburgh ahead of the *Vesuvius*. Later he learned that the new Fulton steamboat was pronounced ready for testing on April 22, 1814, and had made a short run up the Monongahela. It departed Pittsburgh on April 23, with most of the city's citizens assembled along the riverbanks to watch the embarkation, according to the Pittsburgh *National Intelligencer*.

> This morning the Steamboat *Vesuvius*, intended as a regular trader between New Orleans and the Falls of Ohio, left Pittsburgh. A considerable fresh in the river renders it probable that notwithstanding the great size & draft of the vessel she will pass the falls without difficulty, after which she will meet with no obstruction the rest of her passage. . . . The *Vesuvius*, which, with another boat of the same size & construction now building, is to form the 2nd link in this chain of navigation, is of 480 tons burthen, Carpenter's measurement. She has 160 feet keel, 28'-6" beam, & will when loaded draw from 5 to 6 feet of water. . . . In order to witness & ascertain her speed, I crossed the Allegheny, & mounting a very capital horse, I endeavored to keep pace with her along the road which skirts the river. But she moved so rapidly that after riding 3½ miles in 19 minutes I gave up the attempt.[8]

The big steamboat caught up with Shreve's keelboat and passed it. From his position atop the cargo box, holding to the end of the long rudder sweep, Shreve waved to the crew and pictured himself directing the operation of a steamboat of his own. His slow progress—in a keelboat it could take sixty days to go from Louisville to New Orleans even with the river currents to aid the boat's movement—would be transformed to the amazing speed of ten miles per hour or even better. It would be possible, with good luck, to make the whole Pittsburgh-to-New Orleans voyage in three weeks' time. His hopes for the success of the *Enterprise* built to a peak as he saw the masts and smokestack of the *Vesuvius* visible above the trees after the steamboat itself had disappeared around a bend.

As the keelboat entered the Mississippi River, Shreve kept expecting to see the *Comet* puffing its way up the river on a return to Pittsburgh. But he did not see the little steamboat until he was below Natchez. It was

8. Hamlin, *Benjamin Henry Latrobe*, 407–408.

tied at a landing, and the crew, including the captain, were busy working on the machinery. Shreve steered his keelboat over to the landing to see what the problem was. The machinery was giving the crew constant trouble, he learned, especially when it was put under extra load, such as when they had tried to ascend the river above Natchez. The captain, in fact, had already decided that he might as well give up after this trip. He had been approached by the owner of a cotton gin who wanted to buy the steam engine. That would be the end of the *Comet*. Shreve asked if the Fulton-Livingston company men had attempted to stop the steamboat. The captain looked upset. They had examined the *Comet* and decided, apparently, that it was too small to be considered competitive.

Shreve, assailed anew by doubts concerning his wisdom in investing in a steamboat built by French, took the time to learn where the points of weakness in the *Comet*'s machinery were. Then he continued his slow progress toward New Orleans. As he drew near the port city, he met the *Vesuvius* chugging and splashing its way upstream. Passengers waved to the keelboat crew from the deck, seeming to be in high spirits at being aboard for the *Vesuvius'* first scheduled upriver trip. Shreve turned to watch the huge boat move onward. Its progress was slow, and a lot of smoke came from its stacks. He wondered how far up the Mississippi it would be able to go and what its announced destination was. When he arrived in New Orleans, Shreve found out about the plans of the *Vesuvius*. The shipping-news column of the *Louisiana Gazette* for June 14, 1814, carried this item: "*Steam Boat Vesuvius*. The Steam Boat Vesuvius, will positively sail for Shippingport on Sunday the 26th June, unless a full freight should be previously obtained, and of which due notice will be given. All passengers determining to go in her, will please apply early, that suitable stores may be provided. For freight or passage, apply to the Captain on board, or to P. V. Ogden."

The fact that the *Comet* had not been seized in the New Orleans port did not lull him into thinking that he could bring a larger steam-powered craft into New Orleans and load it for an upriver trip unchallenged. Edward Livingston, now a leading attorney in the city and a powerful person politically, had probably been about as disturbed by the *Comet* as by a fly that he could brush from his sleeve. But it was almost certain that a more competitive vessel would be stopped. Shreve decided that when he returned with the *Enterprise*, as he fully intended to do, he should be prepared for legal action by Livingston, representing the Fulton-Livingston interests.

He gave consideration to the matter and then went to the office of a New Orleans attorney noted for his strong-mindedness and individuality, a man not likely to be too much under the influence of Edward Livingston. The man he chose was Abner L. Duncan. In Duncan's office, he made a deal. The two men accepted as a joint goal the success of a campaign to challenge the Fulton-Livingston monopoly, agreeing to fight it all the way to the Supreme Court if necessary, to prove such exclusive rights to be against the public interest. Shreve paid Duncan a retainer of $500, with a bond for $1,500 more to be paid at the successful termination of the suit that was almost certain to be filed. As the two men shook hands on parting, Shreve felt certain he had chosen the right man to represent him and promised that if it was humanly possible, he would return with the *Enterprise* before winter.

Patriotism as well as his business interests had entered into that decision. It was now certain that New Orleans would be under seige before long, and Shreve was impatient to aid his country in the war in the most useful way he could. He felt it to be his duty to return with military and other supplies to aid in defense of the city, for there was a desperate shortage of powder, lead, and guns. The uneasy citizenry had formed military units that were drilling regularly, and they were awaiting the arrival of General Andrew Jackson with his Tennessee volunteers to take charge of the city's defense. But even Old Hickory could do little without supplies.

After his earlier effort to take this same action had been canceled, Jackson was called to new responsibilities. In March of 1814, he demonstrated his military ability in a campaign to put down a Creek Indian uprising in the neighboring Mississippi Territory. Leading a force of two thousand volunteers, Jackson held back until Indian women and children had crossed the Tallapoosa River to safety and then attacked, wiping out eight hundred Indian warriors in the bloody Battle of Horseshoe Bend, in present-day Alabama. The federal government then commissioned Jackson a major general in the regular army and assigned him the responsibility of protection of the Gulf Coast, including the city of New Orleans and the area to the east recently acquired from Spain. While Shreve was in New Orleans, Jackson was near Mobile, not far from Pensacola, where the

British had their base. The people of New Orleans looked daily for news of Jackson's approach to their city, for there were rumors of a great fleet of British ships assembling for the attack.

Shreve felt the growing tension as he prepared to embark with his keelboat for his last upriver voyage under the old, slow, backbreaking methods. The local militia, of which Abner Duncan was a member, told him that war matériel of all kinds were needed, and that if he could get lead, explosives, guns, cannonballs, and other military supplies shipped downriver before the inevitable battle, the people of New Orleans would be grateful. As Shreve departed, it was with a promise to return as soon as possible with a load of war goods. He fervently hoped he would arrive under steam power.

The *New Orleans* had left the city a day or two ahead of Shreve with its usual load of passengers and freight bound for Natchez. It had departed on July 10, with Captain John De Hart as master. But as Shreve's keelboat reached a place two miles above Baton Rouge, he and his crew saw that the *New Orleans* was in deep trouble. The steamboat had stopped at the village of Baton Rouge, on the east bank of the Mississippi, landed some passengers and cargo, and departed late in the day to go two miles to "Mr. Clay's landing," a point on the opposite bank where she regularly took on wood. When the *New Orleans* tied up there, it was dark and raining. De Hart decided to remain docked for the night, planning a departure at dawn. While the crew members carried on the wood that Clay's slaves had cut and stacked to sell to the steamboat operators, the captain attended to some mechanical work. Early in the morning the boiler was fired up, and the *New Orleans* prepared to embark. The engines were started and the paddle wheels turned, but the boat would not move, other than to swing about. Despite the rain, the river had fallen several inches, and the captain concluded that the hull was lodged on a stump. No amount of pushing with poles would dislodge the big boat, but some experimental poking about down in the water determined that the *New Orleans* was indeed hung up on a stump, as the captain suspected. The firewood was taken off to lighten the load. But in the process of trying to free the boat, the planking gave way and water rushed into the hold. Hurriedly, the steamboat was pushed close enough to shore to let the passengers and their baggage be helped to the riverbank. Some of the cargo was also saved, but the *New Orleans* had made its last voyage. Thus ended the career of the first steamboat to ply the waters of any inland river, the boat that had weathered the earthquake on its maiden voyage.

But this was not the only tragedy that summer for the Fulton-Livingston interests, as Shreve found out a couple of weeks later. He and his crew had inched their way beyond Natchez when they encountered the *Vesuvius*. It was not damaged, but it was definitely stalled until such time as the river's waters should rise. Its hull was much too deep for the shifting sandbars of the Mississippi River, and its engine power too weak to control its progress against the currents. The widely advertised trip of the *Vesuvius*, on which it would "positively sail for Shippingport," had ended on a sandbar after making only 700 miles of the scheduled 1,500 miles of the upriver voyage.

This left the Fulton-Livingston group in a bind. The legislative agreements called for service on the rivers, and now, as of midsummer, 1814, there were no steamboats operating on the Mississippi or other inland rivers—unless the *Enterprise* had gone into operation on the upper Ohio. But the Fulton-Livingston interests were left without a single boat to take the place of the *New Orleans* for the rest of the summer and fall. The *Aetna* would not be ready until the spring of 1815. The *Buffalo* was far from ready. Costs had risen dramatically as the War of 1812 progressed, and the company was finding the cost of steamboat construction far above estimates.

There were new conflicts among the company's partners that summer. Latrobe and Fulton argued over what Fulton saw as the excessive costs to be paid for the construction of the *Buffalo*, and Latrobe was forced to resign. The work of completing the steamboat was turned over to Staudinger. Fulton cut off Latrobe's salary of two thousand dollars a year, knowing that the *Buffalo* was far enough along in its construction that Staudinger could easily complete it.[9]

Shreve arrived in Pittsburgh in September. The trip up the Ohio had been made in record time for two reasons: Shreve urged his men on because he needed to make arrangements to get back down the rivers with the munitions, and the water was low enough that poling could be used in many places where slower cordelling was usually necessary. He had seen

9. *Ibid.*, 405.

the *Enterprise* en route to Louisville with a load of freight, captained by Israel Gregg, another of the shareholders. Gregg reported that all was going well and that the steamboat could be turned over to Shreve as soon as the *Enterprise* got back to Bridgeport.

Before he left Pittsburgh to go on to Brownsville, Shreve saw a notice that had been published by Benjamin H. Latrobe under the date of September 1, 1814, from the office of the Ohio Steamboat Navigation Company. In it Latrobe set forth the expenditures on the *Buffalo*, which added up to an amount greatly in excess of the $24,250 he had been allowed. He had invested his personal earnings from steam engines and other projects to the amount of more than $5,000. The notice was to inform all concerned that he was ceasing operations immediately and was willing to put up his personal assets as security on any funds that might be forthcoming from a prospective investor. But no one had come to his rescue. The Fulton-Livingston group had suffered three blows in one short season.

Captain Shreve, hastening home to Brownsville to prepare for his first voyage as master of a steamboat, realized that the Fulton-Livingston group would be fighting for its life. His appearance with the *Enterprise* in New Orleans would not be ignored. He knew that he was in for a battle and was thankful he had had the foresight to enlist the aid of Abner L. Duncan.

7 / **Two Wars to Fight**

Shreve felt a touch of sadness as he directed the docking of the keelboat at the Brownsville wharf at the end of a return trip made in record time. This boat had served him well, and perhaps it would carry another master and crew on a few more short voyages before its planks gave way to the inevitable decay. He was saying farewell to some of his crew, too. A few would turn as he was doing to a new career on board a steamboat; for others, the rough life of the keelboatman was a mold too firmly set for change.

The *Enterprise* would arrive at Bridgeport in a week or two, and from then on there would then be no busier person in all of Pennsylvania than Shreve. He would have to familiarize himself with the vessel and its machinery—and make an improvement to avoid the problems the *Comet* had experienced—before stocking it with munitions at Pittsburgh. In the meantime he could spend some time relaxing with his wife and two young daughters.

The war had not been going well in recent months for the United States. Following Napoleon's defeat and abdication, Great Britain was concentrating on bringing the war in America to an end. In July, 1814,

114

British ships went up Chesapeake Bay and the Potomac to lay siege to the city of Washington, which fell in August. The news of the burning of the Capitol and the White House was only partially offset by the later news that Baltimore had held through a night of bombardment. The necessity of defending New Orleans seemed more urgent than ever.

It was several weeks before the *Enterprise* came chugging and clanging her way up the Monongahela to Bridgeport, where Daniel French and his mechanics waited to make sure she was in good condition before her maiden voyage to New Orleans. News of her approach spread fast through Brownsville, a little town of about seven hundred people in 1814. Shreve hurried down Front Street from his home to cross the chain bridge over Dunlap Creek to Bridgeport, a settlement almost as old as Brownsville but somewhat smaller in population, where French had his shops and wharfage. French had chosen the location so that his steam-engine works would be close to a nearby foundry.

French had generated much excitement when he arrived in town, for he had "big schemes of manufacturing, steamboat building, and navigating the western waters," according to local accounts. He told of his successes in the East with steamboats built under the patent granted him in 1809 and then proposed the formation of two companies that would, he asserted, put Bridgeport and Brownsville into the lead in the steam-engine and steamboat industries. The people considered him "quite a genius in his own way," and soon some of the most influential and wealthy citizens of both towns volunteered to be shareholders.[1] Two corporations were formed. One was for the steam-engine works; the other was the Monongahela and Ohio Steamboat Company, which would build and operate steamboats. Shreve purchased a one-fifth interest in the latter.

When the *Enterprise* was completed, it was tested against a strong current in the Monongahela in which it did three and a half miles per hour upriver and ten miles per hour downstream. It had been well broken in on the rivers most of the summer and fall. When it was back in Brownsville, Shreve insisted upon a thorough overhaul and checking, for he would not start out with so combustible a cargo until the steamboat was pronounced sound from stem to stern. He and Captain Gregg went over the craft carefully, and French's crew went to work to reinforce the hull and repair the

1. Brownsville Historical Society, *The Three Towns: A Sketch of Brownsville, Bridgeport, and West Brownsville* (1883; rpr. Brownsville, Pa., 1976), 51.

machinery. This gave Shreve an opportunity to learn the quirks and eccentricities of the steam-engine assembly.

He was impatient to get started. It was late November when the *Enterprise* finally embarked and steamed down the Monongahela to Pittsburgh for loading with munitions from the North Side Army Ordnance. Shreve was pleased to learn that three keelboats had embarked sometime previously, reportedly in September, each carrying war matériel for General Jackson. He was surprised to find that the keelboat captains planned to stop along the way for trading. To him, the urgency to reach New Orleans was so great that it irked him to be so late in starting. It was December 1 when the *Enterprise* embarked from Pittsburgh.

He made no more stops than were necessary to take on fuel, and given his knowledge of the rivers the *Enterprise* was able to travel at night when the weather was fair as well as in the daytime. His crew were seasoned riverboatmen chosen for their knowledge of the vagaries of the Ohio and the Mississippi and for their ability to adapt to handling the steam-powered craft. Some had been on the *Enterprise* under Captain Gregg; others were of Shreve's own crew. The boat's hull, built by the Brownsville boatbuilders, naturally followed the lines of the type of boat they were accustomed to building—the keelboat. They adapted the design to allow for the placement of the machinery in the hold and for the stern paddle wheel. The weight of the machinery caused the boat to ride somewhat deeper than the keelboats did, and Shreve felt fortunate that the waters had risen enough for quick passage over the Falls of the Ohio. He moved on from Louisville, thoroughly enjoying the speed of transit despite the urgency of his errand.

Not far below the mouth of the Ohio, the *Enterprise* passed the three keelboats traveling in convoy, the boats Shreve knew were carrying munitions. Apparently in no hurry, the men waved as the steamboat passed them, leaning on their setting poles.

Fourteen days after departure from Pittsburgh, the *Enterprise* arrived at New Orleans. The city was in a state of tension, for the British ships and land troops were indeed approaching. The *Enterprise* was worked in gently toward the landing and had scarcely been secured when a uniformed aide arrived with a message from General Jackson. The steamboat, its crew, and its master were all commandeered for military service, and martial law was to be in effect so long as hostilities continued. Shreve was to report to General Jackson at headquarters as soon as he had seen to the unloading of the military stores he carried. Army personnel would assist in their dispatch to the various locations of storage.

Shreve soon discovered that the *Enterprise* was the only steamboat in operation—the only one that Jackson could commandeer for expediting military missions, although one other was in port, the *Vesuvius*. But that ill-fated behemoth, only recently lifted from its sandbar trap above Natchez, had become hung up again. Whether because of the ignorance of the tidal fall in the New Orleans harbor or for some other navigational error, the *Vesuvius* was once again held captive. An old account says she "grounded a second time on the bature, where she lay until the first of March."[2] The batture is the alluvial land between a river at low-water stage and a levee; there the *Vesuvius* could be seen, useless.

The *Enterprise* was thus much in demand by General Jackson for work that it could do in facilitating movement of troops and munitions. Shreve made haste to report to the general at his headquarters at 106 Rue Royale, a three-story building one block away from the Place d'Armes. He found the general still showing the effects of recent bouts with dysentery, his complexion sallow and his body obviously thin under his blue jacket. Jackson's unruly shock of hair was grayer than his forty-seven years would lead one to expect. He was poring over a map on his desk as Shreve was admitted to the room. The bright blue of his eyes as he looked up came as a shock to Shreve, so penetrating were they. Jackson wasted no time on formalities. He spoke appreciatively of the arrival of the munitions and hoped that the *Enterprise* would prove more dependable than the *Vesuvius*. Shreve assured him that he would do his best to keep his steamboat operative. Jackson asked if he had seen the keelboats that were overdue in New Orleans. Shreve reported their whereabouts when he had seen them, and he was then ordered to take the *Enterprise* back up the river, relieve the keelboat captains of their cargo of munitions, and bring the supplies down to New Orleans posthaste.

As he left the headquarters building with his orders, Shreve saw Edward Livingston regarding him coolly. Livingston was wearing the insignia of a colonel. He had made sure he was on hand to meet Jackson when the general arrived in New Orleans on December 2. Offering his services,

2. Scharf, *History of St. Louis*, 1096.

he was immediately made an aide-de-camp to the general and given his official commission. He was at headquarters much of the time, helping to recruit men from the many and varied racial and ethnic groups that made up the population of the New Orleans area—Americans, French, Spanish, free blacks from Santo Domingo, plus peoples of mixed blood.

Out on Rue Royale, Shreve saw men he recognized as belonging to the Lafitte brothers' pirate colony at Barataria, southwest of the city. In 1808 Jean Lafitte had opened a blacksmith shop on Rue Royale, where some of his men fashioned iron grillwork and other iron items so much in demand in the city. It was a known fact, however, that this shop was far from being the real source of the prosperity so evident among the pirates of Barataria. Yet, as Shreve soon learned, the standing of the Lafittes in the city had recently undergone a change. Jean Lafitte had refused to cooperate with the British in their attack upon the port city, an act that had subsequently led General Jackson and other personages in New Orleans to accept him as a partner in the war effort. Had the Lafittes chosen to aid the British, the cause of the Americans might have been lost, for the pirates had many ships and men to assist whichever side they chose to aid.

Edward Livingston, who was the attorney for the Lafittes, had been influential in getting Jackson to see the advantages of accepting help from the pirates, despite the general's outspoken condemnation of piratical activities. Soon after Jackson's arrival in the city, he had talked with Jean Lafitte behind closed doors. Pierre Lafitte, who had been held prisoner in New Orleans for some time, was soon released from jail, and the general was assured of assistance in a naval assault against the British. The presence of many Baratarians in the city immediately became more open and evident.

Since their ships were held in port by the blockade, many sailors were lounging about. Some were engaging Shreve's men in conversation as he returned to the *Enterprise* to prepare to head upriver. The sailors were curious about this steamboat, which was different from the Fulton boats they had seen. Shreve could allow no tours of inspection at that time, however; he immediately gave orders for the boilers to be fired up and began a quick inspection of the machinery. The crew put on board all the firewood available, both to avoid later wood stops and to provide ballast for the upriver trip. When he was satisfied that everything was ready, Shreve ordered the cables released. The crew poled the boat away from the levee, and then, with a burst of heavy smoke and a shower of sparks, the *Enterprise* began to move under power. As the big stern paddle wheel started to turn and the boat moved against the current, the sailors watching from the levee cheered. Shreve was not quite ready to cheer; the upriver strength of the *Enterprise* had not been tested in the Mississippi. His concern over her engine strength increased as he reached the difficult currents at Natchez. But the boat was able to keep moving upstream, although it was obviously a strain on the engines. Fortunately, the keelboats were located just twelve miles above Natchez. Hastily a tow was arranged and the *Enterprise* moved steadily back down the river, like a mother duck with three ducklings.

The little convoy was back in New Orleans in six days from the time of embarkation, having gone 625 miles. Most of the time was consumed on the upriver voyage. Shreve was not too pleased with the performance, but General Jackson was intensely gratified. As the needed munitions were unloaded from the keelboats, Shreve noticed that the Place d'Armes was living up to its name, for it was alive with drilling troops.

Except for a few defectors who preferred British or Spanish rule to American, every man available was on duty, from the city itself and from the plantations for miles around. Slaves were brought in from the plantations to labor at throwing up breastworks in several locations and at moving heavy cannon to positions dictated by the general. The battalions that volunteered to assist in the defense of New Orleans included all the various social elements of the region—pirates, Creoles, plantation owners, and city people; Spanish, French, Americans, and peoples of mixed blood. For once animosities were put aside, as each group followed the orders of General Jackson. Within the battalions, however, there was segregation by class and nationality. One battalion was made up of the free black men who lived at the edge of the city, refugees from Santo Domingo. Older men, rejected for active military duty, had formed emergency troops and were learning to care for the wounded and to fight the fires so likely to break out in time of battle.

Jackson had several missions for the *Enterprise*—mainly to transport troops and supplies to the various entrenchments, several of which were along navigable waterways. An important one was Fort St. Philip, on the east bank of the Mississippi River about halfway between New Orleans and the river's mouth. Upon his arrival, Jackson had gone down to the fort and found it in need of much work to make it an effective blockade to the approach of British ships via the Mississippi. Shreve took men and munitions to Fort St. Philip and to other points the general ordered strengthened. There was no way to be sure which of several routes would be used in the attack. The British could approach from nearly any point of the compass because of the lakes, bayous, rivers, and man-made canals of the area.

Jackson was cheered by the arrival of his lifelong friend, Brigadier General John Coffee, from Tennessee, with his cavalry and followed by a division of three thousand Tennessee volunteers led by another old friend, Major General Billy Carroll. It was well that these men arrived, for on December 23 there was a report of an attack coming from the east via Lake Borgne and a series of canals, bringing the attackers to a point just downriver from New Orleans. Despite Jackson's precautions to cover all possible approaches, they had slipped through and taken over the plantation of Major General Jacques de Villeré, commandant of the Louisiana militia. The Villeré plantation was the farthest downriver of a series of plantations below the city on the left bank. It was bounded at its downriver extreme by a bayou, with a great cypress swamp beyond. The British forces had managed by dint of great perseverance to go through the swamp to the bayou to attack.

The news reached Jackson at two in the afternoon. According to an old account, he was lying on the sofa since he was still not well. But when he heard the news, he leaped to his feet and pounded on the table, crying out, "By the Eternal, they shall not sleep on our soil!"[3] Two hours later he was on horseback, leading his troops. Two miles from the Villeré plantation they halted, overtaken by darkness.

Simultaneously, the schooner *Carolina* went down the river to a point opposite the Villeré plantation and fired at the British in a diversionary action. Jackson's forces then attacked, closing in from several directions. The battle that followed was fought in darkness, and though the Americans eventually were forced to withdraw, it served to make impractical the British plans to advance to New Orleans the next day. The Americans set up a new defense line at Rodriguez Canal, the boundary line between the Macarty and Chalmette plantations, north of the Villeré lands. Jackson took over the Macarty plantation house as field headquarters.

3. J. Fred Roush, *Chalmette National Historical Park* (Washington, D.C., 1958), 20.

Now the danger to the people of New Orleans was all too real. A group of men went to Shreve while he was working over the machinery of the *Enterprise* between missions. They feared for the lives of their women and children, they said, but since the general had requisitioned and appropriated all horses and wagons, they had no means of transporting them to safety. Would Shreve be willing to take the families to a place of safety about fifty miles up the river? Shreve replied that he was willing, but that he and his vessel were under the command of the general and that the committee should check with him. If Jackson agreed, he would take the people. The men departed to see the general and soon reported back. Jackson, busy with many concerns, had listened for only a moment to their request; he gave his consent and turned back to his problems.

With no other orders from the general, Shreve prepared to take the people upriver. The women and children and most of their baggage, including some precious items brought from their homes for safekeeping, were on board the *Enterprise* when a young aide came galloping up with orders for Shreve to report to Jackson. Shreve turned just a moment from checking the machinery. He told the aide that he was about to embark with the women and children as planned, and that he would report immediately upon his return. A look of distress came over the young officer's face. He dreaded the general's fury if he went back to headquarters with that reply. But Shreve proceeded to prepare for embarkation. The aide turned away to report back to Jackson that Shreve had refused to come.

The boat had a head of steam up and crewmen were releasing the cables when four riders galloped up to the landing. The young aide had been correct in his estimate of Jackson's reaction. Now, having experienced his commander's fury, he was not taking no for an answer. He had orders to arrest Shreve and take him back to the general. Shreve had no choice. He stomped away with the soldiers, just as angry as Jackson, calling back orders to his crew to keep up steam and hold the people there— he would return shortly. James Parton's biography of Jackson, published in 1859, gave an account of what happened next.

> Little time elapsed before the enraged Captain stood in the presence of the General. The latter fiercely eyeing Captain Shreve, in a voice husky with intense passion, made the inquiry:
> "By ———, Captain Shreve, dare you disobey my orders?"
> "Yes, by ———, I dare," was the vehement reply of the undaunted Captain.

Jackson could not repress the expression of surprise which spread itself over his face at the unexpected reply of the daring Captain, and in a tone of voice considerably milder than his first inquiry bade Shreve explain his conduct. Upon the explanation given, Jackson dismissed him, simply saying that he had forgotten his promise to the citizens, whose wives and children Captain Shreve then had upon his vessel.[4]

Shreve strode back to the *Enterprise*. Without comment on what had transpired, he ordered his crew to prepare for embarkation. The passengers and their baggage were safely delivered to a plantation, there to remain until the danger was over.

On Christmas Day there was a sudden alarm along Rodriguez Canal, the boundary between the Macarty and Chalmette plantations. The men were working furiously, building breastworks along this grass-grown ditch no longer used as a millrace, for this was the line of defense that Jackson had selected. It was about two miles upriver from the British encampment at the Villeré plantation. The alarm came when a burst of fire was heard from the British forces. It proved to be not an attack but a welcome to a new commander-in-chief, Major General Sir Edwin Pakenham.

But there was no relaxing of the tension, for it was obvious that a battle was imminent. Every available American, black and white, was laboring at lengthening the defense lines, using logs and mud to build more protective walls. Holes were left in the mud-log fortifications to serve as cannon embrasures, and cotton bales were placed in these holes. But in a skirmish on New Year's Day it was learned that the cotton bales were a hindrance in time of battle, for they caught fire and smoldered, blinding the men with smoke. So they were removed.

Shreve was busy with missions for the *Enterprise* all that week. His most dangerous assignment came on January 3, 1815. Jackson called him to headquarters on that day. By then the general realized that the steamboat captain, although eighteen years younger than he, was a match for him in determination and in his demand for respect. As Jackson faced Shreve on that day, it was with an attitude of respect for Shreve's judgment rather than with his usual abrupt commands.

He said, "Captain Shreve, I realize that you are a man who will always

4. Caroline S. Pfaff, "Henry Miller Shreve: A Biography," *Louisiana Historical Quarterly*, X (1927), 201.

do what you undertake. Now tell me, could you get by the British batteries to take supplies down to Fort St. Philip?"

Shreve took a moment to consider what was involved. Then he replied, "If you will give me my own time."

"How much time?"

"Twenty-four hours."[5]

It took less. Shreve put his men to work immediately, suspending bales of cotton over the sides of the *Enterprise*, appropriating them from the many bales stacked on the levee awaiting the end of the shipping blockade. By means of iron hooks and cables, enough bales were put in place to give the wooden steamboat a chance of survival should it be fired upon. By four in the afternoon, this work was done and the supplies so urgently needed down at Fort St. Philip loaded on board. These "supplies" included a big (for its day) "thirty-two pounder" and ammunition for it. Each member of the crew realized that this mission could end in disaster for the *Enterprise*, but not one man refused to go.

When all was ready, the *Enterprise* moved to a point a few miles downriver before sunset to shorten as much as possible the distance that would be traveled under cover of darkness. Too tense to sleep, the men awaited the end of day and the coming of the fog that crept over New Orleans most nights at that time of year. They were instructed that only a minimum of sound must come from the steamboat, and so they made preparations to resort to the use of poles, as in keelboat days, for a part of the passage.

By midnight, the fog was a thick blanket over the river. Under light steam, the *Enterprise* left its mooring, the first steamboat to be employed in running a blockade. After only a short run, the paddle wheel was stopped. No light was allowed on board as the boat drifted on down the Mississippi, helped along only by carefully placed poles. Shreve had memorized the navigational hazards and the course he must follow. The British encampment was just above the English Turn, a bend that called for careful navigation. The men scarcely dared breathe as the *Enterprise* passed the guns directed at them. They blessed the fog that muffled sight and sound, and after minutes that seemed more like hours, they realized they had passed the point of greatest danger undetected.

5. [Treat (?)], "Henry Miller Shreve," 166–67.

A few miles farther downriver the paddle wheel was turning again at full speed. Dawn found the *Enterprise* safely at Fort St. Philip, where there was still a strong possibility of impending attack. The supplies brought by the boat made a major difference in the outlook for the men stationed there, so cut off from the main defenses. The commander expressed gratitude and admiration for the courage of the steamboat's crew in running the blockade to bring relief to them.

With the cargo safely delivered, the crew of the *Enterprise*, with the exception of watch details, rested during the daylight hours. When night came and the fog once more descended, Shreve was ready for the return passage. Since it would be against the currents, steam power would have to be used all the way, even past the British guns. There would be no chance of getting through that passage in silence. The cotton bulwarks might yet be needed. But whatever happened on this return, the assignment had been completed.

He ordered the embarkation, planning on full steam ahead when the real danger zone was reached. There was no way that a steamboat of the early vintage could avoid being heard, and with full steam ahead even the fog might not blot out the sight. So in the darkest hours of the night the guards manning the British long guns heard the clatter of the engines and the groan and splash of the *Enterprise*'s paddle wheel and dimly could see shooting tongues of flame. But steam power and the rate of progress upriver were so new and unfamiliar to the gunners that they could not gauge their firing well. The boat moved rapidly enough that only a few shots struck the bales near the stern and others fell harmlessly into the river. Morning saw the steamboat and all her crew safely back at New Orleans.

As Shreve left the *Enterprise* to report to General Jackson on his successful mission, he saw a group of flatboats tied at the levee. He soon learned that while he was down at Fort St. Philip, on January 4, this flotilla of flatboats had arrived bringing an additional 2,300 Kentuckians, who arrived looking "ill-clothed, ill-fed, dirty and unkempt."[6] But so welcome were they that households had been ransacked to find clothing and blankets for them, and they had been sumptuously fed. It was a little more difficult to find enough rifles for them, for only seven hundred had

6. Samuel Carter III, *Blaze of Glory: The Fight for New Orleans 1814–1815* (New York, 1971), 238.

firearms. Guns were ordered released from an arsenal in the city that the mayor had stocked in case of a slave insurrection. The Kentuckians had already left New Orleans to move to an encampment on Jackson's secondary line of defense when Shreve saw their deserted flatboats.

Jackson was surprised that Shreve appeared at his headquarters so soon. When he learned of the mission's success, he shook Shreve's hand in congratulation. He was impressed with the young man's skill and courage in handling the errand to Fort St. Philip. But he had no more missions for the *Enterprise*, for all attention was now focused on the impending battle, with the various battalions as well supplied and positioned as possible. Knowing that the help of every able-bodied man was needed and feeling a bit useless on board the *Enterprise*, Shreve returned to Jackson on January 7 to ask permission to join the ranks of men ready to face fire. He was assigned to a battery and stationed at a long twenty-four-pounder.[7]

General Jackson was awake long before the mist-ridden dawn of January 8. So were many of his men, for at 2 A.M. word had come from those on watch that the British were launching barges. At five o'clock the fog was very heavy, but not too thick to prevent the sentries from seeing rockets flaring over the British encampment. The enemy troops were advancing. Drums rolled out the call to arms in the American camps. The time for battle was at hand.

In numbers, the British were slightly superior to the Americans, for General Pakenham had over eight thousand men and Jackson about six thousand or perhaps somewhat more. In appearance and training, the British were unquestionably superior. Jackson's men were an oddly assorted lot in a variety of uniforms and nonuniforms. The best trained by military standards were the men of the Fourth and Seventh U.S. Infantry and a detachment of U.S. Marines. There were Coffee's Tennessee Mounted Infantry and foot soldiers from both Tennessee and Kentucky, with most of the men on foot in their frontier buckskins. The free black men from Santo Domingo furnished two battalions, and there was a company of Choctaw Indians. Cavalry troops had come from Mississippi to add to the other mounted troops, who were principally from Louisiana. There were the well-uniformed militiamen of New Orleans, composed in large part of leading citizens, and there were the pirates of Barataria.

7. [Treat (?)], "Henry Miller Shreve," 167.

Shreve took his place with Humphrey's men, seventy feet from the riverbank and charged with guarding the road that paralleled the river just inside the levee. This company was part of General Thomas Beale's command, so placed as to meet the main lines along the Rodriguez Canal at a point vital to defense from land and water attack. Soon British and Americans were engaged in man-to-man fighting, and it appeared for a moment that British Colonel Robert Rennie was about to take over the redoubt at the junction of the lines. He called out to the "Yankee rascals" to cease firing as he mounted the breastwork. Rifle fire cut him down and the tide turned. Shreve, from his position, saw many of the British fall, shot down as they tried to climb the breastworks, the mud rampart that the Americans had built.

In a few hours the Battle of New Orleans was over. The American line had held on the east side of the Mississippi, though across the river the Americans had not fared well. But the victory on the west bank did the British little good, for their losses on the east bank were appalling. The official estimate was 2,600 British killed, wounded, or missing. The defenders of the line at Rodriguez Canal had only seven men killed and six wounded.[8]

After that day, there was almost no fighting except for the bombardment of Fort St. Philip by a small British fleet. The troops in the fort could not reach the attackers on the river with their guns, but they were able to hold the fort, partly due to the reinforcements brought them on January 4 on the *Enterprise*. Shreve took more supplies down to an agreed place just above the fort on January 16. The most important cargo on this trip was a supply of fuses for the thirteen-inch mortars. Enabled to use these guns, the men of Fort St. Philip could reach the British ships with their fire. Withdrawal of the ships came on January 18.

On the next day General Jackson was informed that the British had given up the attempt against New Orleans, and reports came soon afterward that they were renewing hostilities at Mobile Bay. Fort Bowyer, located on the bay, surrendered on February 11. On February 13 came belated but momentous news that had taken almost two months to cross the seas from Europe. The Treaty of Ghent officially ending the War of 1812 had been signed weeks earlier, on December 24.

8. Roush, *Chalmette*, 40.

In the meantime, Shreve had been back at the helm of the *Enterprise*, still under Jackson's command, moving troops, transporting cannons from one place to another, taking the fuses as close to Fort St. Philip as the *Enterprise* could go and stay clear of the British fleet, and keeping the steamboat ready for any other mission the general might order. When peace came, there were still many services in which the *Enterprise* was useful. The *Vesuvius* still lay hung up on the batture, so it was Shreve who was assigned the mission of taking British prisoners down to the gulf for release and exchange for Americans. Then Jackson sent the young captain and his steamboat with troops returning up the Red River to their station at Fort St. Denis, near Natchitoches.

Thus the *Enterprise* was the first steamboat to enter that river, which, 1,300 miles in length, is a major tributary of the Mississippi. Rising in the Texas Panhandle near the border of New Mexico, the Red River forms the southern boundary of Oklahoma and then cuts across the southwestern corner of Arkansas before entering Louisiana. It cuts a diagonal line from the northwestern corner of Louisiana to the Mississippi River at a point about halfway between Baton Rouge and Natchez, its mouth being 244 miles by river above New Orleans. To take troops on the steamboat to Natchitoches, about in the center of Louisiana, was no easy task.

On entering the Red River, Shreve found much driftwood, and when he reached Natchitoches, he saw an unforgettable sight—the greatest mass of driftwood he had ever seen. This was the foot of the natural phenomenon known as the Great Raft. It blocked upriver navigation except by very small boats for the rest of the river's length. For as long as there had been trees growing along the mudbanks of the upper Red River, flooding had torn whole trunks loose and washed them down the river. More driftwood piled against the first snags, especially just above Natchitoches, an old settlement—the oldest in Louisiana—that had grown up where the French had maintained a fort since Louis de St. Denis established one there in 1714. At that point, changes in the riverbed aided in stopping the downriver progress of the logs and limbs and whole trees that were carried down the muddy stream. For hundreds of years the wood had been accumulating, with occasional sections breaking loose at the foot to go farther down the river and break up.

When Shreve first laid eyes on the raft in 1815, it extended as far as he could see up the river and many, many miles beyond. There were narrow waterways and bayous along the edges through which small boats might be paddled, but to take the steamboat farther up the Red would be impossible. The Red River Raft went on and on, a long, long island made up of piles of huge "jackstraws" that had lain so long undisturbed that some of the wood had rotted and sprouted vegetation.

In addition to his mission up the Red, there were nine trips to Natchez and back. By the time martial law was finally lifted on March 12 (about the time the *Vesuvius* floated free), Shreve and his commander, Andrew Jackson, had become well acquainted. Each man respected the other, and an enduring friendship developed despite the age difference between them. When Jackson sought election to the presidency in 1824, he had no more staunch supporter than Shreve, by that time himself a man of influence.

A news item that appeared on July 1, 1815, in *Niles' Weekly Register*, the national news bulletin published in Baltimore on "South st. next door to the Merchants' Coffee House," provides a summary of how the *Enterprise* served Jackson after the Battle of New Orleans.

> Brownsville, May 3.—By a letter from an officer of the steam boat ENTERPRIZE, of this place, we are informed that she was at Natchez on the 24th of March, having subsequent to the 14th of January made from New Orleans, five trips to the Balize [old name for one of the channels through the Mississippi delta], and one to the rapids of the Red River [at Alexandria]. Her last trip from New Orleans to Natchez, was made in *four* days, distance of *three hundred and thirteen miles*, against the strong current of the Mississippi, without the aid of sails, her rigging having been previously laid aside. She will make two more voyages between the last mentioned places, and then take her departure homewards.

With military duties ended, Shreve began to think of his return to Brownsville. He saw two hindrances to taking a load of freight up the rivers. One was the capability of the *Enterprise*. He knew her strengths and weaknesses well after all his military missions. There had been many times that the steamboat's engines were strained to move her against river currents, when he had been forced to contrive easier routes than the main channel. He needed the income from a paying cargo, but he had no wish to start upriver only to meet with a fate similar to the one the *Vesuvius* met when it lost the struggle against the tricky currents above Natchez. The navigation of that part of the Mississippi would demand careful planning.

The other hindrance was the Fulton-Livingston claim to exclusive rights of steamboat navigation. During the months of involvement in the defense of New Orleans, this consideration had been put aside. Edward Livingston and Shreve's attorney, Abner Duncan, were both serving as aides to General Jackson. Neither lawyer had distinguished himself during the actual battle on January 8. Abner Duncan had been in some disgrace through acting too hurriedly upon a rumor that the state legislature was about to surrender New Orleans to the British rather than fight. The rumor was not entirely unfounded, but the surrender Duncan reported did not take place, and the lawyer suffered some humiliation. As for Livingston, who had made himself so conspicuous when Jackson first arrived in the city, he contrived to plead illness, and on the day of battle was seen sitting on his balcony at home in his dressing gown.[9] When the smoke of battle cleared, Livingston once again made himself conspicuous; Shreve learned he was telling his friends that the *Enterprise* would be in for trouble should it defy the monopoly and attempt to leave with cargo or passengers.

Shreve discussed the situation with Duncan. What the attorney said made him thankful that he had had the foresight to enlist Duncan's aid. The lawyer told him that when word came that the *Enterprise* was on her way down the rivers, he had been contacted by Livingston, as had all the other lawyers of New Orleans. All but Duncan had agreed to join with Livingston in helping maintain the monopoly. Duncan refused, saying he had already agreed to represent Shreve. Livingston then offered Duncan three thousand dollars if he would remain silent.[10] Duncan's total fee from Shreve had been agreed upon as two thousand dollars, with the maximum contingent upon a successful defense. Duncan showed himself to be an honorable man in refusing the Livingston offer, and Shreve was most grateful for Duncan's loyalty. The two planned what action might be expected as the *Enterprise* was readied for departure and how Duncan would handle any eventuality.

The river was rising, but very slowly. When it had at last risen enough to free the *Vesuvius*, that steamboat began service between New Orleans and Natchez, replacing the sunken *New Orleans* without any problem.

9. Charles B. Brooks, *The Siege of New Orleans* (Seattle, 1961), 271.
10. [Treat (?)], "Henry Miller Shreve," 170.

But in the case of his own boat, it was not this segment of the river that worried Shreve. With his knowledge of the rivers, he was concerned about the waters above Natchez. He reasoned that if the rise in water level would continue into flood condition, he could find deep enough water away from the currents to take the steamboat up to the Ohio. Snows were melting in the north, feeding the Mississippi-Missouri-Ohio system, and there seemed to be a major flood coming. Shreve watched the high-water mark on the posts at the riverfront each day. More rains were predicted as April ended. He would wait a little longer rather than risk loss of the *Enterprise*, although he was more than anxious to go home.

As he waited, the newspapers carried a story of interest. Robert Fulton, working on his warship in New York for the United States government, had to take time out in January, 1815, to go to court in New Jersey as a witness for John R. Livingston in a suit over the legality of the monopoly. Fulton's errand was successful, but he became chilled while waiting in the damp hallways of the state capitol. En route to his home, he was riding the Hudson River ferry when it was caught in ice and detained several hours. Fulton stood in the icy winds, and when he reached home, he was ill with pneumonia. He went out against his doctor's advice to check the progress of his ship and became more ill. He died on February 24, 1815.

Now that both Robert Livingston and Fulton were dead, Shreve thought, perhaps the monopoly battle would not materialize. False hopes, Duncan told him. Edward Livingston, representing the estates of the men, would be no less determined. Furthermore, Livingston had enlisted the aid of John R. Grymes, considered by many to be the ablest attorney in New Orleans, to assist him in the prosecution.

On April 24, the new Fulton boat, the *Aetna*, arrived in New Orleans to end her maiden voyage. Her crew reported the rivers to be near flood stage above Natchez. Shreve purchased his cargo for Pittsburgh and proceeded to load it, at the same time advertising for passengers and other freight. He announced that embarkation would take place on May 6, 1815, with fare to Pittsburgh at $160.[11] On the morning of that day, as the crew was getting up steam preparatory to starting up the Mississippi, a deputy appeared with papers preventing the embarkation under the state law

11. Gould, *Fifty Years on the Mississippi*, 199.

that permitted only steamboats licensed by the Fulton-Livingston group to operate in Louisiana waters. Shreve was fully expecting this; he immediately contacted Duncan, who had bail ready. To Livingston's frustration, the *Enterprise* was on her way upriver before he could take another step to prevent the embarkation.

The Battle of New Orleans was over and won, and the War of 1812 concluded. But Shreve's other war was still in progress. His small victory on May 6, 1815, was only the first skirmish.

8 / **Triumph and Tragedy**

Henry Shreve was surprised at the enthusiasm with which he was received in Louisville. The people there saw his return on the *Enterprise* as an omen of great things to come, of their deliverance from the problems of inadequate transportation. His triumphant arrival at Louisville was on May 31, 1815, as master of the first steam-powered vessel to have ascended the Mississippi and Ohio rivers all the way from New Orleans. Having skirted the difficult passages by taking advantage of the flood situation, he had completed the voyage in twenty-five days. This was an amazement to people who were accustomed to a three-month time lapse between embarkation from New Orleans and arrival at Shippingport. The voyage of the *Enterprise* from New Orleans to Pittsburgh would take a total of only about thirty-six days. But it was not only the speed that cheered the people; in addition, the costs of bringing freight upriver would be reduced. In the July 1, 1815, issue of *Niles' Weekly Register* the editor enthused: "How do the rivers and canals of the old world dwindle into insignificance compared with this, and what a prospect of commerce is held out to the immense regions of the West by the means of these

132

boats. It is thought that the freight from New Orleans to Louisville (at the falls of the Ohio) will soon be reduced to $3.50 per hundred weight."

Shreve did not entirely share the enthusiasm. He was almost certain that had he been forced to come upriver at a time when he could not ride flooded fields and swamps, the *Enterprise* could not have made it. At the Falls of the Ohio, the boilers had been fired up to the limits of safe pressure, but the *Enterprise* could not make it over the rough passage on her own. Captain Joseph Swagger of Louisville recalled that passage some years later and told of it in an interview for the Louisville *Courier* in the 1880s. "There were quite a number of us watching her make the attempt," he recalled, "and when she failed we volunteered to warp her over. We sank the anchor at the head of the Falls and connected it by a two-inch cable, with the capstan on the front, and wound her over by hand."[1] Once over the falls, the *Enterprise* was docked at Louisville to unload freight and passengers at that city.

The citizens were not disturbed by any doubts about either the steamboat or its future, and Shreve said nothing to dampen their enthusiasm. They gave the young riverman a hero's welcome, for not only had he been the first to guide a steamboat the full upriver distance from New Orleans, but they had also had news of the role Shreve and the *Enterprise* had played in the Battle of New Orleans and of his daring stand against the wealthy easterners who sought to hold back steamboat progress. A public dinner was held, with toasts offered in praise of the young captain and in prediction of a great future for Louisville because of the coming of the steamboat. But Shreve was not ready to say that their hopes could be justified immediately, for his confidence in the *Enterprise* was limited. He did assure the people, however, that there would soon be better steamboats to replace this one. He did not announce his own plans, but he was ready to be the builder of that better steamboat.

In a few days, the *Enterprise* was en route again, making stops wherever freight was to be delivered. The bulk of the cargo was destined for Pittsburgh. With the *Enterprise* in ballast, Shreve was back in Brownsville-Bridgeport on June 26. The Brownsville *Telegraph* in its next issue carried this item:

1. Gould, *Fifty Years on the Mississippi*, 189.

Arrived at this port on Monday last the steamboat Enterprise, Shrieve, of Bridgeport, from New Orleans in ballast, having discharged her cargo at Pittsburgh.

She is the first steamboat that ever made the voyage to the mouth of the Mississippi and back. She made the trip from New Orleans to this port in fifty-four days, twenty days of which were employed in loading and unloading freight at the different towns on the Ohio and Mississippi. So she was only thirty-four days in actual service in making her voyage, which our readers will remember must be performed against powerful currents, and is upwards of 2,200 miles in length.

Shreve had been gone from home a long time—nearly eight months: He found that his third child and first son had arrived on April 8. The baby, named Hampden Zane Shreve, was not very robust, and the father's concern for this longed-for son was great. The little girls and Mary were well and glad to know that father and husband would be at home for some time to come.

For Shreve had determined that he would not leave on another voyage until he was master of his own steamboat, built to his plans and specifications. He had spent so much time and traveled so many miles on board the *Enterprise* that he was probably as experienced in steamboat operation as any man on the inland rivers. He knew what was needed, and he would build the type of vessel that would stand the best chance of being profitable to operate.

He turned the *Enterprise* over to his partners to put in the care of a new master. He also warned against sending the steamboat all the way to New Orleans because it was unlikely she would be able to repeat her feat of completing the round trip. The steamboat was turned over to Captain Daniel Worley. Unfortunately, the *Enterprise* was in operation only a few months longer, for she was wrecked at Rock Harbor, at the end of the Kentucky chute near Shippingport, a route that Cramer warned was passable only in high water. Thus ended the saga of the historic steamboat.

Soon Shreve met with his partners in the Monongahela and Ohio Steamboat Company to discuss his new plans. Another boat similar to the *Enterprise* was nearing completion at Bridgeport, the *Dispatch*, and his partners were disappointed that Shreve did not share their enthusiasm over it even though its machinery had been tested and found to operate as planned. The newspaper duly reported: "We are happy to learn she is likely to answer the most sanguine expectations of the ingenious Mr.

French, the engineer on whose plan she is constructed. It is expected when her works are in complete operation, she will pass through the water at the rate of nine miles an hour."

Shreve was not interested in taking over operation of the *Dispatch*, which was even smaller than the *Enterprise*. But he had been unable to convince his partners that a boat that could carry so small a payload was not likely to be able to compete with the big Fulton boats. Israel Gregg took the new steamboat down to New Orleans after first operating it on the Pittsburgh-to-Louisville route, going on the longer voyage when the upper rivers began to be blocked with ice. He arrived in New Orleans, according to old port registries, on February 13, 1816. He took on a cargo of sugar and molasses that he intended to take back up to the Ohio River ports. But Edward Livingston had no intention of allowing this. He had the marshal, with appropriate legal papers, on hand to force the unloading of the cargo. Gregg was ordered to leave the waters of Louisiana without cargo or passengers under threat of confiscation of the *Dispatch* should he defy the order. He was also told the steamboat would be confiscated if it reappeared in New Orleans.[2]

Niles' Weekly Register for June 1, 1816, reviewed the incident.

> *Steamboat navigation.* Mr. Livingston, of New-Orleans, under a law of the state of Louisiana, as the assignee of Fulton and Livingston's *exclusive right* to navigate the *Mississippi* and its *waters*, by *steam*, so far as respects the navigation from *New-Orleans* to and up the *Red river*, has prevented the steam-boat Despatch, of Pittsburgh, from taking a return cargo at New-Orleans, though, it appears, she is worked by machinery quite distinct from that used under the aforesaid patent. He has, however, *permitted* her to go out of the limits of the state without incurring a penalty. The procedure appears likely to create much sensation in the "western world."

When Shreve learned of Gregg's treatment, he realized that the Fulton-Livingston group were not yet convinced that they would have to make concessions because of popular opinion. Duncan wrote him of the outcome of his own case in the Inferior Court of Louisiana; the judgment had been in favor of free and open navigation of the rivers. Fulton-Livingston, represented by attorney John Grymes, immediately filed an appeal. Duncan was willing to continue as Shreve's attorney and was sure he could again win a favorable judgment. But Grymes and Livingston were power-

2. *Ibid.*, 143.

ful adversaries, with full knowledge of any and every possible legal ruse to employ. They also were politically eminent in New Orleans, influential despite popular opinion against the monopoly.

It was with full realization of the risks he was taking that Shreve prepared to begin construction of a steamboat of his own design, one that he believed would be practical and that he fully intended to use in the trade between New Orleans and Louisville. The expense involved was much more than he could cover alone. In proceeding he would need partners and consequently would be risking not only his own financial security but theirs also. It would be difficult to find partners willing not only to risk backing new, untested ideas in steamboat design, but also to invest despite the legal opposition sure to be encountered.

He did not underestimate the difficulties. His fellow members of the Monongahela and Ohio Steamboat Company looked at his drawings and listened to his explanations of the diagrams. Shreve wanted to build a steamboat such as none of them had ever seen. The hull, the machinery, the arrangement of passenger and freight space—everything was different. The men questioned every departure from accepted design and shook their heads in disbelief.

They had never seen steamboat machinery such as Shreve proposed to build. It was very different from the bulky assemblage on Fulton steamboats and even more compact than those French had designed. Shreve had decided to go to a truly high-pressure engine in order to provide sufficient power to move a large steamboat of high tonnage against the river currents with which he had so many years' experience. His engine would be similar to the Evans engines in the pressure produced, at least one hundred pounds per square inch, but different from them in several respects. The connections to the side paddle wheels would also be unique. The Shreve design used a "cam cutoff," which was expected to save three-fifths of the fuel. In French's engines, the cylinder took the vibration, whereas Shreve had so designed his engine that the vibration was "given to the pitman"—the *pitman* being a term used for a connecting rod to the cranks.[3]

Some writers report that this steamboat was to have four boilers, each equipped with a flue. Instead of being placed in the hold as in all earlier steamboats, they were to be placed upon the deck and set in pairs with a

---

3. [Treat (?)], "Henry Miller Shreve," 168.

tall stack rising from each pair. Although four boilers and the double stack are proven features of later boats built by Shreve and he is credited with these innovations, there is no proof that they were included in his first steamboat. There is agreement that Shreve's plan included at least two boilers equipped with flues and placed on the deck in horizontal position. Also confirmed is a horizontal positioning of the cylinder, said to be twenty-four inches in diameter with a six-foot stroke. The entire machinery unit would be of much less weight than either Fulton's or French's. Shreve's machinery was said to be only one-twentieth the weight of Fulton's.[4] This was possible because the heavy beam and flywheel of other steamboats were eliminated and because the cylinder for a high-pressure engine was of much smaller size and operated without a bulky condenser chamber.

To accommodate his machinery and allow room for passengers and freight, Shreve had also redesigned the hull, decks, and superstructure. The boat would be very large, capable of carrying a burden of four hundred tons. This size, the designer argued, would make the new boat highly competitive in freight and passenger service, unlike the little *Dispatch*. The hold would be used primarily for freight and decked over, with passenger accommodations built at a higher level. The passengers would thus ride above the machinery, in luxurious cabins with a view of the rivers.

It was this addition of a second deck that raised the eyebrows of the men of the Monongahela and Ohio Steamboat Company. The reaction was that the whole concept was outlandish and that the boat would be top-heavy and likely to tip over in a good stiff breeze. Patiently, Shreve explained that although the boat might appear top-heavy to the observer, in reality it was not, because of the concentration of weight in the lower sections. No breeze encountered in a river could possibly overturn it. It would ride like a waterbird, and what waterbird, with most of its bulk above the water, ever had trouble balancing itself? He further defended his hull design with the plea that a riverboat should not look like an oceangoing vessel but should be created expressly for the shallow-water conditions it would encounter. It should be patterned after a keelboat in this respect, designed to ride over many of the shallows of the rivers, and it should not be slope-sided, like an ocean-sailing ship.

4. Frederick Brent Read, *Up the Heights of Fame and Fortune and Routes Taken by the Climbers to Become Men of Mark* (Cincinnati, 1873), 73.

He chose to use side paddle wheels, believing that the pair of side wheels would give more power in combating the currents than the stern wheel used on French's *Enterprise*. The dimensions of the proposed steamboat would be about 140 feet in length and 25 feet in width. This would make it shorter than the *New Orleans* by about 8 feet and narrower by 7½ feet. Yet, Shreve's boat was estimated to be capable of carrying more tonnage—403 tons compared to 371 for the *New Orleans*.[5] The greater capacity was due to the increase of deck space through the superstructure.

But all of his explanations failed to convince Shreve's partners of the feasibility of his designs. They were not interested in investing hard cash in a steamboat that was so radical a departure from the boats already on the rivers. Tradition has it that all of Brownsville-Bridgeport was soon deriding the scheme, laughing about the top-heavy craft. But all the derision did not change Shreve's mind. He was convinced that his plans were sound, and if the Monongahela and Ohio Steamboat Company did not want to build the boat, he would sell his own shares and form a new company, a company made up of investors who could see the logic in his ideas.

He purchased a large building lot near his home on the opposite side of Front Street, probably for the purpose of having a construction and storage area.[6] This would be his home base for his new independent operation. But he could not go far in developing his engines or the boat itself without adequate financial backing. With a no-confidence vote from Brownsville, he would look elsewhere. His search took him to Wheeling, at that time in the state of Virginia, in the summer months of 1815. There Shreve talked to George White, owner of a boatyard on the bank of Wheeling Creek, near the site of old Fort Henry. George White did not laugh. He not only agreed to supervise the building of the unusual boat but also to take a one-fifth investment share. Another citizen of Wheeling named Noah Lane also bought shares in the new steamboat. These men were not only willing to invest but were enthusiastic about it. They wanted to name the boat for Andrew Jackson, who was an immensely popular national hero in the western states since the Battle of New Orleans. Shreve admitted to a liking and admiration for General Jackson,

5. Hunter, *Steamboats on the Western Rivers*, 77.
6. Fayette County Land Records, Book I, 381–82, Fayette County Courthouse, Uniontown, Pa.

but he insisted that his first steamboat would be named for his boyhood hero, George Washington. The *Washington* it would be.

Back in Brownsville, Shreve found that two of his old friends, also experienced boatbuilders, were willing to take a chance on his ideas. After all, everything Shreve had attempted so far had come out well. Perhaps those who were laughing now would someday be wishing they had stopped laughing long enough to recognize a real opportunity. The two who were willing to invest were Neal Gillespie and Robert Clark. With his own shares, Shreve now had the five-man company he sought. His partners had, however, taken the precaution to seek a legal opinion on the Livingston claims; they were advised the monopoly was not valid.[7]

Construction began in Wheeling with the laying of the keel on September 10, 1815. Woodsmen brought in timbers from the forests nearby for most of the framing, but George White also built into the *Washington* some of the aged timbers from old Fort Henry. After seeing the laying of the keel and making sure that White knew exactly how the *Washington* was to be built, Shreve saddled his horse and rode back over the road to the ferry at West Brownsville. Soon he was across the Monongahela and checking on the castings he needed to get his engine under construction.

Daniel French shared the skepticism of many other people about the safety of developing such high pressure as Shreve proposed for his boilers. His own engines developed forty or fifty pounds per square inch, and to him the doubling of that seemed risky. But Oliver Evans had demonstrated over and over in his steam-powered flour mills that the release valves made the engines safe and that the development of more power was a real advantage. He claimed that the amount of pressure built up was under control at all times.

As early as 1805, Oliver Evans had prepared a book on the subject of high-pressure steam engines titled *The Young Steam Engineer's Guide*. He explained (and demonstrated many times) how a cylindrical boiler with the "ends closed with half globes" could withstand pressure up to over a thousand pounds per square inch in a cylinder fifteen inches in diameter, with the amount of pressure allowable decreasing as the diameter of the boiler increased. The construction Evans recommended for boilers

7. "Washington Steamboat," in J. C. Comstock (ed.), *West Virginia Heritage Encyclopedia* (Richwood, W.Va., 1976), XXII, 4865–69.

was of "wrought iron sheets one quarter of an inch thick, thoroughly riveted together."[8] He claimed that these boilers would be safe and that if a weakness somewhere in the construction were to develop, the riveting would weaken first and allow the steam to escape gradually and harmlessly.

"Then we may safely conclude, and say, that it has been proved in practice that these boilers cannot be exploded to do any serious injury," Evans wrote.[9] Later, he was proven to be wrong, but at the time his arguments were convincing. Shreve was certain in his mind that he had no choice. The high-pressure engine was a necessity in order to enable a steamboat of commercial size to progress upstream against the unpredictable currents in several segments of the Mississippi River. His engine, however, was not a copy of Evans' engines but had been developed from his own ideas. Aware of the public concern over the safety of high-pressure engines, he was careful to include in his plans valves to release pressure automatically should it rise above a certain limit. He spent most of the time that winter of 1815–1816 in Brownsville working on the construction of his engines.

News about other steamboats served only to spur Shreve onward in his efforts to complete the *Washington*. One item was that the *Aetna*, Fulton-Livingston's third steamboat on the western rivers, which had arrived in New Orleans a week before Shreve left that port with the *Enterprise*, was the only steamboat in operation in the Natchez–New Orleans trade. The ill-fated *Vesuvius* had caught fire late in the summer, supposedly from the firebox of the boiler down in the hold. The flames consumed the boat to the waterline, destroying the valuable cargo as well as the steamboat. (The hull was later raised and rebuilt, the machinery repaired, and the *Vesuvius* put back into service until worn out in 1819.)[10]

The shippers of New Orleans were losing confidence in steamboats, and the *Aetna* paid the consequences. According to a letter of January 28, 1842, written by Captain Robinson De Hart, the *Aetna* spent the summer towing ships from the mouth of the Mississippi up to New Orleans. In the fall of 1815 the owners of the *Aetna* decided to attempt to repeat the feat

8. Gould, *Fifty Years on the Mississippi*, 151–52.
9. *Ibid.*, 152.
10. Dunbar, *A History of Travel in America*, 393.

of the *Enterprise* with their steamboat. They took on about two hundred tons of freight and booked a few passengers. "Above Natchez," De Hart recalled, "she had to depend upon driftwood, and occasionally lying by two or three days, at civilized settlements getting wood cut and hauled; broke a wrought water-wheel shaft near the mouth of the Ohio, and laid at Henderson nearly fifteen days trying to weld it, and at last had to end the passage to the falls with one wheel in sixty days."[11] But the *Aetna*, first Fulton boat to manage the upriver trip, made the necessary repairs at Louisville and then went downriver with three hundred tons of freight in seven days.

As for the *Buffalo*, others took over completion of the boat after Benjamin Latrobe was forced to give up through lack of funds. The architect and engineer went back to Washington, invited to draw up plans for the reconstruction of the Capitol, the White House, and other buildings damaged or destroyed in the War of 1812. He had seen the *Buffalo* well on her way to completion, with the hull launched in May of 1814, and when others took over the vessel under the sheriff's hammer, it was soon ready for operation on the run between Pittsburgh and Louisville. It was described as a "fine and uncommonly well built vessel of two hundred and eighty-five tons burden. . . . She has two cabins and four state-rooms for private families and will conveniently accommodate 160 passengers with beds."[12] There was also another steamboat, the *Harriet*, on the Fulton-Livingston stocks at Pittsburgh, intended principally as a freight carrier for the upper Ohio.

Nicholas Roosevelt had been granted a patent for the invention of the side paddle wheels on December 1, 1814. But he had about as much luck in making his patent hold and collecting royalties as he had had in getting satisfactory payment from Robert Fulton. Perhaps Roosevelt learned of the construction of the new side-wheeler at Wheeling the winter of 1815–1816, for he ran an advertisement in several newspapers early in 1816. In it he announced that he held the patent for the invention of "Vertical Wheels, as now generally used for Steam Boats throughout the United States," and that persons who wished to use such wheels would need to secure a license from him. Failure to do so would lead to prosecu-

11. Read, *Up the Heights of Fame and Fortune*, 72–73.
12. Gould, *Fifty Years on the Mississippi*, 104.

tion, he concluded.[13] But Shreve, who was building his steamboat with "vertical wheels," must have decided to proceed without applying for a license from Roosevelt. There is no record of his having made an application, nor is there record of a suit by Roosevelt against him or anyone else. Thus, Roosevelt, although he no doubt fumed and fussed, again was left with no more satisfaction than having had the legal right granted to him.

About the time that he was completing the building of the machinery for the *Washington*, Shreve decided to move his family from Brownsville to the vicinity of Louisville. There would no longer be anything to hold him in the Brownsville area, and it was likely that his big steamboat would be unable to come upriver farther than the Falls of the Ohio except in times of very high water. Therefore, he set out for Louisville to make preparations for moving his family to Kentucky.

He found a location for his new home just below the falls, at Portland, a mile or two below Shippingport. The plans under discussion for the eventual building of a canal to bypass the falls favored its running from Portland to Louisville, leaving Shippingport on a man-made island. Shreve decided that Portland would be the most desirable location for his family, since his steamboat would be at one end of its regular run there and he could spend time between voyages with his family. He had a house constructed for his wife, the two little girls, and his infant son. The move was made to Portland before or about the time of the completion of the new steamboat.

In the meantime, the people of Wheeling found the construction of the *Washington* at their town a fascinating subject for observation and conversation. No steamboat of any kind had been built there previously, and this boat was obviously quite different from the Fulton and French steamboats the people had seen in operation on the Ohio. Some took an attitude of skepticism and even ridicule as they saw the ungainly double-decked framing take shape. But others had great faith in Shreve, who was a hero to many of them. If the young captain believed in this awkward-looking steamboat, they would have confidence in it, too.

The women of Wheeling got together at their sewing club and made a flag for the *Washington*. On it, they embroidered the figure of a goddess

13. Dunbar, *A History of Travel in America*, 399–400.

lying on her side, holding in her right hand a trumpet and in her left an unfurled scroll. She represented Fame, they said. The ladies were whole-heartedly on Shreve's side in his battle against the Fulton-Livingston interests, which they realized was not yet won. The *Washington* was certain to head into trouble at New Orleans. In designing the banner, the ladies also had in mind the War of 1812 and its struggles; on the scroll they embroidered these words: OUR FRIENDS SHALL NOT WITHHOLD WHAT WE HAVE WRESTED FROM OUR ENEMIES. On the other side of the flag they had appliquéd the last words of James Lawrence, commander of the *Chesapeake* and hero of the War of 1812—DON'T GIVE UP THE SHIP. This phrase had become a watchword in the latter part of the war, and the ladies of Wheeling felt it was still a suitable motto for Shreve in his battle with the Fulton-Livingston interests. The women knew of how two vessels, the *Dispatch* and one other, had been forced to embark without cargo. Shreve assured the ladies that when the *Washington* returned, it would be with a paying load.

In the spring, he loaded all his machinery aboard a flatboat and took it down the Monongahela and Ohio rivers to Wheeling. As he superintended the assembly of the machinery and its installation in the *Washington*, afloat now near the mouth of Wheeling Creek, he had to put up with people who told him what was wrong with his boat and why the whole assembly was doomed to failure. But Shreve proceeded according to his plans. Each day the number of scoffers and jeerers and criers of doom increased, despite the loyal supporters who pointed out the merits of the odd-looking steamboat.

People were more inclined to look on in silence or even make an attempt at an expression of sympathy when they learned that down in Louisville Shreve's little son, not yet a year old, had died. Shreve did his best not to show his grief. As it turned out, little Hampden Zane Shreve was his only son.

On May 25, 1816, when the *Washington* was nearly ready for testing, a long article appeared in *Niles' Weekly Register* signed by Oliver Evans of Philadelphia. Evans' words were reassuring to Shreve, who undoubtedly had his moments of wondering at his own foolhardiness in risking his own and other people's money on an untried idea. Evans wrote, "I have ever been convinced that this principle [high pressure in steam engines] properly applied to propel boats, would render all other application useless, because the engine is much lighter, requiring only half the fuel, and finally be worth millions annually to my count." He went on to tell why he himself had not completed a boat he began at Pittsburgh in 1812: He had immediately become so involved in legal defense of his right to build such a boat and to operate it upon the inland waters "as to dry up all my resources so that I was forced to abandon my steam boat to the depredations of time and the weather which has destroyed it. Thus the good people were deprived of the benefits so much longer." He went on to question the right of government to grant monopolies that were against the public interest. Shreve was thoroughly in agreement and pleased to see the ideas on which he was staking so much put before the public.

That same week the *Washington* was ready for its first test under steam power. Everything worked as well as Shreve had hoped, and there were only minor adjustments to be made. Embarkation on her maiden voyage to New Orleans was posted for Monday afternoon, June 3.

The people of Wheeling turned out en masse to watch the departure of the steamboat they felt to be their own. With the ladies' banner streaming and black smoke pouring from the two stacks, the *Washington* headed down the Ohio. *Niles' Weekly Register* for July 20, 1816, carried an account of the embarkation reprinted from a St. Clairsville, Ohio, paper of June 6.

> On Monday evening last the steamboat *Washington* sailed from Wheeling for New Orleans under command of Captain Henry M. Shreve. She got underway about five o'clock and in forty-five minutes she made nine miles, since which time she has not been heard from.
>
> The steamboat *Washington* was built at Wheeling by George White; her keel was laid on the 10th of September last. In August all her timbers were growing in the woods. She is 148 feet in length. Her main cabin is 60 feet; she has three handsome private rooms besides a commodious bar room. She is furnished and equipped in a very superior style. Gentlemen from New York who have been on board of her assert that her accommodations exceed anything they have seen on the North river. She is owned by Messrs. Neal Gillespie and Robert Clark of Brownsville, Messrs. Noah Lane and George White of Wheeling, and Captain Shreve. Many who have seen and examined her pronounce her the finest steam vessel on the western waters. Her steam power is applied upon an entirely new principle, exceedingly simple and light. She has no balance wheel, and her whole engine possessing a power of one hundred horses, weighs only nine thousand pounds. It is the invention of Captain Shreve.

The light weight of the machinery was considered a major step forward. One early writer, Frederick Brent Read, contrasted the weight of the

Washington's engine to that of Fulton's engines and commented: "The alterations and improvements by Captain S. made the engine essentially a new machine; and in the course of a few years, no other model was used west of the Alleghanies. If Fulton's inventions entitle him to the great fame awarded by the world, why should not equal merit be accorded to Captain Shreve, whose improvements superseded all others more than fifty years ago?"[14]

There were twenty-one passengers aboard as the *Washington* started her downriver voyage. The evening of the next day she dropped anchor at Marietta, Ohio. Although the old accounts of what happened next are somewhat confusing, apparently the *Washington's* stop at Marietta was of longer duration than would be needed simply for loading and unloading of passengers and cargo. Perhaps Shreve had detected some mechanical function in need of checking or even a casting in need of replacement. But in any event the next move downriver was only about five miles, to a settlement on the Ohio side of the river known as Point Harmar. Apparently Shreve was not yet satisfied with the mechanical operation of the boat, for the boilers were allowed to cool down and an overnight stop made so that work could be done.

In the morning, the fires were again built and the water in the boilers heated. Steam pressure was up when the anchor was raised and the boat began to drift. The machinery was about to be engaged to start the turning of the paddle wheels when some difficulty arose. The river's current carried the *Washington* over toward the Virginia shore, out of the deep channel toward Muskingum Island's shallows. The crew and some of the passengers gathered on the rear boiler deck while the problem was being attended to.

All seemed to be in readiness, and the crew began to pull in the kedge, the light anchor used in warping, which had been thrown out to assist in getting the big vessel moved out to deeper waters where the paddle wheels could be set into motion once again. But just as the wheels were about to be put into action, one of the boilers burst. Scalding water and steam shot out at the crew and passengers gathered on the deck. Screams filled the air, and the force of the explosion threw several people overboard, Shreve among them. Some of the passengers jumped into the river for fear the whole boat was about to explode. Crew members hur-

14. Read, *Up the Heights of Fame and Fortune*, 73.

ried to shut down the engine and drop the anchor. Soon small boats arrived to rescue people from the river and to aid the victims of the steam and scalding water. News of the disaster spread quickly, and doctors and other people from Marietta came to help in the emergency. Injured people were cared for on board the *Washington*, for the steamboat was undamaged except in the boiler area.

Shreve, who had been knocked unconscious by the explosion, awoke to find himself in his bunk. His physical pain brought awareness of what had happened, and when he learned the full consequences of the disaster, his mental distress overshadowed the pain of his injuries. He was told that six passengers had died, mainly from breathing the scalding steam in the first moments after the explosion. The ship's carpenter and the cook had also been killed, and one deck hand had been lost in the river. The *Washington*'s engineer and Shreve had been injured, as had four passengers, one of whom died several days later.[15]

The days that followed the disaster were the most difficult in Shreve's life, a time when he must have often been tempted to give in to despair and discouragement. An added irritant, once he was up and about again, was the "I told you so's" from the criers of doom. Many assumed that the explosion would lay to rest forever the foolishness of using high-pressure engines on a steamboat and that Shreve would concede that he had been mistaken. The remarks may have had the opposite effect, kindling renewed determination in him to prove the soundness of his steamboat design.

At the first opportunity, he and his engineer carefully examined the mechanisms of the *Washington* to determine the cause of the tragic accident. Shreve was convinced that there was no reason for it to have happened if the machinery had been operating normally; safety valves were provided for just such a situation as a buildup of steam beyond the time when it was ready for release. They deduced that the problem must have been in the safety valves themselves, for all else had been functioning perfectly. These valves were brought into operation by the lowering of a weight at the end of an arm suspended from the valve head. The weight had failed to shift as it should have under extreme pressure, they discovered. Perhaps the tilting of the boat as it brushed the sandbar after it

15. James T. Lloyd, *Lloyd's Steamboat Directory and Disasters on the Western Rivers* (Cincinnati, 1856), 55–57.

had drifted shoreward had been responsible for the sticking of the valve. At any rate, Shreve saw how the apparatus could be altered to prevent that from ever happening again, an insurance against an explosion occurring unless someone deliberately blocked the release valve (something steamboat operators were later to do frequently, especially on boats with low-pressure engines, in attempts to build up more operating power).

Shreve resolved that there would never be another explosion on one of his steamboats. There never was. But records show there were many more steamboat explosions in subsequent years on other operators' steamboats, with the loss of more than a thousand lives by 1852. Carelessness was cited as the cause of more than 90 percent of boiler explosions.[16]

The horror of the explosion and its aftermath made this period a time of agony for Shreve. But when he was able to look at the situation more objectively, he could see that the principles upon which his machinery operated were sound because with the exception of that one safety valve, the mechanisms functioned as he had foreseen they would. He would not stop now, he decided, for he still felt that he could demonstrate that steamboats were practical for the inland rivers. Not to try again would have the effect of retarding economic progress in the West. Another consideration was the financial loss to his partners and to himself and his family. He moved the *Washington* down to Louisville to begin the work of putting the steamboat back into first-class condition.

Work proceeded, including the reconstruction of each of the safety valves and their testing. By August, 1816, Shreve knew that he and his steamboat were ready to try again. The *Washington* made test runs up the Ohio, but the water was too low for passage over the falls.

16. Scharf, *History of St. Louis*, 1109.

9 / **The Way Is Opened**

When the river began to rise in early September, Shreve advertised for passengers and freight. He could understand why no passengers applied, and much of the freight had to be underwritten at his own expense and risk. He realized that he would have to prove to people the efficiency of the craft, and he knew also that Edward Livingston would use whatever legal action was possible to delay the departure of the *Washington* from New Orleans with return freight. But he would not do as others had done and capitulate to the Fulton-Livingston demands, regardless of how long he had to remain in the port city.

On Tuesday, September 24, 1816, the *Washington* was piloted through the Falls of the Ohio and embarked for New Orleans. With her DON'T GIVE UP THE SHIP banner streaming in the breeze but without the enthusiastic crowd of well-wishers present at the first start, the steamboat began her downriver voyage. She moved along swiftly, free of any mechanical difficulties and aided by the currents. On Monday, October 7, less than two weeks from the day of passage over the falls, the *Washington* tied up at New Orleans.

In compliance with the law, Shreve took his manifest to the custom-house to file and pay his wharfage fees. He refused to pay the additional fee demanded by the Fulton-Livingston people. He returned to the *Washington* to find that a crowd had collected, some to admire this largest,

finest boat yet to appear in New Orleans and others to make less compli-
mentary remarks about its appearance. Pushing his way toward Shreve
was Edward Livingston, who obviously had just had a conducted tour of
the *Washington*.

Livingston's words to Shreve that day were noted at the time and have
often been repeated since. He said, "You deserve well of your country,
young man, but we shall be compelled to beat you if we can."[1]

Attorney Abner Duncan was wholehearted in his admiration of his client's vessel. He was also concerned, however, about the legal actions.
John Grymes had found what he believed to be violations of technicalities
in the proceedings of the court in the earlier trial, and it was on these that
he was basing his plea for hearings in the higher courts. There had been
postponements and delays. Meanwhile, Livingston was proceeding as if
he were on solid legal footing, demanding the exorbitant fees from each
and every steamboat operator arriving in New Orleans unlicensed by
Fulton-Livingston. The *Oliver Evans* (soon to be renamed the *Constitution*), built by Oliver's son George for some Pittsburgh investors, had arrived in New Orleans in April. It was compelled to depart without doing
business there—or anywhere else within the territorial waters of Louisiana. Again, the newspaper editors of inland America expressed indigna-
tion at interference with the progress of trade.

Shreve went ahead with the business of preparing to take on freight
and passengers for a return trip, but this was soon interrupted. Rumors of
an impending arrest of Shreve spread quickly in the little city. The levee
all along the waterfront from the markethouse at the east end of the
square to beyond the west end was nearly always crowded with people
marketing everything from fresh fish to tinware. This day they were hard
put to protect their wares from being stepped on by the curious crowd
that had collected to see Shreve's arrest—to see the resistance they
hoped the young boatman would make.

Shreve climbed the long slope of the levee to its crowded top and
pushed his way toward the gangplank to the *Washington*. The marshal
was waiting there for him with a seizure warrant for the steamboat and a
demand for bail. Shreve was prepared, having already consulted with
Duncan about this eventuality. Duncan had advised him to resist payment of bail but not of arrest. He was to allow himself to be taken off to

1. [Treat (?)], "Henry Miller Shreve," 168.

jail. Loud were the catcalls of the crowd, which was largely sympathetic to the young man who had become a hero in New Orleans at the time of his operation of the *Enterprise*. The marshal himself seemed a bit embarrassed at having to follow through with the arrest. Some of the people were so angered at what was happening that they were about to take violent action to aid Shreve, but he asked them to hold back, assuring them that he himself was not at all upset and that justice would win out.

The marshal had fully expected Shreve to comply with the request for bail and did not want to take him to jail. Instead, the marshal proposed, they should go to Livingston's office to talk the matter out. Livingston admonished Shreve that he was fighting a losing battle and dismissed him.

Shreve and Duncan immediately planned their next step. Duncan filed a countersuit, arranging for an almost immediate court hearing. He contended that the same amount demanded in bail—ten thousand dollars—was due Shreve from Livingston in damages for detention of the steamboat. A jury was impaneled and quickly reached a verdict in favor of Shreve.

No doubt Livingston fumed at this turn of events. He and John Grymes met to discuss the next step. As Shreve was taking on freight and passengers for his departure on the upriver voyage, they called him to their office. They had a proposal that they believed would be of mutual benefit. If Captain Shreve would "instruct his counsel to so shape the defense as to cause a verdict to be rendered against him" and place his *Washington* in the Fulton-Livingston line of steamboats, the company would in return reward him with a half interest in the company itself.[2]

Shreve was tempted. This could mean an end to his financial problems—which were becoming severe at this point before he had realized any profit on his steamboat. It would mean a comfortable living for his family and himself and an end to this war against the powerful Livingston group. He would no doubt become a wealthy man. But the monopoly would continue to stifle all independent efforts at opening the rivers to free navigation. As Frederick Brent Read put it in retrospect, "The issue was one of vast moment to the millions who received benefits of the free navigation of the Mississippi and its branches."[3]

"No, thank you, gentlemen," was the essence of Shreve's reply, given

2. *Ibid.*, 240.
3. Read, *Up the Heights of Fame and Fortune*, 76.

after thoughtful consideration. The offer was repeated, but he stayed with his decision. He had not gone into this long struggle solely for personal financial gain.

The *Washington* arrived back at Shippingport in November. Now the people were truly impressed. Even the most persistent doubters began to backtrack a little, conceding possible haste in their earlier judgments. The *Washington* had made the voyage to New Orleans and returned under normal river conditions, under steam power alone, demonstrating that it was indeed a practical means to carry on two-way, long-distance commerce.

Ice in the Ohio that unusually cold winter of 1816–1817 held the *Washington* at Shippingport until March. But this time, when Shreve advertised his next embarkation, he had a favorable response in freight shipments and in passenger listings. On March 3, 1817, the steamboat departed for New Orleans with a full load of cargo and at least a portion of her cabin space occupied. Nine days later, on March 12, the *Washington* docked at the port city.

Now the legal battle began in earnest. The court records tell the story of what happened. The suit, filed on March 22, 1817, was entitled *Heirs of Fulton and Livingston* v. *Henry M. Shreve*, and it was heard by Dominick A. Hall, judge of the United States District Court for the Louisiana District. The petition filed by Livingston and Grymes stated that in 1811 the Territory of Orleans had granted the Fulton-Livingston interests "the sole and exclusive right and privilege to build, construct, make, use, employ, and navigate all and every kind and species of boats, vessels, or watercraft which may be urged or impelled through the water by the force of fire or steam, in all creeks, rivers, bays and waters whatsoever in and within the jurisdiction of the said territory." Furthermore, the act had specified that anyone not properly authorized by the Fulton-Livingston group would not be allowed to operate a steam-powered vessel in the Territory and that for each violation the sum of five thousand dollars was to be forfeited, along with the steamboat itself. The petition went on to maintain that "one Henry M. Schreeve, a citizen and inhabitant of the state of Ohio, well knowing the premises and without being authorized properly . . . did on the seventh day of October, One Thousand Eight Hundred and Sixteen, use, employ, or navigate a boat or vessel called The Washington . . . on the river Mississippi within the limits and jurisdiction of the said late territory of Orleans, now state of Louisiana contrary to the true intent of the law before recited." Shreve was further accused of repeating his offense on March 12 and therefore being liable to a fine of ten thousand dollars plus his steamboat.

In the ten days between his arrival in port and the filing of the petition, Shreve had been taking on freight and listing passengers for a return to Shippingport. The prey was about to escape, Livingston saw, and so the court pursuit was hasty.

On the day the suit was filed, Shreve and Duncan consulted. Duncan, realizing that public opinion was on their side and that a bit of drama might help their case more than hinder it, advised his client to allow himself to be arrested by the marshal and this time to insist on being taken to jail and incarcerated. And so the marshal, protesting that actual impoundment was not necessary, took Shreve off to the jail upon the captain's insistence. The bystanders who had gathered to watch the excitement jeered at the officer assigned this unpleasant duty. Court records dated March 22, the day the suit was filed, show that the arrest took place, with bail set at ten thousand dollars.

But Shreve was released the next day.[4] A later entry (for April 10) in the court records suggests that he may not even have paid bail. At any rate, Duncan had again justified his fees, and on the following day, Monday, March 24, Shreve could board the *Washington*, which was loaded and ready for departure.

Extracts from his logbook for that return voyage were later published in the *Louisiana Gazette*.

> Monday, March 24, 1817, sailed from New Orleans to Louisville, Kentucky, at 5 P.M.
> March 25, spoke steamboat *Harriet*, at noon, 50 miles up the coast.
> March 29, arrived at Natchez at 2 P.M. (314 miles)
> Thursday, April 3, spoke a brig from Cincinnati by Cypress bend.
> Off Arkansas River, Sunday.
> Monday, 7th, off Chickasaw Bluffs at 5 P.M.
> Tuesday, 8th, spoke off Plum point, keel-boat *Western Trader*, bound for Nashville.
> Wednesday, 9th, spoke off Island 21, barge *Eliza Mary*, Captain Butler.

4. J. Fair Hardin, *Northwestern Louisiana: A History of the Watershed of the Red River, 1714–1937* (Louisville, 1937), 239–45.

Thursday, 10th, touched at New Madrid.
Friday, entered the Ohio. (1009 miles)
Saturday, touched at the mouth of Cumberland.
Monday, 14th touched at Henderson.
Thursday, 17th, off the mouth of Indian Creek at 8 P.M.; spoke the *Buffalo* for New Orleans.
Arrived at shipping port after a passage of 24 days.[5]

The era of the steamboat had arrived at last when the *Washington* came steaming toward Shippingport. To have made the upriver voyage in only twenty-four days attracted national attention and was considered a marvel as well as indisputable proof that the steamboat was now truly master of the Mississippi. "This was the trip that convinced the despairing public that steamboat navigation would succeed on Western waters," wrote E. W. Gould in his history of navigation on the Mississippi. *Lloyd's Steamboat Directory* (1856), in describing the *Washington's* successful navigation of the Mississippi and Ohio rivers, noted that "this feat . . . produced almost as much popular excitement and exultation in that region as the battle of New Orleans."[6]

And so a grand occasion was planned in celebration, held on April 23, the Wednesday following Shreve's arrival in Louisville. A Louisville newspaper of April 26 reported, "The citizens gave Captain Shreve a grand dinner on Wednesday at Union Hall in honor of the quick trip he made with the steamboat *Washington* from New Orleans at this port, in the unprecedented time of 24 days." There were many toasts and tributes, of course, and one was a letter read at the dinner and presented to Shreve as a memento of the occasion.

> Sir: The undersigned, in behalf of their fellow citizens of Louisville avail themselves of this occasion to express their sincere gratification of your speedy return to this place, and beg you to accept their congratulations at the very expeditious voyage you have performed from Louisville to New Orleans and back. While they view with the liveliest interest the revolution that the application of steam to the navigation of our rivers is effecting in the commercial relations of this country, they fully appreciate your exertions for the success of an undertaking once deemed by many to be of doubtful issue, but whose prac-

5. Comstock (ed.), New Orleans *Louisiana Gazette*, May 6, 1817, reprinted in "Washington Steamboat," 4867.
6. Gould, *Fifty Years on the Mississippi*, 105; Lloyd, *Lloyd's Steamboat Directory*, 45.

ticability they deem by you in particular to be established in certainty, and felicitate themselves in being the organ through which is made known the esteem in which your undertakings are held by their fellow citizens.

Levie Taylor
James A. Pearce.
Louisville, April 21, 1817.[7]

Then it was Shreve's turn to rise and respond. People noted his modesty in acknowledging their tributes, but they looked at each other in disbelief when they heard the young captain state that the trip from New Orleans to Louisville would some day be shortened to ten days. But that day came not many years later, and in 1853 a new record was set of four days and nine hours running time.[8]

When the banquet took place, Shreve was already preparing for another voyage to New Orleans. He was, of course, concerned about his court case, but he had confidence that it was in the hands of an excellent advocate. The *Washington*, this time with a full complement of freight and passengers, soon embarked for New Orleans.

Shreve was proud of the record time his steamboat made on that downriver trip. His pride added zest to the ad he placed in the *Louisiana Gazette* on May 6.[9]

FOR LOUISVILLE, Ken.
The Steam-Boat
Washington
CAPT. SHREVE

Arrived last evening after a passage of seven days from Louisville, being 6 days under way, having touched at Henderson for cargo, where she was detained a day and night. She will be ready to receive cargo, on Wednesday 7th, and will positively sail on Thursday 15th. For freight or passage apply to Messrs. Flower and Finley, or to the captain on board. Any person having freight on board will attend immediately to receive it.

A meeting with Abner Duncan was of first priority when the steamboat's business had been attended to. Duncan was jubilant. On April 21, two days before the festive banquet in Louisville in Shreve's honor, the

7. Reprinted in Comstock, "Washington Steamboat," 4866–4867.
8. Gould, *Fifty Years on the Mississippi*, 166.
9. Reprinted in Leonard V. Huber, *Advertisements of Lower Mississippi River Steamboats* (West Barrington, R.I., 1959), 3rd page (unpaginated).

case had been heard. This time it was permanently laid to rest, and the Fulton-Livingston group would no longer be an obstacle to Shreve. Judge Dominick Hall was undoubtedly aware of the protests by steamboat operators in the East who were plagued by the Fulton-Livingston monopoly and its exorbitant licensing fees in the state of New York. Controversies over the issue were constantly in the news, and public opinion was turning increasingly against the granting of monopolies restricting the use of anything so patently a public convenience as a river. But thus far the eastern judges had upheld the constitutionality of the monopoly when it was challenged in court. New York's Chief Justice James Kent, a supporter of states' rights, ruled in March, 1812, against a rival steamboat operator sued by Fulton, judging the monopoly not to be in contradiction to the Constitution. The landmark decision that Congress could regulate interstate trade was not made until 1824 in the case of *Gibbons* v. *Ogden*, a decision that carried with it the ruling that rivers on which interstate traffic was carried were not subject to regulation by any state.

It is likely that Judge Hall did not want to contradict the eminent James Kent, a highly respected jurist. But public opinion in Louisiana had swung to a point where it was much in favor of free use of the waters, and Hall would not find much approval except from Livingston and Grymes if he ruled in their favor. The court record suggests that he sought a way out of his dilemma and found it: "Monday, April 21st, 1817. The Court met according to adjournment. Present: The Honorable Dominick A. Hall. No. 1003 The Heirs of Fulton & Livingston, citizens of New York vs. Henry M. Shreve, citizen of Kentucky. It appearing after arguments of counsel and the examination of the record in the case, that the court has no jurisdiction of the same, it is therefore ordered, adjudged, and decreed that the petition of the Pltffs be dismissed with costs."[10]

Judge Hall's decision to get rid of the case on the grounds that neither party was a resident of Louisiana may have been dodging the issue, but the public interpreted the end of the litigation as a complete victory for the free navigation of the rivers. No doubt Livingston and Grymes sought ways of activating the suit again, and it is known that in 1818 they were attempting a suit against the steamboat *Constitution*. But about this same

10. Hardin, *Northwestern Louisiana*, 243.

time, the Fulton-Livingston group was also selling its vessels to other companies because of the overwhelming competition.

Shreve's steamboat *Washington* moved freely in and out of the port of New Orleans, and other steamboat owners also defied the Fulton-Livingston monopoly. The interpretation of Judge Hall's decision among the boatbuilders on the Ohio River was that it was tantamount to a decision overruling the legality of the monopoly. Steamboat building immediately took a great spurt, with several builders copying the *Washington's* design. Shreve was hailed as a great benefactor to the people of the inland states.

The nineteenth-century historians of the subject unanimously affirm that from the time of Judge Hall's dismissal of the charges against Shreve, the waters of Louisiana, as well as all the rest of the western rivers, were free and open to navigation by anyone who wished to "urge, impel, or drive through the water by the force of steam or fire any vessel," despite several additional, rather feeble efforts by the Fulton-Livingston heirs to uphold the monopoly.

With convincing evidence that a steamboat properly designed and equipped with powerful machinery could master the upriver currents, boatyards from Pittsburgh on down the rivers went into full operation. Throughout the steamboat age, most of the vessels were built along the Ohio between Henderson, Kentucky, and Pittsburgh. In this area, especially, there was a new burst of activity in each and every boatyard in 1817, and in 1818 production more than tripled the 1817 totals.[11]

The old Fulton-Livingston yards at Pittsburgh, however, were no longer occupied by the Ohio Steamboat Navigation Company. Troubles appear to have accumulated for all the Fulton-Livingston operations west of the Appalachians. The *Buffalo*, for example, was soon "sold at sheriff's sale, at Louisville for $800." The *James Monroe*, a small Fulton steamboat, was acquired by "a company at Bayou Sara, and run in the Natchez trade."

An issue of the *Louisiana Gazette* in 1818 carried this announcement: "The stockholders of the Natchez Steamboat Company met yesterday. The subscription to stock having been completed amounted to one hundred thousand dollars. The company in November last purchased the substantial steamboats New Orleans and Vesuvius and propose to keep

11. Fred Erving Dayton, *Steamboat Days* (New York, 1925), 336.

them engaged in the trade between this place and New Orleans. These boats were originally built under the sanction of the New york patentees, Messrs. Livingston and Fulton, and will possess whatever advantages may be derived from the establishment of their rights."[12]

It is doubtful that the Natchez Steamboat Company got a bargain. The *Vesuvius*, although she made a trip to Shippingport early that summer, was old and had gone through so many damaging accidents that her useful life was at an end. Thus, "on examination subsequent to the sale she was pronounced unfit for use, was libeled by her commander, and sold at public auction."[13] The *New Orleans*, built in 1817, was a replacement for the original boat of that name. This steamboat was in somewhat better condition than the *Vesuvius* but had the machinery of the original *New Orleans*. It served its new owners only until the next February, when it sunk for the second and last time. As for the rights that the buyers acquired, they meant little following the settlement of the suit against Shreve.

Perhaps the Natchez Steamboat Company stockholders were caught in the wave of enthusiasm that followed the runs of the *Washington* in the spring and summer of 1817. The wharf register at New Orleans, on which were entered the first arrivals of any new steamboat in that port, gives a graphic overview of the development of steamboating. In 1812, the *New Orleans* was the only entry, and in 1813 there were none. The year 1814 saw the arrival of the *Vesuvius* and the *Enterprise* (for some reason the *Comet's* appearance at the New Orleans levee was overlooked on this record). The *Aetna* was the only new steamboat in 1815, the year that Shreve was planning and beginning work on the construction of the *Washington*. In 1816, the *Washington* was the third steamboat to arrive at the port city, after the *Dispatch* (French's boat) and the *Zebulon M. Pike*. In 1817, the year of the *Washington's* repeated successes, six new steamboats arrived at New Orleans, including George Evans' *Constitution*. Another to arrive in 1817 was the steamboat that had brought so much distress to Benjamin Latrobe, the *Buffalo*.[14]

The year 1818 saw twelve new steamboats registered at New Orleans. According to E. W. Gould, "The steamboat ceased to be a novelty on the Mississippi in 1818 and became a recognized agent of the commerce of the

12. Gould, *Fifty Years on the Mississippi*, 231, 105.
13. *Ibid.*, 101.
14. *Ibid.*, 240–41.

valley." In 1819, seventeen new steamboats were registered in New Orleans. On May 6, 1820, the *Louisiana Advertiser*, listing the names and destinations, noted that there were twenty-three steamboats tied up at the port of New Orleans at that time. In addition, as Gould wrote, "The year succeeding the introduction of steamboats, 1817, New Orleans chronicled a large increase in its receipts of produce." The dollar value of "produce received at New Orleans from the interior" was $8,773,379 for 1816–1817. For 1818–1819 it almost doubled, reaching $16,771,711. In 1821, there were 287 steamboat arrivals at the port city as the boats made repeated trips throughout the season, bringing in a reported 54,120 tons of cargo.[15]

The sudden expansion of steamboat operation was not confined to the New Orleans trade. There were a number of new steamboats, and some older ones, plying the Ohio River between its many and growing settlements and even venturing up the small rivers to serve inland communities. The *Zebulon M. Pike*, a keelboat converted to steam power, is of special note. It had the distinction of being the first steamboat to make it to Louisville from farther downriver, arriving from Henderson, Kentucky. The *Pike* first docked at New Orleans on October 2, 1816, one week ahead of Shreve's arrival there for the first time with the *Washington*. Going back up the Mississippi, the *Pike*, which had a low-pressure engine, used a combination of keelboat methods of propulsion and its inadequate steam power. Later, using this same slow method, the *Pike* went up to St. Louis from Louisville under Captain Jacob Read, making it there on August 2, 1817. This was a day that went down in St. Louis history, for never before had a steamboat arrived at that city's riverfront. The *Pike*, running only in daylight hours, took six weeks to make the trip.[16]

The newspapers carried notices of other new ventures by steamboat owners. *Niles' Weekly Register* for December 12, 1818, announced one with particularly ambitious plans. "The new Steam-boat *Johnson*, built by Col. Johnson of Kentucky, passed Shawneetown the first of October—She is intended as a regular trader from Kentucky on the Mississippi and the Missouri, as far up as Yellow Stone River." This ambition, to go up the Missouri River to the Yellowstone (its confluence with the Missouri is in

15. *Ibid.*, 112, 204–207.
16. *Ibid.*, 102–103.

extreme northwestern North Dakota) was beyond any steamboat's demonstrated capability at that time. But there was under way in 1818 a United States government plan to take a fleet of steamboats up to the Yellowstone, a distance of 1,760 miles from St. Louis.[17]

All the news of steamboat capabilities, initiated by the success of the *Washington*, had influenced government and United States Army planners in their decision to substitute steamboats for keelboats in the "Yellowstone Expedition." This was a project intended to improve relations with the Indians who dwelt in the lands along the Missouri River and who were actively and destructively showing their resentment of the many fur-trading expeditions into lands they considered theirs. Indian interference with fur traders was a significant threat to the rapidly growing trading companies.

The plans for the Yellowstone Expedition were begun in 1815, when President Madison recommended the establishment of military posts in the northwest as a defense against British encroachment in fur-trading areas used by American companies during the War of 1812. The idea of improving relations with the Indians, and perhaps even securing their cooperation with American agents, was originally a secondary goal. In 1817 James Monroe succeeded to the presidency and continued the planning of the expedition, but now with solving the Indian problem as the main concern. The goal was to establish a military and trading post at the mouth of the Yellowstone River; when this was seen to be highly impractical or even impossible at the time, the projected fort or post was to be built on the Missouri River in central North Dakota. The name Yellowstone Expedition was retained and organized to start up the Missouri River from St. Louis in 1819, with Major Stephen H. Long in command. A fleet of five or six steamboats was to be constructed to transport men and supplies. The planners, based in Washington, D.C., were obviously in total ignorance of the difficulties a steamboat would face in attempting to navigate the muddy and unpredictable Missouri River.

At the time the plans were formulated, no steamboat had as yet ascended the Missouri River even a few miles. There was no absolute certainty that even a steamboat like the *Washington* would be capable of conquering that unruly river. But in the spring of 1819, a little flotilla of

17. Stanley Vestal, *Mountain Men* (Boston, 1937), 6.

steamboats, including the *Johnson*, was going down the Ohio and up the Mississippi to St. Louis.

One of them, the *Independence*, a small steamboat of only fifty tons burden, arrived with sufficient time to go on a trading voyage as a test run up the Missouri River to Franklin, the westernmost settlement in 1819. Franklin was newly settled, having originated as a shipping point for salt from the Boon's Lick springs, but it already had a newspaper, the *Missouri Intelligencer*. The issue of May 28, 1819, carried a feature story announcing the arrival of the *Independence*.

> With no ordinary sensation of pride and pleasure we announce this morning the arrival at this place of the elegant steamboat, *Independence*, Capt. Nelson, in seven sailing days, but thirteen from the time of her departure from St. Louis, with passengers and cargo of flour, whisky, sugar, nails, castings, etc., being the first steamboat that ever attempted to ascend the Missouri river. She was joyfully met by the inhabitants of Franklin, and saluted by the firing of cannon, which was returned by the Independence. The grand *desideratum*, the important *fact*, is now ascertained that steamboats can safely navigate the Missouri.

A week later, the steamboat *Expedition* also made the 220-mile voyage to Franklin. But Franklin, about halfway across the present state of Missouri, was far from the mouth of the Yellowstone. The *Independence* returned to St. Louis to await the rest of the flotilla before attempting the long-distance voyage. It was planned that another steamboat, the *Thomas Jefferson*, would lead the expedition because it was named for the man who had promoted the Louisiana Purchase. As the steamboats started into the Missouri River, the occasion was celebrated with "martial music, display of flags, and firing of cannon."[18] But the *Thomas Jefferson's* engines were not powerful enough for it to hold the lead. As it foundered, the *Expedition* and the *Independence* moved ahead. The ill-fated *Jefferson* plodded along as best it could until it struck a snag and and had the distinction of being the first steamboat to sink in the Missouri River. The *Calhoun*, the *Exchange*, and the *Johnson*, deep-hulled boats needing six feet of water for flotation, proved incapable of ascending the Missouri and dropped out at various points well below Franklin. The *Expedition*, a boat of 120 tons burden, continued a short distance above Franklin but then had to transfer its cargo and passengers to keelboats. The *Independence*

18. Gould, *Fifty Years on the Mississippi*, 115.

succeeded in ascending the Missouri to the great bend of the river, where Kansas City is now. At that time, the only sign of civilization in the area was Fort Osage, a military and trading post on a bluff above the south bank of the river, just below the bend. Fort Osage was the terminal point of the *Independence*'s upriver voyage.

The third and most successful of the Yellowstone Expedition's steamboats to ascend the Missouri River for an appreciable distance was the *Western Engineer*, a steamboat unique for all time. It was built under army supervision at an arsenal on the Allegheny River at Pittsburgh, from whence it headed for St. Louis amidst cheering and the firing of a twenty-two-boom salute from its guns, one boom for each of the twenty-two states of the union. Bringing Major Long himself, it was the last of the expedition's steamboats to arrive at St. Louis. It reached Franklin late in June, 1819, and was accompanied by even more excitement than the *Independence*. The *Western Engineer* was the only one of the 1819 steamboats able to go as far up the Missouri as Council Bluffs, where there was a new military post. This was the point at which the expedition's grandiose plans had to be abandoned because of the effects of the Panic of 1819.[19]

The *Western Engineer* was of a very special design. Its hull depth, high-pressure engine, and stern paddle wheel turned out to be just what was needed in Missouri River steamboats. But one problem with the high-pressure engine slowed progress on the river. Not using a condensing system, the engine drew a constantly new water supply into the boilers from the river; the *Western Engineer* had to make many stops along the way to allow the boilers to cool down so that they could be cleaned of the mud that was brought into them with the Missouri River water. The hull was quite flat-bottomed, drawing only nineteen inches of water. It was also copper-clad, an excellent protection against the many snags that made steamboat travel in the Missouri dangerous. It was about seventy-five feet in length and only thirteen in width. The type of stern paddle wheel on the *Western Engineer* proved most practical in Missouri River steamboats, which were usually smaller than Mississippi steamboats.

But it was its outward appearance that made the *Western Engineer* so memorable to all who saw it. The designers wanted to make this steam-

19. Robert G. Athearn, *Forts of the Upper Missouri* (Englewood, N.J., 1967), 5.

boat an object likely to inspire fear and awe among the Indians and arouse in them a respect for the white man, who was master of the boat. So the craft was designed to give it the appearance of a tail-lashing, puffing dragon, a denizen of the river such as had never before (and has never since) appeared. In June, 1819, a St. Louis newspaper described the *Western Engineer*.

> The bow of this vessel exhibits the form of a huge serpent, black and scaly, rising out of the water from under the boat, his head as high as the deck, darted forward, his mouth open, vomiting smoke and apparently carrying the boat on his back. From under the boat, at its stern, issues a stream of foaming water, dashing violently along. All the machinery is hid. Three small brass field pieces, mounted on wheel carriages, stand on the deck. The boat is ascending the rapid stream at the rate of 3 miles an hour. Neither wind or human hands are seen to help her; and to the eye of ignorance, the illusion is complete, that a monster of the deep carries her on his back, smoking with fatigue, and lashing the waves with violent exertion.
>
> Her equipment is at once calculated to attract and to awe the savage. Objects pleasing and terrifying are at once before him:—artillery; the flag of the republic; portraits of a white man and an Indian shaking hands; the calumet of peace; a sword; then the apparent monster with a painted vessel on his back, the sides gaping with port-holes, and bristling with guns. Taken altogether, and without intelligence of her composition and design, it would require a daring savage to approach and accost her with Hamlet's speech:
> "Be thou a spirit of health, or goblin damn'd,
> "Bring with thee airs from heaven, or blast from hell;
> "Be thy intents wicked or charitable,
> "Thou com'st in such a questionable shape,
> "That I will speak with thee—"[20]

To Shreve, who was largely responsible for the surge of confidence in the steamboat that led to such expansive efforts, the lyricism of the newspaper editors and the fantastic adaptations of his inventions must have been rather amazing. But he was not, in 1818 and 1819, sitting around reading the newspapers. He believed that the way had been opened for the steamboat age, but he was also working on new projects that would assure its continuance.

20. *Niles' Weekly Register*, July 24, 1819.

10 / **The Steamboat Era Established**

Captain Shreve kept the *Washington* busy carrying freight and passengers between Louisville and New Orleans for the remainder of the 1817 season, wasting no time in exultation over the acclaim of the public. As soon as profits warranted, he organized a company to finance the construction of another steamboat that would incorporate some of the improvements his active mind was constantly devising in both the power plant and the design of the steamboat itself. His double-decker design was now widely accepted and copied by other builders, and he had no trouble with derisive onlookers or doubtful potential investors. He was able in 1818 to build a large brick warehouse in Portland to facilitate the handling of his freight.[1]

That year saw boatbuilders more or less copying his designs at Pittsburgh, Wheeling, Cincinnati, Louisville, Henderson, Frankfort, and New

1. H. McMurtrie, *Sketches of Louisville* (Louisville, 1819), 165.

Albany. Shreve chose New Albany as the site for building his next steam-boat. It was in Indiana, almost directly across the Ohio River from his home in Portland (now part of Louisville). His partner in this venture, the building of the steamboat *Ohio*, was James C. Blair, probably a member of his wife's family.

The *Ohio*, begun in 1817 and completed early in 1818, was of 443 tons burden and thus was even larger than the *Washington*. In operating the *Washington*, Shreve found that certain portions of the fireboxes, because of the intense heat to which they were subjected, had to be replaced often. He devised an improvement for the *Ohio* and his later steamboats to lessen the heat exposure through the use of double flues and changes in the firebox construction. Old descriptions say the "boilers were supplied through the 'aftstands,' thereby further reducing fuel consumption, and also preventing those stands from being burned out every few months."[2]

Construction of a somewhat smaller steamboat, the *Napoleon*, with a burden of 322 tons, began at a boatyard on the south side of the river at Shippingport shortly after work started on the *Ohio*. For the *Napoleon*, Shreve had other investment partners, Louisville residents named Miller and Breckinridge. He was a busy man indeed, taking his *Washington* on as many voyages as could be squeezed into the remaining weeks of 1817 and going from one boatyard to the other between voyages to check on the progress of the two steamboats. As the spring of 1818 came, both were in the final stages of construction.

Shreve's new boats and others being built at this time were similar to the *Washington*. In them the hold was reserved for freight and for part of the machinery (although eastern steamboats continued to have their passenger accommodations in the hold, following Fulton's plan). On the main deck, the boilers and the fuel supply were just forward of the big paddle wheels, which Shreve had placed slightly aft of the boat's center. Sometimes behind these but more often aft on the upper deck was the ladies' cabin, designed with an open aisle and curtained-off sleeping bunks in two tiers along each side. The upper bunks, since ladies were not expected to climb into them, were reached by means of a staircase and platform built behind each row. All the center aisle space was needed for the complicated process of becoming clothed in the fashions of the

2. Dorsey, *Master of the Mississippi*, 133.

day. Washing facilities, at the end of the cabin, were crude even in the best of boats.

The men's cabin, forward on the deck, was larger, and since there were always more male passengers than female, the space in it was utilized to accommodate a maximum by having three tiers of bunks. Only the center tier could be entered easily. The men assigned to the bottom tier were at floor level and had almost to roll into their sleeping spaces. The passengers with top tier bunks had to climb up to them the best they could. There were crude washing facilities and small water closets. Passengers with foresight brought their own towels and toilet articles; those lacking in foresight or fastidiousness either did without or shared the articles hung near the pitcher and basin for common use. The meals were served in the center aisle of the gentlemen's cabin, and this assured that no man stayed abed to doze away the morning hours.

When the steward had the table prepared and had checked to see that all was in readiness, he sent a boy to announce to the ladies in their cabin that a meal was about to be served. The ladies filed in and took places at the table. After they were all seated, a bell was rung as a signal that the men also were at liberty to come to the table. The food was served family style, and often the person who held back out of politeness found himself facing empty bowls and platters. According to travelers' reports from those early steamboat days, conversation ran a poor second to the business of eating.

Between meals, many of the gentlemen patronized the barroom, which was at the forward end of the gentlemen's cabin. Tables were set up for the card games always in progress. In good weather, many hours could be whiled away by both ladies and gentlemen in watching the passing scenery, but other than that there was little for the ladies to do. They often felt uncomfortable outside the cabin. There were usually deck passengers on the steamboat, lounging about wherever there was space and not noted for their culture and gentlemanliness. These deck passengers earned part of their low-cost fare by assisting in loading the firewood on board whenever there was a wood stop.

Fares for cabin accommodations, including meals on board the steamboats, were published in *Niles' Weekly Register* for January 9, 1819, and they were typical of the time. Upriver passage was, of course, more expensive than passage downriver, since the voyage required more days on board. The passage from New Orleans to Natchez was $30. To go to the mouth of the Ohio, an intermediate point where some passengers changed to steamboats with other destinations, cost $95. To Shippingport from New Orleans was $125. One could go all the way downriver from Shippingport to New Orleans for $75. Children from two to ten years old traveled at half fare and those under two years at quarter fare. The fare for "way passengers" was figured at 12½ cents per mile up- or downriver. Servants were charged at the same half-fare rate as children.

Early in the steamboat era, settlers along the shores found that they could have a cash income by cutting wood from the forests and stacking it at the river's edge to sell to the steamboat operators. A cord of wood usually brought from two to three dollars. If the wood stop lacked a deep enough drop-off for the steamboat safely to move in close, the wood was stacked on a raft and moved to deeper water for loading onto the boat. By 1832, it was estimated there were almost as many men working as woodcutters as there were men on steamboat crews—4,400 woodcutters to 4,800 crewmen.[3]

Many of the steamboats, especially the more successful ones, were, like Shreve's, equipped with high-pressure steam engines. But this was not universally true of the new steamboats being constructed. The heavy, cumbersome low-pressure engines were less efficient, but in the minds of many people the term *high pressure* meant high likelihood of explosion. No doubt the explosion on the *Washington* early in her career contributed to this fear, and regardless of how many safe voyages she made, the fear persisted.

Less than a year after the *Washington's* accident, there was another spectacular explosion on a high-pressure steamboat, one constructed by George Evans but never operated by him. On June 7, 1817, *Niles' Weekly Register* carried a report of it.

> *Steamboats.* A steam boat called the Constitution (late the Oliver Evans) burst her boiler nearly opposite St. Francisville, on the Mississippi, by which every person in the cabin, 11 in number, at breakfast, were scalded to death.
> Such dreadful accidents may go so far to reduce the confidence of the people in these invaluable boats (under proper management) as to destroy a great part of their usefulness. Those who are conversant with the subject assert that such accidents always come out of carelessness. How sober and discreet ought they

3. Gould, *Fifty Years on the Mississippi*, 125.

to be who have charge of machinery capable of accomplishing such terrible mischief in a moment!

This accident took place on May 4, 1817, while the *Constitution* was ascending the Mississippi. In addition to those in the cabin who were scalded and died instantly, many died by drowning after jumping overboard. The final number of casualties was much larger than in the *Washington's* explosion: thirty lives were lost on the *Constitution* to ten on Shreve's boat.[4] No official statement of the accident's cause is available, but as the editor of the *Register* inferred, it may well have been sheer carelessness. This theory is supported by the observations of a passenger on the rebuilt *New Orleans*, a German traveler named J. G. Flugel, in his diary.

> May 4. At 7 o'clock this morning the steamboat "Washington" passed. Last year the boiler of this boat blew up near Marietta, doing great damage. . . . Just as I turned in the direction of the front door I perceived 1½ miles up stream a large white cloud, which seemed to me something unusual. It rose distinctly, as the blue horizon and the color of the Mississippi contrasted with the white cloud. About 1½ hours later, Mr. Stirling, a merchant from St. Francisville, crossed the river with several doctors to give relief to the distressed. I understand that the cylinder of the steamboat "Constitution" burst, scalding a number of passengers. They had to draw her by means of ropes to the shore. There is a continual crossing of the river all day to see the distressed. Eleven persons are dangerously scalded. Two of them were deprived of their senses. It is said that the Captain challenged the "Washington" to a race. A few minutes after he had challenged her the destruction took place. This evening eight of the sufferers were dead.[5]

On this date the *Washington* was nearing the end of her second downriver voyage in the spring of 1817, and she arrived at New Orleans the following day, having set a new record. Whether Shreve was aware of the fate of the *Constitution* or the racing challenge as he proceeded downriver is not recorded.

At this time and even earlier, Oliver Evans, by then in his sixties, was carrying on a writing campaign to educate people in the principles of steam-engine operation and to overcome the fear of high-pressure engines. He felt that this fear was unjustified and based upon a fallacy and

4. Scharf, *History of St. Louis*, 1108; Lloyd, *Lloyd's Steamboat Directory*, 55–57.
5. Quoted in Lyle Saxon, *Father Mississippi* (New York, 1927), 203.

that if the navigator did not abuse or become careless with the engines, there was little likelihood of an accident. The fallacy Evans perceived was the idea that the pressure in so-called low-pressure boilers was less likely to cause explosions. His contention was that there was more likelihood of an accident on a low-pressure steamboat than on one equipped with a high-pressure engine because the operators of the low-pressure engines often found the power production inadequate. Sometimes they made the safety valve ineffective by weighting it down and ran at pressure almost as high as that in engines intended for higher pressures. This frequently brought on explosions in steamboats with low-pressure engines.

Evans, a resident of Philadelphia, saw many of the eastern steamboat builders continuing to use the type of engine, with only minor changes, that Fulton had used. Some of these steamboats built along the east coast were taken by the coastal route to New Orleans to be put into service in the Mississippi River. Most of the western or inland boatbuilders used high-pressure engines, as Shreve did in all his boats. Oliver Evans felt very keenly about the continued rejection of the high-pressure engine in the East. One of his articles, appearing in *Niles' Weekly Register* for August 30, 1817, began: "*Safe Steamboats.*—Citizens attend! Surely the sum of death and misery, occasioned by the explosion of the boilers of steam engines on board of boats, is now enough to arrest your attention, if you ever intend to travel in steam boats. This discovery has recently been so openly attacked that the inventor is compelled to defend it."

He explained the principle on which his high-pressure engines, invented forty years earlier, operated, using far less fuel and being of much less weight than the low-pressure engines with condensers. "I have since gotten into operation seventy or eighty steam engines constructed on the eternal and immutable principles and laws of nature," he wrote. These engines were "so combined and arranged that it is nearly beyond the art of man, either by neglect, design, ignorance, or malice to explode them," he said, and he went on to claim that "no accident has ever happened with any of my engines to do injury." (This statement leaves unanswered the question of what happened to the *Constitution*, with its Evans-built engine likely to have been designed by Oliver Evans.)

Evans then told of the manner in which an accident could take place with no loss of life and minimal damage to a high-pressure steamboat. There would be, he said, a gradual loss of steam pressure through the weakest point of a boiler. He cited an accident on board a steamboat in which the steam escaped so harmlessly that the passengers were not even aware of the break except for noticing that the engines had lost their power. He highly recommended the "self acting safety valves" with which this steamboat was equipped and explained how the valves should be regulated for safe operation.

A low-pressure condensing engine could be extremely unsafe, he maintained, when the operator, to get more power, blocked the safety valve. In this situation, "with any other than a circular type of boiler [the type used only with high-pressure engines] he [the operator] can obtain no safety, because he cannot prevent the steam from rising in two or three minutes to a pressure that will explode his boiler, in case the valve be not lifted to let the steam escape." The boiler Evans recommended was fifteen inches in diameter with half-globe ends; it would hold 1,300 pounds of pressure per square inch of its inner surface area, he claimed. Larger diameters could not withstand as much pressure to the square inch. There was a much greater margin of safety in pressure in a high-pressure engine than in a low-pressure one, he argued, and hence a greater leeway in operation. At the end of his article, Evans offered five dollars to any newspaper publisher who would reprint his article and mail a copy to him, so anxious was he to convince the public of the safety of the high-pressure engine. Throughout the later years of his life (he died in 1819 at the age of sixty-three) he carried on his newspaper campaign.

Shreve needed no further convincing, although he used his own ideas in construction of his high-pressure steamboat engines. Many others were also convinced that high-pressure engines were necessary and that they could be operated safely, and before many years had passed, the high-pressure engine became standard.

There was one notable exception, and that was the largest steamboat of all built in this period, a time when bigger and bigger boats were being built for the Mississippi River. The colossus was the *United States*, of seven hundred tons burden and equipped with low-pressure engines. As might be expected, the huge boat was designed and built by eastern craftsmen, although the actual work was done at Jeffersonville, Indiana, in 1819. A New York shipbuilder named Vandusen had contracted to build the *United States* for a New Orleans owner. He ordered two Watt and Boulton engines for it, which came by sailing ship to New Orleans in 1820.

The engines were held at New Orleans while the hull was completed. The New York contractor made some of the same mistakes his fellow eastern boatbuilders made, using a deep hull design and making the boat too heavy in weight. "Her planking and timbers were of immense thickness, twenty inches of solid wall so as to make her snag proof," wrote E. W. Gould. When the hull was finished at Jeffersonville, it was worked down the rivers to New Orleans by "sweeps" to have the machinery installed. The port registry lists her first arrival in New Orleans on March 17, 1820, with Captain Samuel Hart as master. "She made several voyages between New Orleans and Louisville, but was of so heavy draft and slow speed that she did not prove a success," according to Gould. "In 1823, while lying up at Withers' saw mill, just above the city, the batture caved in and sunk her."[6]

The *Washington*, the *Ohio*, and the *Napoleon* made an impressive fleet of steamboats for Shreve. In May and June of 1818, he acted as captain of the *Ohio* on its maiden voyage to New Orleans, where it arrived for the first time on June 9, according to the registry. His old friend from Brownsville, Captain Israel Gregg, was at the helm of the *Napoleon* when it followed downriver a few days later, arriving on June 19 at New Orleans.

Shreve seems to have taken a turn·at being master of each of his boats, checking them constantly for smoothness of operation and possible defects. The *Washington* was not cast aside in favor of the newer steamboats, however, and there are enough reports of her appearances to show that her route varied from time to time. The St. Louis *Gazette* of March 3, 1819, noted the arrival on March 1 of the "large and elegant steamboat *Washington* from New Orleans, which city she left on the first of February."[7] In November, 1820, John James Audubon, traveling to St. Louis on a steamboat descending the Ohio, near a point called Chain of Rocks about twenty miles above the Ohio's mouth, noted in his journal, "The old *Washington* Steam Boat came alongside us Took 70 barrels of salt, rais*d* steam and made herself fast about 2 miles below."

The veteran steamboat was capable of ascending the Missouri River and was in fact among the larger of the steamboats to do so. The Missouri was still considered a challenge to any steamboat at that time. The Franklin *Missouri Intelligencer* carried this story on April 30, 1821:

6. Gould, *Fifty Years on the Mississippi*, 110, 154–55.
7. *Ibid.*, 113.

Steam Boat Navigation of the Missouri. It affords us great pleasure to state, as an evidence of the facility with which the Missouri may be navigated by the aid of steam, that the large and elegant Steam Boat WASHINGTON, Capt. SHREVE, arrived at this place on Wednesday the 25th inst. at 10 minutes past 7 A.M. having left St. Louis on the Thursday preceding, at 17 minutes past 10 A.M. and performing the trip (a distance of about 220 miles) in six days, against a stream the most rapid, perhaps in the world. She is destined for the Council Bluffs, being laden with provisions for the army. After remaining at Franklin about fifteen minutes, she proceeded on her destination. The time usually consumed by keel boats the same distance is from twenty to thirty days. The practicability of navigating the Missouri, with safety and facility, may be considered as established beyond the possibility of doubt. This fact is of immense importance to Missouri, whose mighty stream has, heretofore, presented obstacles to the successful prosecution of commerce.

But time was bringing inevitable rot to the *Washington's* timbers. The life of a steamboat spared from piercing by a snag or burning was about six years at the most, and in 1822 the time had come for the grand old steamboat to retire. The *Ohio* and the *Napoleon* were in service for about the same length of time.

Even while the *Washington* was still scheduling regular voyages, the prediction that Shreve made when he completed her first upriver voyage from New Orleans that so impressed the public seemed likely to come true. The *Washington's* time of twenty-five days, her master had predicted, would be cut in half. That prediction was no longer an unlikely goal when this item appeared in *Niles' Weekly Register* for July 3, 1819: "The steam boat James Ross lately made a passage from New Orleans to Louisville, about 1500 miles, in 14 days! What a progress is this against the currents of the rivers of the west—what a field does it present to the speculative mind, disposed to anticipate the future of things!"

At that time, Congress was taking much interest in the rapid expansion in the West. There was concurrently a growing conviction that waterways that abutted more than one state should be under federal jurisdiction, thus avoiding the problems that had arisen from the granting of exclusive privileges in the segments of the rivers within the boundaries of any one state. John Marshall's decision in the *Gibbons* v. *Odgen* case had not yet established the principle of federal control of interstate waterways, but the public was ready for such a decision. In the meantime Congress evidenced a tendency toward regulation of interstate commerce when, in

March of 1819, it passed an act empowering the Post Office Department to employ one or more steamboats to carry interstate mail on the Ohio and Mississippi rivers.

Shreve kept a keen eye on the news of the day and immediately applied for assignment under this act. He contracted with the boatbuilders at New Albany to construct a small packet specifically for the purpose of carrying the mail. The *Post Boy* was completed in a few months' time and was the first steamboat under contract by the Post Office Department, going into operation on its route before the end of 1819. One stipulation by Congress was that the cost was not to exceed that of carrying mail by land. This was an easy requirement to meet, and the *Post Boy* moved up and down the rivers regularly, stopping to leave and pick up mail sacks at many landings. The *Post Boy* worked the Ohio River primarily, and it was not until May 22, 1821, that its registration in the port of New Orleans appeared as a first arrival. It was a small boat of two hundred tons, operated at the time of the New Orleans registry by Captain H. N. Breckinridge, one of Shreve's partners in the building of the *Napoleon* and possibly also of the *Post Boy*.

There was a trend toward specialization of purpose as the number of steamboats increased. Some were built entirely for cargo transport, and in 1818 for the first time one was built exclusively as a passenger vessel. This was a small steamboat, the *General Pike*, which "measured 100 feet keel, 25 feet beam . . . drew only 39 inches of water," and had accommodations for a hundred passengers.[8] Although the *General Pike* went farther afield later, it was built at Cincinnati especially for the route from Louisville to Cincinnati and thence upriver to Maysville, Kentucky. For the use of the passengers there were the usual ladies' cabin aft and the larger gentlemen's cabin forward. But in addition, there were more than the usual number of small staterooms to accommodate couples or family groups, marking the start of a trend that would lead to the replacement of the less private large cabins. The *General Pike* had one group of six staterooms and another group of eight at the ends of the main cabins. Between the groups of staterooms was a public room or "saloon," forty feet long by eighteen feet wide. Subtracting the eighteen feet from the stated width of

8. *Ibid.*, 107.

the steamboat, twenty-five feet, one can see that these first staterooms were far from commodious.

As soon as it was clear that the *Washington*'s days on the rivers were ended, Shreve began to plan a replacement, and included in his planning was a better way to accommodate passengers. The passenger trade had increased to become a highly lucrative aspect of the operation of steamboats.

The vast interior of the United States in the 1820s was still almost innocent of a road long enough or passable a sufficient number of months of the year to be termed a highway. The steamboat held first place as a dependable means of transportation; it carried much of the mail as well. The same short span of years that saw such rapid increase in the rate of steamboat building following Shreve's demonstrations with the *Washington* also saw accelerated population growth in the part of the United States served by the inland rivers. There were eighteen states when the *Washington* was launched, with Indiana admitted as the nineteenth in that year of 1816. By 1821, with the admission of Missouri after a long debate over slavery, there were twenty-four states; all of the new ones except Maine were in the central part of the continent, with its abundance of rivers and streams.

In all of the interior states, new and old, the most rapidly growing cities were located along navigable rivers. Most of the business in each of the cities centered around the wharf. Products of the farms were brought by small boats or by wagon to the riverfront area; processing plants and warehouses appeared in each town to handle the cargo shipped out or brought in via steamboat. Even the social life revolved around steamboat arrivals. From Pittsburgh to New Orleans, at large city riverfronts as well as at every little settlement and plantation landing, the sound of an approaching steamboat brought out the people. The mellow steam whistle did not come until the 1840s, but the keelboat's bugle or gun had been replaced by a hoarse, one-note steam blast that could be heard for a long distance and was a magnetic signal.[9]

These trends toward increased passenger service and freight tonnage on the rivers were important factors behind Shreve's plans for a replace-

9. Harry Sinclair Drago, *The Steamboaters: From the Early Side-Wheelers to the Big Packets* (New York, 1967), 1.

ment for the *Washington*. Many ideas for improvements had occurred to him in his years as a steamboat operator, and the best of them were incorporated in his design. The resulting steamboat, the *George Washington*, became the prototype for the "floating palace" of the Mississippi River. It would be the culminating achievement of the portion of his career devoted to steamboat building and operation and would earn for him the name of Father of the Mississippi Steamboat.

People had laughed at the clumsy appearance of his first steamboat. Nevertheless, in a few years almost every steamboat built for the passenger and freight trade on the Ohio or Mississippi was patterned after the double-decked design that had called forth such derision. As the framing for the new *George Washington* took shape late in 1823 at a Cincinnati boatyard, there were again those who jeered at Shreve's novel ideas. This boat rose three decks high—certain to tip over, some said. On top of the second or boiler deck, the framing for passenger accommodations showed a complete departure from earlier boats. Shreve liked the idea of more private quarters for couples and families, such as the *General Pike* had. He went farther. He conceived a long series of such small private rooms, each with its windows opening onto a covered veranda. A passenger might spend his time gazing at the passing scenery from his stateroom or, if he preferred, go out for a stroll on the walkway. The deck above the main passenger accommodations, known as the hurricane deck, was topped with a pilot house, set far back on the steamboat. From this vantage point, the steamboat's pilot and other crew members could command a view of as much length of river as needed in navigation of the big vessel.

This whole structure was set upon a hull that was shallower than any heretofore used on a steamboat, measuring slightly over eight feet at its deepest point. The underside was a complete departure from the Fulton steamboats, with the greatest portion of it nearly flat. It was the precursor of the standard hull of the later steamboat era. People commented that the *George Washington* appeared to ride *on* the water and not in it. Shreve viewed its hull design as the best possible answer to the shifting sandbars and shallows so often encountered in the inland rivers.

The keel, scarcely perceptible along the underside of the hull, was 152 feet in length, about 12 feet longer than that of the *Washington*. The new boat was a full 5 feet wider, measuring 30½ feet beam. But its tonnage was about 50 tons less, only 355, because of the increased emphasis on passenger service.[10] The side paddle wheels, larger than any on Shreve's other boats, were completely enclosed and moved somewhat farther toward the stern.

Looking at this huge creation, skeptics asked how all this structure was to keep from tipping over. Wouldn't the pilot find himself suddenly diving into the river if a sudden wind hit the boat broadside? How could the boat keep from swaying?

Shreve ignored the skeptics, but he carefully explained the principles of the design to his partners in the investment. Given the weight distribution, it would be impossible to capsize this steamboat unless one took it out into the open ocean and exposed it to a gale. And there was no intention for it to leave the inland rivers. He explained the mathematical principles upon which he based his statements. The sturdy trussing, known as the hogging frame, again employing mathematical principles in the diagonal bracing, would prevent swaying. Even if the steamboat had a full complement of passengers and all of them went to watch at the rail on the same side of the upper deck, the steamboat, with ballast or cargo in the hold, could not capsize, Shreve assured his partners. He was right. It never did.

In his earlier steamboats, Shreve had increased the number of engines to four and the boilers to eight, with all of them powering the pair of side paddle wheels. In the *George Washington*, each paddle wheel had its own set of boilers and engines and complete mechanism, all placed on the deck so that there was no longer any part of the machinery in the hold. Two huge stacks, bound together with metal bracing for stability, rose for smoke release, and there were additional, smaller steam stacks. The idea of the separate complement of boilers and machinery was to make it possible to maneuver the steamboat more easily in the rivers. Each paddle wheel turned independently of the other and could be reversed in direction for turning the boat about in a minimum of water distance. This made the side-wheeler equal or superior to the stern-wheeler in maneuverability while sacrificing none of the power advantages of the pair of side-wheels.

There were other mechanical improvements, the results of Shreve's

10. Hunter, *Steamboats on the Western Rivers*, 77.

many hours of study and observation. The *George Washington* was the product of his critical analysis of all the steamboats he had designed and operated in the past eight years plus adaptations and improvements of ideas he had seen used in other builders' steamboats. When the *George Washington* was completed late in 1824 or early 1825, it was pronounced the finest steamboat on the rivers.

With his increased emphasis upon passenger accommodations, Shreve employed the stateroom idea as he had seen it used in the *General Pike*, but he amplified it to provide many more private accommodations. There are some writers who credit him with originating both the stateroom idea and the term. *The Crisis*, a historical novel written by the American author Winston Churchill and published in 1901, contains a passage of dialogue about Shreve.

> "Jinny," said the Captain, "did you ever know why cabins are called *staterooms*?"
> "Why, no," answered she, puzzled.
> "There was an old fellow named Shreve who ran steamboats before Jackson fought the redcoats at New Orleans. In Shreve's time the cabins were curtained off, just like these new-fangled sleeping-car berths. The old man built wooden rooms, and he named them after the different states, Kentuck, and Illinois, and Pennsylvania. So that when a fellow came aboard he'd say: 'What *state* am I in, Cap?' And from this river has the name spread all over the world— *stateroom*."[11]

Shreve (who was far from being an "old man" in 1824, at thirty-nine years of age) may have named the cabins after states on the *George Washington*, but the idea probably came to him because they were already known as staterooms. The term was in use for private accommodations before that time.

Fortunately, there was a passenger aboard the *George Washington*, an English gentleman, one W. Bullock, who kept a journal of his travels in 1826 and 1827. In his "Sketch of a Journey Through the Western States of North America," Bullock recorded his impressions of travel aboard Shreve's finest steamboat.

> On the 3rd of April we left New Orleans, in the beautiful steam-boat George Washington, of 375 tons, built at Cincinnati, and certainly the finest freshwater vessel I had seen. River boats, like these, possess the advantage of not having

11. Winston Churchill, *The Crisis* (New York, 1901), 273.

to contend with ocean storms, as ours have, and are therefore built in different manner, having three decks or stories above water. The accommodations are much larger, and farther removed from the noise, heat, and motion of the machinery; wood being the only fuel made use of, they are consequently not incommoded by the effects of the dense smoke, so annoying in some of our steam vessels. The accommodations are excellent, and the cabins furnished in the most superb manner. None of the sleeping rooms have more than two beds. The principal are on the upper story, and a gallery and verandah extends entirely round the vessel, affording ample space for exercise, sheltered from sun and rain, and commanding, from its height, a fine view of the surrounding scenery, without being incommoded by the noise of the crew passing overhead. The meals furnished in these vessels are excellent, and served in a superior style. The ladies have a separate cabin, with female attendants and laundresses; there are, also, a circulating library, a smoking and drinking room for the gentlemen, with numerous offices for servants, &c. &c. They generally stop twice a day to take in wood for the engine, when fresh milk and other necessaries are procured, and the passengers may land for a short time. The voyage before the introduction of steam, was attended with much risk and labor, and occupied ninety days, from New Orleans to Cincinnati, for small vessels; the same voyage (1600 miles) is now performed, with the greatest of ease and safety, in eleven or twelve days, against the stream, and the descent between the above places is done in seven days; each vessel taking several hundred passengers, besides her cargo of merchandise. The rate of travelling is extremely moderate in proportion to the advantages of the accommodation. We paid about 8£ each from New Orleans to Louisville (1500 miles), which includes every expense of living, servants, &c. In ascending this magnificent river, the Mississippi, of which the Ohio may be considered a continuation, is navigable for the largest vessels, at high water, from the Gulf of Mexico to Pittsburgh (2212 miles). The traveller is now enabled, without the least danger or fatigue, to traverse the otherwise almost impassable and trackless wilderness, and wilds that abound the western states of America, and this, without leaving his comfortable apartment, from the windows of which he can enjoy the constantly varying scenery, so new to European travellers.[12]

Shreve saw the fulfillment of his prophecy of a return trip from New Orleans to Louisville in only ten days accomplished by one of his own vessels, for Bullock, after describing the scenery en route, recorded that "the tenth day brought us to the flourishing commercial town of Louisville, in Kentucky, 1542 miles from the sea, considered as second only to Cincinnati in the western states." At that point in his travels (he was actually at Shippingport), he left the *George Washington* and went by coach to the

12. Thwaites (ed.), *Early Western Travels*, XIX, 128–29.

Louisville riverfront, where he and other passengers bound for Cincinnati or other upriver ports boarded another steamboat.

Bullock also commented on an important development well under way in the late 1820s—the long-awaited construction of a canal to bypass the Falls of the Ohio: "On our road from Shippingport, at the foot of the falls, we had an opportunity of examining the fine canal and locks, now constructing at great expense, to enable vessels of all dimensions to navigate the river at all seasons. It is a great work, and calculated to be of considerable advantage to this country." Construction of the Louisville and Portland Canal had started in 1825 under the auspices of a private company. Much slave labor was employed in the digging, which had to be done with scoop shovels drawn by horses or mules and by hand labor. The route, as Figure 13 shows, left Shippingport set apart on a man-made island. Boats entered the canal just above Portland and left (on the upriver route) at the Louisville riverfront. The work was completed in 1830 at a cost of about $740,000, and it immediately relieved the situation that had so long impeded commercial shipping on the Ohio River.[13]

By the time of the dedication of the canal in 1830, Shreve was already deeply involved in the next phase of his life, that of improving the navigability of the rivers. His first ideas in that direction began to appear in letters he wrote around that time.

His *George Washington* was a great success. Its innovations were soon being copied by other builders, and the ultimate result was the huge floating palace that Currier and Ives prints of the race of the *Natchez* and the *Robert E. Lee* made famous. The three "stories" of Bullock's account no longer seemed in the least outrageous after only a few years; in fact, as the hulls grew broader, with side extensions, and even shallower, the superstructures rose higher. By 1850 freight space on the main deck had been increased by the expedient of raising the boiler deck to twelve or even more feet above the main deck. Upon the hurricane deck, where the pilot house stood on the *George Washington*, a long, narrow cabin was added to house the officers, and the pilot house set atop that as a final story. This addition came about the time that Texas became the twenty-eighth state of the union in 1845, and someone pinned the name "texas"

13. Works Projects Administration Writers' Program, *Kentucky* (New York, 1939), 180, 186.

on this last of the staterooms. By that time, the regular staterooms had private outer doors leading to the gallery and a walkway decorated to the extreme with miracles of wood turning.

So Shreve's ideas had blossomed and flourished. As Frederick Read wrote in 1873: "His daily experience, aided by his habits of close practical observation in all matters pertaining to steam navigation, guided by sound judgment and great sagacity, enabled him, through a long course of years, to be of far more essential service to his country than Fulton ever was. His originality in steamboat improvements is far more manifest at this late day, and his innovations were manifestly the result of his own reflections, since we know that he was unaided by the counsel of scientific friends."[14]

It must have been with great satisfaction that Shreve saw his ideas being adopted and the steamboat as he had conceived it becoming the means of the rapid economic growth of inland America. But his mind was occupied with another problem even before he built the *George Washington*. It was the problem with which he was most closely involved during the greater part of the steamboat era, the matter of making the rivers safer for navigation. When the time came for action, he was ready with an important new invention vital to safe navigation.

14. Read, *Up the Heights of Fame and Fortune*, 80.

11 / **Captain Shreve Faces New Challenges**

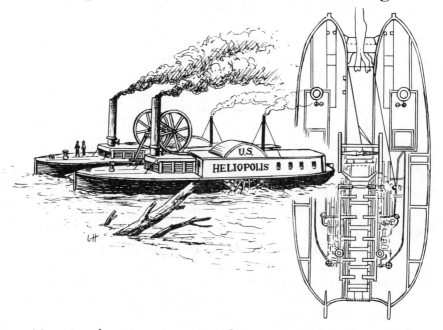

More steamboats meant more accidents, many of them due to lurking, treacherous snags. "Three steam boats have been lost in five months, in the Mississippi, in consequence of running foul of great trunks of trees called 'sawyers,'" reported Niles in his *Register* of June 27, 1818. He went on to plead, "Will not the increased navigation of this mighty stream soon justify an attempt to clear it of such serious incumbrances—or is it practicable to do it?"

Captain Shreve believed the answer to Niles's question on practicability was yes. In his off-hours, he sat with paper and pencil and sketched workboats that might be used to pull up the sunken trees and root masses. He favored this idea—clearing the rivers—rather than altering steamboat design drastically to protect the boats, such as another steamboat builder did in 1820. That designer built a "snag room" at the front of his steamboat *Columbus*. The *Columbus* hit a snag, but it did not sink, because water was prevented from going farther into the hull than a sealed-off space near the prow.[1]

1. *Niles' Weekly Register*, April 8, 1820.

Shreve felt this wasted valuable cargo space and did nothing to prevent the ripping of any other part of the hull. His mind went beyond such protective devices to the possibility of ridding the rivers of the menacing snags. Hoping to succeed with this approach, he had plans for a snag boat drawn up as early as 1821.[2]

He reasoned that speed of travel could be greatly increased if the rivers themselves were made safer. It was extremely hazardous in many segments of the rivers to operate a steamboat at its maximum speed in full daylight or to run at moderate speeds at night. Even an experienced pilot could be taken by surprise, with no time to turn the boat from the piercing limbs of a huge snag, for the river channel was ever shifting and far from a stable, static body of water in which hazards could be depended upon to remain stationary. As sands shifted, new snags were freed to rise. The pilot might pass over an unruffled surface going downstream and on his return meet with disaster at the same location. It is difficult today to picture the size of those underwater trees, for today's forest trees do not compare with the first-growth giants that became snags in the rivers, many of them three to six feet in diameter and imbedded in the channels to a depth of ten to fourteen feet.[3]

In the 1820s, the rivers were "booby-trapped" to an extent difficult to imagine in later years, with snags skirting the banks of mainland and islands and apt to be encountered at every bend. Losses amounted to millions of dollars in cargo and vessels and to unknown numbers in lives. Steamboat captains began to demand that the federal government take steps to make the rivers safer, since it was claiming jurisdiction over rivers of interstate length. Two conditions brought action from Congress in 1824. One was the landmark decision by the Supreme Court in the *Gibbons* v. *Ogden* case, confirming federal jurisdiction over interstate waterways. The other was the need to keep the rivers open for military transport since there were few roads between the Appalachians and the Mississippi River and almost none beyond the river. The number of western army outposts was growing; most were located on or near a river.

John C. Calhoun was secretary of war in 1824. Reflecting upon problems in transportation that had surfaced in the War of 1812 and in Indian

2. Henry M. Shreve, *Memorial: Official Evidence in Support of the Claim of Capt. Henry M. Shreve on the United States Government for Its Use of His Patented Invention of the Steam Snag Boat* (St. Louis, 1847), 3.

3. [Treat (?)], "Henry Miller Shreve," 246.

campaigns subsequent to that war, he urged congressional action to open the way to improvements in the Ohio and the Mississippi and possibly also in the western rivers, such as the Arkansas. Congress passed an enabling act on May 24, 1824, and appropriated seventy-five thousand dollars for that purpose. The United States Army engineers were to be in charge of the projects.

Feeling that experienced riverboat captains would be most likely to have practical suggestions to offer, the chief of engineers, Major General Alexander Macomb, sent them a circular, dated June 1, 1824.

> Sir: The Act of Congress of the 24th of May, 1824, having made an appropriation for the improvement of the Mississippi, by removing all trees which may be fixed in the bed of the river, commonly called planters, sawyers, or snags, the Secretary of War is desirous of availing himself of your skill and experience in the navigation of the river, and requests that you will present such suggestions as may occur to you, as to the best means of carrying into effect the intentions of Congress. He particularly desires your opinion, whether the river could be freed, advantageously, by dragging the trees or snags from their bed, and what would be the best mode and time of doing so; or whether it would be practicable to saw them off at a depth so low as not to endanger the navigation of the river at the lowest water; and what would be the best mode and season of the year for effecting the same; what would be the effect of passing heavy rafts of timber down the river; and what would be the best form or mode of constructing the rafts for the purpose of removing the impediments to the navigation. Any suggestions on these or any other points, having relation to the subject, and accompanied by estimates of the probable cost, will be acceptably received by this department; the communications to be addressed to the Secretary of War; and endorsed "Engineer Service."[4]

Shreve was, of course, among the boat operators to receive a copy of this circular. As he wrote later, he had in 1821 designed "a machine for sawing off snags and sawyers under water, which consisted of a twin boat connected with a wheel and windlass worked by manual labor."[5] On July 5 he wrote his reply to the secretary of war. He stated his firm conviction that clearance of the rivers was indeed possible and made several suggestions about how the task should be approached. He offered to submit a model of his 1821 plan for inspection by the engineers.

To this offer, he received no reply. But soon an advertisement was

4. *Ibid.*, 243.
5. Shreve, *Memorial*, 3–4.

mailed to him stating that the secretary of war would pay a premium of one thousand dollars for the best plan of removing snags, sawyers, and planters. Shreve felt that his invention was worth more than the offered one thousand dollars, and since acceptance would make the idea the property of the United States government, he did not send his model for consideration.

Soon afterward, he learned that the award went to a Kentuckian named John Bruce and that Bruce was under contract with the federal government to begin the work. For sixty-five thousand dollars Bruce had agreed to remove all the obstructions from the channel of the Ohio River for its entire length and also from the Mississippi River from the mouth of the Missouri to the Balize.

Bruce had built a twin-hulled steamboat with a single paddle wheel between the hulls to propel the boats.[6] A windlass and capstan were hand operated. But he soon found that his boat was impractical and incapable of pulling up many of the snags. Working under the superintendence of Major Babcock of the Corps of Engineers, Bruce worked with flatboats, levers, chains, and handsaws. At the end of two years, he was still working in the Ohio River between Louisville and the Mississippi, where he and his crew had spent the whole frustrating time and the entire appropriation. The Mississippi River, which was much more snag-infested, had not yet seen any efforts at improvement. It was obvious that Bruce was not going to be able to fulfill his contract. The work was at a standstill.

In 1824, the same year that the call had gone out for ideas on snag removal, there was a significant political contest. General Andrew Jackson, then senator from Tennessee, was nominated for the presidency by the Democratic party. In Louisville, Shreve campaigned wholeheartedly for the man who had been his commander during the War of 1812. He was among those most disappointed when, despite Old Hickory's ninety-nine electoral votes to John Quincy Adams' seventy-eight, the presidency went to Adams as a result of the vote in the House of Representatives, where the election was decided since no candidate had a majority of all votes cast by the electors. At that time there were twenty-four states in the union, and the congressmen, voting by states, cast thirteen votes for Adams.

6. The description of Bruce's snag boat is from a report dated February 23, 1843, George W. Hughes of the Topographical Bureau, based on a description written by Bruce in 1824. The report is included in Shreve, *Memorial*, 16–17.

When the problems on snag clearance came up, John C. Calhoun had become vice-president under Adams, and the new secretary of war was James Barbour. Barbour was perplexed at how to quiet the clamor in the West arising from the failure to accomplish the snag clearance of the Mississippi. He consulted with Calhoun, who recalled the interesting proposals contained in the letter from Shreve when the first call went out for ideas. He suggested Shreve be contacted, although Shreve's political leanings were well known. Shreve was soon offered the office of United States superintendent of western river improvements. The commission, dated December 10, 1826, was signed by President Adams.

Shreve had much to ponder. Acceptance of this commission would alter his life drastically. Financially, he would be the loser, for he would no longer be free to develop his line of steamboats and continue their profitable operation. But he was never one to turn away from a challenge. No one realized more than he did how necessary it was to clear the rivers of snags, and no one was more certain that the job could be done. He saw the offer of the superintendency as a great opportunity. Steamboating could not develop its potential unless the rivers were made safer.

Henry Shreve was now a man of mature years for those times, entering his forties, heavier than he had been in his youth as a result of the less physically demanding life he had led since his success with the *Washington*. He was well known on the rivers as a man of strong convictions, with the ability to take command of any situation in which he found himself and of any working crew. Jackson's earlier estimate of him as a man who would do whatever he undertook and do it well was shared by many people.

And yet, popular opinion was against the idea that *anyone* would be able to rid the Mississippi of those huge and numerous snags. Bruce's work had demonstrated the magnitude of the job, and he had not even begun work on the Mississippi. But Shreve, if he had any doubts, pushed them aside despite popular opinion. His inventive mind was exploring the many possibilities as he wrote his acceptance of the commission on January 2, 1827.[7]

His agreement with the government was not in terms of a contract for a stated amount of work for a stated sum but to work for a salary of six dol-

7. [Treat (?)], "Henry Miller Shreve," 245.

lars per day.[8] He immediately built a snag boat on the plans and model he had proposed a few years earlier, similar to Bruce's but with the paddle wheels on the outer sides of the twin hulls. He began working with it at the lower end of the Ohio River, near Chain of Rocks, where Bruce had left off.

Shreve needed only a few weeks of actual experience on the job to make him realize that the manually powered mechanisms for freeing or cutting the snags were inadequate. Speaking of himself in the third person, he later wrote, "Believing that a more economical and effective machine might be devised for accomplishing the object, he turned his attention to the subject and after much thought the idea occurred to him of a twin-snag boat, so connected and combined with the windlass and pulley and the snag beam, aided by the momentum given to the boat by the continuous action of the paddle wheels, as to afford the best, if not the only means of breaking off, uprooting and raising snags from the bed of the river."[9]

Through the early months of 1827 the lamp often burned until late at night in the captain's quarters. Shreve needed to study the problems of how best to apply steam power to breaking off and lifting the massive underwater trees with which he had to deal. He later recalled that he had great difficulty in designing the steam-powered snag boat "so that the concussion between the snag and the snag-beam would not dislocate the boilers of the boat."[10] At last, satisfied that he had perfected his plans, he was ready to build a model. In October he wrote to the War Department explaining his ideas and seeking authorization from the secretary to build a full-scale snag boat following his plans.

His letter was full of optimism and confidence, but the people in Washington did not share his mood. Even in talking with other steamboatmen, Shreve met with headshaking instead of encouragement. Most of them believed that snag removal was an impossibility. They could not see how steam power could be applied as Shreve proposed without the twin snag boat itself being wrecked in the attempt.

For a time it seemed that no one but Shreve himself had any faith in the invention he had so carefully diagrammed. A fellow steamboatman

8. Shreve, *Memorial*, 3.
9. *Ibid.*, 4.
10. *Ibid.*

wrote to the War Department: "It is said that the present Superintendent (Capt. Shreve) has it in contemplation to construct a large and powerful steamboat, for the purpose of cutting out the snags, and pulling them out by the force of steam. Now, those projects are only calculated to get through the appropriation, without anything like the object contemplated. All machinery, whatever, whether used by lever or steam power is considered by persons who are well-acquainted with the Mississippi river navigation, as a useless expenditure of time and money."[11]

But Shreve's ideas had been scorned before. There were a few steamboatmen who recalled this and who also recalled his subsequent successful demonstrations. A group of them drew up a petition to the secretary of war requesting that Shreve be empowered to proceed with construction of his snag boat.

The secretary himself could not conceive of how Shreve's invention could succeed. Shreve wrote again, explaining the principles upon which the snag boat would operate. The tone was so confident that, coupled with the petition, the secretary began to feel that perhaps he should obtain agreement at least to allow Shreve to build and demonstrate his snagboat. He was perhaps also influenced by continuing reports of steamboat disasters from encounters with snags. Losses were mounting as the number of steamboats on the rivers increased. He gave in. On June 27, 1828, he wrote Shreve granting him permission to construct the snagboat at government expense. But the authorization was heavily loaded with restrictions and conditions. The tone of it was far from confident. If the snag boat proved a failure, the secretary warned, Shreve would find himself charged with the expense of it personally.

What the War Department lacked in confidence, Shreve more than compensated for. He immediately and jubilantly began construction of the first of his steam-powered snag boats, the *Heliopolis*. Construction was at the boatyard of Dohrman and Humphries in New Albany. While the carpenters were busily constructing the sturdy hulls and connecting beams, engines for the boat were being readied across the river at Louisville by mechanics Shreve had learned to trust at the foundry of John Curry. Assisting Shreve in supervising the work were two of his old friends who were also steamboat captains, Abraham Tyson and John Kill-

11. [Treat (?)], "Henry Miller Shreve," 246.

ingham. Even the official inspector, a Captain Moffet, had a part in the work, since he was also the blacksmith who forged the chains and fastenings. Moffet gave the *Heliopolis* his official approval on July 22, 1829.

As the diagram from Shreve's later patent application (see Figure 14) shows, the snag boat consisted of twin steamboat hulls, each 125 feet in length and 25 feet of beam, connected by two tiers of beams and fitted with a large pulley wheel, cables, chains, and other mechanisms for snag removal from the rivers. Shreve himself said of his invention, "The machine is beautifully simple and most powerful in its operation and produces the effect intended in the most admirable manner."[12]

Each hull had a paddle wheel on the outer side and its own boilers and steam engine. These were coupled in such a way as to be usable with combined force. The snag beam, connecting the two hulls at the bow, was at the waterline, "wedge-shaped, and in the exact centre of percussion, so that a blow with it produces no jar whatever, and consequently does not, as predicted, disturb in the least any of the machinery connected with the boilers or engines."[13] This snag beam was shaped from heavy timber, two and a half feet thick, assembled with bolts and with the front edge, the smallest part of the wedge, rounded. The whole was sheathed with plate iron one quarter of an inch thick, and extended through the hulls of the boats to the outer wall framing. Just aft of this was a bulkhead similarly sheathed and inclined, to aid in getting the timber on board the boats for sawing.

Forward of the paddle wheels was the main windlass, resting on a diagonal framing on each boat, holding it twenty feet above the water. The shaft was sixteen inches in diameter in the center, tapering to ten inches at the ends. Heavy chains were released or wound up with the use of this windlass. An eighteen-foot wheel was at each end of the shaft to carry cables and lines, and the whole was connected with the steam-engine machinery. In operation, the boat moved toward a snag at full power, so directed that the snag beam would hit the tree trunk. The effect was either to snap off the trunk just above the spreading of the roots or to dislodge it entirely from the muddy river bottom. In either case, the windlasses then operated to haul up the trunk onto the rollers that carried it along.

12. Henry M. Shreve, "Specifications Forming part of Letters Patent No. 913, Sept. 12, 1838" (U.S. Patent Office Washington, D.C.), 1.
13. [Treat (?)], "Henry Miller Shreve," 246.

The root mass, if it came up, was cut off and dropped in deep water to sink well below any point where contact with a boat was probable. The trunk of the tree was sawed into lengths that could be handled, and since it was too water-soaked to be put in the fuel stacks for the steam engines, it was dropped overboard to float downriver for others to retrieve and dry out for firewood or to pass off to the sea. The entire operation of removal of a large snag required about forty-five minutes.[14]

The *Heliopolis* was put to work and had soon cleared out the remaining snag-ridden miles of the Ohio River. It entered the Mississippi on August 29, 1829. A newspaper report in 1830 reflected the successful operation of the snag boat over the next months.

> Capt. Shreve has perfectly succeeded in rendering about 300 miles of river as harmless as a mill-pond, and will in the course of the short period remove every obstruction from Trinity to Balize. [Trinity was located about six miles above the mouth of the Ohio, where the boats from the Ohio and Mississippi exchanged cargoes.] His plan is to run down the snags with a double steamboat; the bows are connected by tremendous beams, plated with iron; he puts on a heavy head of steam and runs the snag down; they are found uniformly to break off at the point of junction with the bottom of the river, and float away."[15]

Shreve himself wrote later, "With that boat your memorialist broke off and raised snags—consisting of trees sixty feet long and three and a half in diameter, implanted twenty feet in the bed of the river, with the greatest ease."[16]

As soon as the successful performance of the *Heliopolis* was reported to the secretary of war, Shreve suggested the building of a second snag boat, a duplicate, to hasten the work. Congress was impressed with what had been accomplished, and in 1831, the *Archimedes* was built and launched. Shreve took over as master for operations in the Mississippi River, assigning operation of the *Heliopolis* to an experienced assistant, Captain Israel Moorhead, to attack the job of river clearance in the Arkansas. Two more snag boats were authorized for construction in 1836, both also basically identical to the *Heliopolis*. The first snag boat operated so satisfactorily that even Shreve could find only minor changes to make for its improvement.

14. Shreve, "Letters Patent," 2.
15. Gould, *Fifty Years on the Mississippi*, 244.
16. Shreve, *Memorial*, 5.

A newspaper report from the time summarized the progress made by Shreve and Moorhead.

> The captains and crews of the snagboats Archimedes and Heliopolis, under the superintendence of Capt. Shreve, are progressing rapidly in removing obstructions to the navigation of the Western waters. The Heliopolis, Capt. Moorehead, has ascended the Arkansas River about 20 miles, and after removing all the snags in that distance, on account of low water has returned to the Mississippi, and it will in the course of the week have cleared the channel of the Mississippi between Helena and the mouth of the Arkansas River. The business, as it now progresses, is effectually done. During the year 1831, Capt. Shreve continued on down the river, and made the cut off at the mouth of Red River. Capt. Moorhead continuing during 1831 and 1832 to work down to that river, removing all the snags that presented themselves.[17]

That "cut off at the mouth of the Red River," a type of canal, was the one segment of his river improvement work that gave Shreve reason to regret his labors. Just as is common today when a government-backed project is proposed, people found reasons to object and complain about many of the engineering projects on which Shreve worked. But the Red River cutoff was the source of more complaints than any other, and Shreve himself was disturbed at the unexpected river changes that resulted. So unpopular was the cutoff that for years, Shreve's name brought a negative reaction to some people of the area who completely overlooked the good work he had done. A biographer of Shreve writing in 1927 asked a steamboatman of her day whether he had ever heard of Shreve. "Of course," he answered disapprovingly. "He made the Red River cut-off."[18]

The 1820s and 1830s were years when cutting a canal was considered a likely solution for many transportation problems. Americans, especially in the developing land between the Appalachians and the Mississippi, were desperate for ways to ship their growing production. Railroads were not yet built, and they seized upon the idea of cutting canals to connect navigable riverways. The Erie Canal opened in 1825, and immediately afterward work was in progress to cut canals from rivers emptying into Lake Erie to connect them with tributaries of the Ohio. It was soon possible to go by boat, changing vessels at each waterway, from New York City to cities on the Ohio River and thence downriver to New Orleans, making

17. Gould, *Fifty Years on the Mississippi*, 244.
18. Pfaff, "Henry Miller Shreve," 206.

use of the network of canals. The long-planned and much-needed canal around the Falls of the Ohio, the Louisville and Portland Canal, became a reality in this period. Its formal opening took place on December 5, 1830.

Canals also seemed the answer to avoiding many miles of river in places where the channel had been cut in horseshoe bends, with a mile or less of land separating the ends of the horseshoe. Cutting canals across these narrow necks could save many miles of travel. It was proposed to Shreve that he cut such a canal connecting the ends of a horseshoe on the Mississippi just upriver from the mouth of the Red River to save thirty miles of river travel. He cut this canal in 1831.

But the canal disturbed the Father of Waters in a manner Shreve had not foreseen. Silt in great quantities was carried downstream and dropped where the Red River currents joined the Mississippi. There the mud built up, forming bars that blocked large portions of the mouth of the Red. Complaints were many and vociferous. Dredges were put to work immediately to reopen the Red River to traffic, but the bars tended to re-form and dredging had to be continued at intervals. Blame was heaped upon Shreve's head for making the cutoff.

In the summer of 1832, Congress passed an act that renewed Shreve's appointment as superintendent of western river improvements, assigning him the sole responsibility for supervision of improvements in the Mississippi, Ohio, and Arkansas rivers. The same act altered the financial arrangements, putting Shreve on an annual salary of three thousand dollars instead of the former six dollars per day, a substantial increase for those times. Shreve drew up plans for projects in those three rivers, assigning the *Archimedes* to some work needed on the upper Ohio. More large steamboats used the Louisville-to-Pittsburgh segment following the opening of the Louisville and Portland Canal, and engineering work was needed in some places to accommodate them.

In 1828, Colonel Charles Gratiot replaced Alexander Macomb as chief of engineers and thus became Shreve's direct supervisor. A letter from Gratiot (now a brigadier general) dated September 5, 1832, gave Shreve reason to alter his plans for 1833. For many years the people of northwestern Louisiana had been petitioning Congress for assistance in opening the Red River to traffic above Natchitoches, where the immense formation of driftwood known as the Great Raft almost filled the channel. Gratiot's letter concerned the raft and brought to Shreve's mind his first view of it, which he had gained when sent to Natchitoches with the *Enterprise* on military transport duty for General Jackson.

Shreve recalled how the raft so blocked the river that no steamboat could progress any farther upstream. Goods had to be transferred to small keelboats that made their way by skirting the raft, cutting into the many bayous, which had increased in number because of diversion of river water blocked from the main channel by the Great Raft. Small keelboats and canoes could travel the bayous, but the waters were too shallow for steamboats. Often the crews of the small nonmechanical boats found that driftwood had blocked the mouth of a bayou since their last passage, converting the bayou to a lake. Occasionally, passage could be made to the opposite bank of the Red between sections of the Great Raft, for the formation was not entirely solid. From time to time a section, which might be a half mile or so in length, would break away at the foot of the raft, causing variations in the location of the foot. But each year more driftwood came down from the upper reaches of the Red, adding to the total length of the Great Raft at a faster rate than segments broke away.

No one knew how old the Great Raft was. The Red River's upper course was through the alluvial soil and forest lands of northeastern Texas. Trees rooted in the loose soil were easily washed free when rivers rose in floodtime and in seasons of heavy rains. The trees thus freed often piled up one upon another at a bend in the river—and there were many bends. The resulting buildup of wood collected more branches and silt. The long-term effect was that as the wood decayed, new growth sprouted upon it, becoming trees that rooted in the original driftwood. The top growth was mostly willows and cottonwood.

Shreve learned that land development along the Red River was delayed because prospective farmers saw no way to market the cotton or other products that could be grown in the rich soils upriver from the raft. Bordering the raft, the numerous bayous that had formed as the channel was filled and waters diverted, had led to the flooding of many hundreds of acres that could otherwise be productive.

For some years, a group of residents in the area had been petitioning Congress for aid in opening the river, but since the population was sparse, Congress paid little heed until the Red River assumed greater importance around 1830. Eastern Texas along the upper Red River was officially a part of Mexico, although there were many Americans who went there to live following the bestowal of a land grant by the Mexican government to Stephen F. Austin in 1821. The United States was known to be casting an acquisitive eye upon this area, which would be far more accessible if the Red River were opened.

This was also the period of forced removal of many of the eastern Indians to Oklahoma, then called Indian Territory. The Red River was the boundary between Indian Territory and Texas. It assumed new importance because it was logical to maintain a military post in Indian Territory that could be reached via the Red River. The first military post so located was Fort Towson, established in May, 1824, about 1,100 river miles above the mouth of the Red, on the east bank of Gates Creek about six miles north of the Red.[19] This was about 200 miles as the crow flies above Natchitoches but nearly 700 miles by winding river. The worthy representatives in Congress believed that better transportation to Fort Towson was vital to protecting American interests in Indian matters and in the Mexican-Texas situation. So inaccessible had Fort Towson been that it had been abandoned in June, 1829. It was burned shortly thereafter, but the recent turn of events had made it advisable to rebuild and restaff Fort Towson at a location south of Gates Creek in 1831. An effort to remove or bypass the Great Raft to allow steamboats to reach Fort Towson now became important in national defense, and pleas for funding no longer fell on deaf ears.

Before Shreve received his first letter from Gratiot on the subject, an expedition of military men had gone to survey the situation. They concluded that removal of the Great Raft was next to an impossibility and that perhaps canals could be dug to make a steamboat channel bypass. The officer in command was one Lieutenant W. Seawell of the Seventh Regiment Infantry, temporarily on engineer duty.[20] Lieutenant Seawell directed the digging of a short experimental canal near a trading post known as Coate's Bluff, where the city of Shreveport is now. Seawell saw no way that the Great Raft could be removed and conceded that the canal system would be costly indeed, both to construct and to maintain.

19. Robert W. Frazer, *Forts of the West: Military Forts and Presidios and Posts Commonly Called Forts West of the Mississippi River to 1898* (Norman, 1965), 125.
20. Registry for 1831, *American State Papers: Documents of Congress of the United States*, Vol. V: *Military Affairs*, Pt. 4, p. 669.

The members of Congress were unsure of how to proceed. Even were the mudbank canals to be dredged out successfully, they would be in constant need of redredging. General Gratiot wrote to Shreve asking if he could visualize a better way of attacking the problem. Did Shreve think there was any possible way of removing the Great Raft? Of course, any proposals would have to be made with the limitations of the budget established by Congress in mind. The letter, dated September 5, 1832, ended with a suggestion: "It is believed that the small steamboats at present engaged on the Ohio might, as soon as their operations on that river are closed, be despatched to the Red river to make trial of the proposed project by commencing at the foot of the raft, and removing the timbers of which it is composed in detail throughout to its head. This, however, must be considered by you as but a mere suggestion for the present, as no further measure in the matter will be taken until your communication in answer is received."[21]

Shreve received the letter in his Louisville home. He was rather surprised at the suggestion of deployment of some of his equipment to the Red River, for his newly renewed contract specified only the Mississippi, Ohio, and Arkansas rivers for his work area, and furthermore, his Ohio River work was incomplete. Apparently the War Department assumed enlargement of his area of responsibility and wanted the Red River improvement to take precedence. Shreve felt a quickening of his pulse, for he never could resist a challenge, and removal of the Great Raft would most certainly be a challenge.

But he knew what his snag boat could do, and he believed it could pull that raft apart and set those logs free to float on downriver to the sea. It might take a while—he began to make estimates. Then it occurred to him that the freed logs would collect at a bend or around a snag rather than going on with the current, and the raft would gradually rebuild itself farther downriver. Yes, the *Archimedes* could pull the raft apart, but he would also have to dispose of the driftwood. Perhaps clearing the banks below the Great Raft of protruding trees and snags would allow the logs to float on to the Mississippi. But opening a clear channel would have to be the first step. He sat down to write his reply to General Gratiot on September 29. His letter read, in part:

21. Hardin, *Northwestern Louisiana*, 252.

To accomplish that object, I would recommend that the banks of the river should be cleared of all the trees that are now on its banks in and near the water, which are so situated as to be liable to obstruct the free passage of the floating timber as it passes down the stream, after it may have been removed from the lower end of the raft. By this means the masses of timber which now form that great raft, after being loosened from the lower end, will find its way to the Mississippi river, and from thence to the Gulf of Mexico, and will not be liable at any other point to form similar rafts.[22]

General Gratiot took this letter as Shreve intended it—an acceptance of the challenge. He wrote a letter back to Shreve on February 8, 1833, that began with the summary command, "You will proceed with as little delay as possible after the receipt of this, with such of the boats, machinery, etc. under your command as may be used with advantage, [to] the great raft on Red River, La., and commence operations on its removal."

The expenditure allowed for the removal of the raft was what remained of a $25,000 appropriation by Congress before Lieutenant Seawell's expedition. The amount left was $22,628. Shreve was informed that of this amount, $965 had already been spent to pay a "balance due under the former superintendent." This left him $21,663, which he was cautioned to be careful not to exceed.[23]

Correspondence between Louisville and Washington was frequent for the next month or two. Shreve could not simply drop all his other responsibilities and spend his full time preparing to go to the Red River. He would have to make assignments for continuation of work in other locations. Fortunately, he was familiar enough with the Red River and its valley to enable him to anticipate some of the problems that would be sure to arise. In a letter written on February 24, he specified which of his vessels he would take and also stated: "The great raft is in so remote a part of the country that I cannot receive monthly remittances. It is therefore necessary that I should take with me the necessary funds."

To this, General Gratiot responded on March 6, stating that the necessary funds were being forwarded to Shreve in Louisville. In another letter came orders for work with the *Archimedes* on the upper Ohio, although Shreve had specified that snag boat as the one he was repairing and pre-

22. *Ibid.*, 252–53.

23. Robert B. DeBlieux (comp.), "Excerpts from Correspondence Between Captain Henry Miller Shreve and His Superior, Brigadier General C. Gratiot, 1832–33," *North Louisiana Historical Association Newsletter* (April, 1966).

paring for the heavy duty that would be demanded of it in Louisiana. It vexed the captain to have the personnel in Washington allow themselves to be so remote from actuality as to overlook such details as that one snag boat could not be in two locations simultaneously. He nevertheless was patient in his expression of his reactions in a letter he wrote from Louisville on March 23, just preceding his departure on the new assignment.[24]

> SIR: Your letter dated the 27th ultimo, acknowledging the receipt of my reports of work done in the month of December last, and suggesting the employment of the steam snag-boat Archimedes above the falls of the Ohio, and asking the privilege to build repairing docks, and authorizing the working of the Archimedes &c. has been received.
>
> I have to inform you that the expedition to the Red river will prevent that boat from working above the falls in Ohio, as contemplated, as she is the most important boat I have for removal of the raft. She arrived here on the 20th instant. The crew which was in her since June last has been paid off; her engines have undergone the necessary repairs, and she is now in readiness to leave for Red river. Two of the other three steamboats are also ready. The other will be repaired and ready for the 26th. On that day I shall probably leave. I have all the stores on board, and the men shipped. Nothing except a failure of my receiving the funds by that day will delay me longer. I have applied the balance remaining in my hands from the Ohio and Mississippi, to make the necessary repairs of boats, and purchase of stores for subsistence. I hope, however, no delay will take place on that account. I find public opinion much against the probability of removing the raft; but I am of a different opinion, and believe that I shall succeed. However, I am not yet discouraged. Your letter of the 6th instant, informing me of a requisition in my favor for $21,663, and yours of the 8th, relating to my request to have copies of surveys and reports of the raft in Red river have also been received.
>
> I am, &c.
> HENRY M. SHREVE

He had risen to a challenge. He stood almost alone in the opinion that the Great Raft could be removed. He heard many a discouraging word as "public opinion" was expressed, but this was not new in his life and experience. Shreve's indomitable spirit was aroused, and it would take more than mere public opinion now to turn him away from the challenge of the Great Raft.

24. Hardin, *Northwestern Louisiana*, 254.

12 / **Attack on the Great Raft**

Natchez lay shrouded in predawn mist on April 3, 1833, when Captain
Henry M. Shreve directed the small steamboat *Java* to the shadowy
riverfront of Natchez-Under-the-Hill. A sister steamboat, the *Souvenir*,
cut its engines and moved into place behind the *Java*. Just down the river
the *Pearl*, the third of the working steamboats of the flotilla, was tied, and
looming large and shadowy beyond it was the snag boat *Archimedes*, with
its great eighteen-foot wheels rising nearly as high as its smokestacks. The
Archimedes and the *Pearl* had arrived at the Natchez rendezvous point
thirty-six hours ahead of the *Java* and the *Souvenir*.

All of these steam vessels were the property of the United States Corps
of Engineers. With them, plus a fleet of keelboats and rafts and 159 men,
Shreve was prepared to tackle the job of removing the Great Raft of the
Red River, despite the skeptics who declared it could not be done. Natchez
was the last stop above the mouth of the Red River, and Shreve called the
halt for final checking of equipment and supplies. Near the end of the day,
he sat down at the table in his quarters to write a short letter to General
Gratiot. He posted the letter, and at six in the evening steam was up on
all four vessels.

The three steamboats that accompanied the steam snag boat bore little resemblance to the *George Washington* and other passenger liners except in their operating machinery. There was no air of luxury and no fine carpets, silver service, or any of the other refinements on the *Java*, the *Pearl*, and the *Souvenir*. The accommodations were strictly utilitarian, for these were working steamboats. They were smaller in size than the passenger boats, required less depth of water for flotation, and were built with sturdiness in mind, for they worked as supplements to the snag boat and took much battering against floating logs. In such work as dredging, lifting, and pushing operations, the small steamboats moved about like workers of a bee colony about the "queen" snag boat.

On the evening of April 3, darkness was already closing in as Shreve blew the three long blasts that signaled that the fleet was to move out into the Mississippi and head downstream. The men would be leaving the familiar world behind them for several months. At the mouth of the Red, the steamboats would take flatboats and keelboats in tow for the journey upriver to the site of the Great Raft.

In his note to General Gratiot posted in Natchez, Shreve estimated the little fleet would reach the foot of the raft on April 9.[1] The actual arrival was two days later, on the morning of April 11. All through the hundreds of miles of ascending the rusty red, twisting river, Shreve made notes and map sketches of river conditions and his course. The Red was within two feet of its all-time high-water mark; it was obvious that if he tried to clear the banks of trees as he had outlined in his earlier plans, formulated in Louisville, much of the cutting would have to be done underwater. It could be months before the water dropped to normal or low level. Shreve reconsidered his plans. Would it be possible to find a way to dispose of the great mass of material he would pull from the raft other than releasing it to float down the river?

As the *Java* moved up the river, Shreve noted and mapped the many bayous and overflow outlets along the Red. Some of these would be isolated lakes as the water level dropped, but he had no proper map to indicate which were permanently open channels. In fact, the full course of the Red River, including its source, was still unknown. The same Major Stephen H. Long whose aborted Yellowstone expedition had brought the first steamboats up the Missouri River had turned from that expedition to

1. Hardin, *Northwestern Louisiana*, 254.

an attempt to locate the source of the Red River. In what is now Oklahoma he charted some streams that he thought might be the source of the
Red. None could be selected just for its color, for all of them ran through
the red soil that gave the water its rusty hue. Long and his men followed
one such stream for two hundred miles, having been told by Indians that
this was indeed the Red River, only to find that it was the Canadian, a
tributary of the Arkansas. "In a region of red clay and sand, where all the
streams become nearly the color of arterial blood, it is not surprising that
several rivers should have received the same name," wrote one of the
men of the Long expedition.[2]

The Red River's banks and those of the tributaries that fed into it were
nearly all composed of this loose, red soil. Not only did this affect the
color of the water, but the loose soil also allowed whole trees to be torn
from the banks and carried downstream whenever floods came. Over the
many centuries, the trees thus washed downstream had accumulated to
form the Great Raft. The raft in turn affected the flow of the water, slow-
ing the current to sluggishness and blocking the channel 'so that water
spread into the bayous. The Red's main channel was inclined to shift
frequently, and the river was by 1833 a network of side channels, or
"chutes," and bayous.

The strange nature of the Red River is evident in the rough sketch
Shreve prepared and included in his later report to the army engineers
(see Figure 16). The drawing is a detail of the segment of the Red blocked
by the Great Raft as he found it in 1833. Shreve estimated the raft's length
at 160 miles; others have said it was closer to 200 miles long. The turns
and twists of the river made determination of the length difficult.

The flotilla made a brief stop at Alexandria, having covered about one-
third of the distance upriver to the foot of the Great Raft. Alexandria, a
settlement almost as old as Natchitoches, is in the geographical center of
the state of Louisiana. It began at the time of early French explorations as
a trading post located where rapids—or the "Rapides"—disturbed the
otherwise gentle flow of the Red. In 1833, Alexandria showed promise of
becoming a metropolitan center for central Louisiana, already boasting its
own bank and the College of Rapides, where the well-known Reverend
Timothy Flint of Massachusetts was a teacher.[3]

2. Grant Foreman, *Adventure on the Red River* (Norman, 1937), 9.
3. Timothy Flint, *Recollections of the Last Ten Years in the Valley of the Mississippi*, ed.
George R. Brooks (Carbondale, Ill., 1968), 230, 324n.

After the Louisiana Purchase, a large number of American families had come to Alexandria and homesteaded in the pine forests of the area on both sides of the river. They added a new element to the mixture of cultures that already included French, Spanish, black, and Indian. A crowd of people representing all of these cultures came to the riverfront to see the curious, double-hulled steam snag boat that tied up there briefly and the little fleet of steamboats that accompanied it. They talked of how all the Red River settlements would grow when the river was open to steamboat traffic all the way to Fort Towson, although, as always, there were those who seriously doubted that the Great Raft could be removed. But even some of these doubters were impressed by Shreve's confident manner; it was clear that when he gave an order, he expected it to be obeyed. His physical presence was also impressive, for though he no longer had the slender, youthful build that had characterized him in earlier days, he had gained a solidity that commanded respect.

Beyond Alexandria there was but one settlement, Natchitoches. As he approached the village, named for a tribe of the Caddoan confederacy, Shreve had a surprise. When he brought the *Enterprise* to this town twenty years before, he had docked the steamboat almost in the heart of the settlement. But now the main channel of the Red River had shifted, leaving Natchitoches without a riverfront. The people had not yet adjusted to the idea that this was a permanent change, for it had taken place just a year earlier, in the high waters of 1832, when the Red had cut a new main channel five miles to the east. This alteration weakened the residents' confidence that as the Great Raft was removed, Natchitoches would become a major city of Louisiana. In place of a navigable river, they were left with a quiet loop of water that took on the nature of a lake. This was a real blow to the aspirations of the citizens of the old settlement; its *raison d'être* was seriously threatened.

The fleet continued on upriver about ten miles. The recent floods had loosened the lowest sections of the Great Raft, breaking them off to form again in bayous or inlets or to stop against other snags at riverbends. The foot was somewhat farther upstream than at last report. On the morning of April 11, opposite Loggy Bayou, they reached the mass of timber.

Shreve wasted no time. He was eager to test his expectations of how the *Archimedes* would dig into the Great Raft. By ten o'clock he had chosen the place he considered right for the first attack, and the work began. The full force of the snag boat was applied against one log after another until a section of the raft separated from the main body. The old, rotted wood gave way quite easily.

He was pleased and at the same time a little perplexed. He now had to dispose of the driftwood in a different way from the one he had planned. All the way upriver he had been concerned about it. He wanted to clear the banks for at least fifty miles below the foot of the raft so that the drift-wood could float freely. But the water level had not yet begun to drop. Too many willows and other trees that leaned out over the water when it was at normal level were now deep in the water; bank clearance was not prac-tical. He wanted to have a clear channel 130 feet or wider to enable the old logs to float freely.

As soon as work began, he learned that the current was too sluggish to carry off the loose logs. As he pondered the situation, an idea occurred to him. There were all those bayous branching off from the river. Why not force the floating timber into the bayous and let them fill up? This would dispose of the wood and at the same time hold the river's flow into its proper channel. Before the first day of work came to an end, the little steamboats were forcing the freed material into a bayou.

At day's end he wrote a report to General Gratiot to send on its way the next morning. Five miles of the raft had been loosened on that very first day! He tried not to let his jubilation or an air of "I told you so" creep into his correspondence. But the going was easy and he was even more certain of success. He assured the general that the Red could be made safe for steamboat navigation and spoke of being able to remove the whole raft in sixty-six days.

But the foot of the raft was less compact and more rotted than the struc-ture was a few miles farther into its body. The work had gone on for about three and a half weeks when Shreve again reported to headquarters. He told of how he had found the solution to the problems of disposal but was slightly less optimistic in his estimate of working time needed.[4]

> Great Raft, Red River
> 8th May, 1833
>
> SIR: I have the honor to inform the department that I have progressed through the raft about forty miles: in the main bed of the river, in that distance, thirty-one sections of the raft have been removed by drawing them out log by log, and

4. Hardin, *Northwestern Louisiana*, 255–56.

separating them in such manner as to pass them down the bayous that lead to the swamps and into the low bottoms that are found on either the one or the other side of the river, near the whole distance from the foot of the raft to this place. The willows and other timber that lean over the water are all cut away; the islands have been cleared of timber by hauling the trees out by the roots, so as to make the navigation good as far as I have proceeded.

I shall probably not be able to reach Coate's settlement this season; however, I shall make every exertion in my power to do so; if I succeed, the steamboat navigation will be extended about eighty miles higher up the river. The keel-boat navigation at the same time will be shortened round the raft about two-thirds in distance. What portion of the whole labor and expense will then be completed, I am not now prepared to say, but, previous to my leaving the raft, I will be so well informed, that I may make a rough estimate. As relates to the practicability of effecting a complete and permanent improvement, there is no longer a doubt; I view it certain of success; nothing but a sufficient amount of funds, with enterprise and the requisite skill, is required to render the navigation as safe and certain at all stages of water through the raft as it now is from the Mississippi to its foot.

I should have made more frequent communication to the department had it not been for the impossibility of sending letters to Natchitoches without despatching a steamboat to that place until I had proceeded thus far up from whence I am able to send by land.

The health of the men has been good, the work is now progressing much faster than when I first commenced the operations.

I am, &c.
Henry M. Shreve
Superintendent, & c.

A week later, on May 16, Captain Shreve wrote again: "I am now about fifty-five miles up from its foot, at the junction of Bayou Pass a Gola, which passes out from the main bed of the river on its right bank and falls into bayou Pierre; it is about as large as the main river; I am now engaged in removing some rafts in it, by which means I shall open its channel in such a manner as to be a safe deposit for the raft in the main bed, perhaps for twenty miles above."[5]

The crew were by then working in the full heat of summer in a steamy climate in which the humidity was close to 100 percent. Most of the men spent hours in the water, often with the full force of the semitropical sun beating down upon them. These were men from the Ohio River valley,

5. Ibid., 256.

unaccustomed to southern summer weather, particularly in a swampy region. They were working through a region of low hills forested with long-
needle pines and scrubby oaks of the variety known as blackjack, but
down on the river the bluffs and rolling land held in the steaminess of the
Red's floodplain. Besides the climate, the crew had to deal with animal
life to which they were unaccustomed—"alligators, snakes, and noxious
animals," in the words of Timothy Flint in a letter written while he was
teaching in Alexandria.[6]

Directing his men on the job, Shreve was constantly on the move, en-
ergetic, and bathed in sweat himself. He kept the snag boat continually
busy ramming at the mass of logs. Shouting men pulled the logs away and
pushed them on toward the swamps and bayous. Steamboats puffed about
busily, prodding, pushing against the logs, packing them tightly in their
new formations in the bayous.

On the *Archimedes*, machinery growled and groaned as the "choc-
taws," the huge ancient logs and root masses, were broken loose. "Haul
in!" was the shout and the windlass screeched as the engineer set the
wheels turning to pull in the cable. The *Archimedes* strained and tilted,
but again and again it was the winner in the battle against the huge snags.
Its steam power set the giant saw wheel turning, and with agonized
squeals and wails the great chunks of tree trunk and root were cut to a size
that could be floated away under control.

Men on rafts pushed and prodded at the released ancient wood, forming it into new, small, manageable rafts that could be nudged and bumped
by the little, steamboats until they entered a bayou. There the men in
smaller craft kept them moving on in. When the bayou seemed full, a
steamboat would push and shove at the mass, going as far in as the water
depth permitted before backing off. Thus the bayous were filled and the
water flow was changed. The waters in the main channel grew deeper,
and the current increased from a sluggish quarter mile per hour to about
three miles per hour.

Shreve described the work to General Gratiot.

> One of these bayous, the Pass a Gola, was as large as the river; it has been
> filled full of timber from the raft, a distance of about four miles, and so drove in
> by running a steamboat frequently against the timber as it was conveyed in,

6. Daniel Dennett, *Louisiana as It Is* (New Orleans, 1876), 30; Flint, *Recollections*, 232.

that near all the water was immediately forced down the old bed of the river. To complete the improvement, all these bayous must be stopped up in such a manner as effectually to prevent their washing any longer, and draining off the water from the old bed of the river, which has sufficient capacity to carry off the whole volume of water, so soon as the timber that has grown up in it since the formation of the raft is cut away and the raft removed.[7]

In late May he looked back downriver with satisfaction. Mile after mile, where there had been the horrible, blockading Great Raft and only sluggish water alongside it, there was now open river where the *Java*, the *Pearl*, and the *Souvenir* could move about freely. But, although he would have liked to continue the work, Shreve had to face the fact that he must be satisfied with what had been accomplished to date until cool weather returned. By the end of May, twenty-five men were ill. It was obvious that the crew could not hold up under the even steamier days sure to come in July and August, and if illness spread, even June would not be a work month. Progress had slowed because of the lack of manpower and also because the farther upriver the work progressed, the more solid and difficult to penetrate was the Great Raft. It was built up with soil and tangled growth that made every mile of advancement like thirty miles at the beginning.

On June 5 Shreve wrote that he was within three miles of the Caddo agency, just downriver from the point he had earlier referred to as "Coate's settlement," seventy miles into the Great Raft. It was an area into which Caddoan Indians had moved; at the time of their arrival they had been squeezed between French settlements to the southeast and Spanish settlements to the west. Believed to have come originally from the Southwest, the Caddoans who settled in the Red River valley lost many of the nomadic tendencies of plains Indians and built more or less permanent villages. One of these settlements was on a bluff above the river where Shreve's men were working, on the southwestern bank. Like other Caddo villages, it was made up of groups of dome-shaped huts of mud and straw, arranged in a circle with a large building that served as a community house in the center. In the open space about this central building the ceremonial dances and other rites took place.[8] The inhabitants of the Caddo villages had organized governments and abided by a code of laws. They

7. Hardin, *Northwestern Louisiana*, 257–58.
8. Works Projects Administration Writers' Program, *Louisiana* (New York, 1945), 361.

were generally peace-loving and willing to discuss problems with the whites who came into their area, treating them courteously until given reason to be antagonistic. Often they honored the white visitors with ceremonial feasts.

A United States Indian Agency cabin, a fairly new one, was at the edge of the village that Shreve was approaching. The Indians themselves, of the Kadohadachos tribe of the Caddoan confederacy, had not been in that location long, having come there around 1800. They had been forced to move southward from lands north and east as Osage Indians responded to pressure to leave Missouri by taking land near the Arkansas-Oklahoma line where the Kadohadachos had been established. The United States government had granted them the land between the Red River and the Sabine to the west, land also claimed by Mexico.[9]

But the floods of the Red River and the swampiness endangered crops and health. The Mexican government, wishing to build up a population friendly to itself in Texas, invited the Caddos to take lands west of the Sabine, and some had already left. When the United States government opened the agency on the Red, the remaining Indians became hopeful of being paid for their land. In their dealings with the Indian agent, they were represented by a white man named Larkin Edwards, said to have come to Louisiana with the Indians when they moved southward from Arkansas. Edwards had married a Caddo woman when his first wife died.

A few other white people had come to live at a place named Coate's Bluff, just upriver from the Caddo village, now in Shreveport at the east end of Olive Street. The news that the Great Raft was about to be removed was already attracting more white settlers, and it was expected that the government would soon purchase the Caddo lands to expand the settlement area. Word of government plans to open more land always brought a stream of restless American frontiersmen and their long-suffering wives and families, regardless of how raw the frontier might be.

Not quite all of the land was to become United States government land. The people of the Caddo village considered Larkin Edwards to be their friend, and when they learned that he, growing old, planned to remain on the Red River, they offered him a gift of a section of land of his own choos-

9. Holice H. Henrici, *Shreveport Saga* (Baton Rouge, 1977), 34.

ing. This section was not to be included in the cession to the government. It was payment in appreciation to Edwards for acting as the interpreter and friend of the Indians in many situations during the years he had lived among them.

In mid-June, Shreve made the acquaintance of Larkin Edwards, his grown sons Larkin, Jr., Newton, and John, and his daughter, Mary Irwin, married to a gunsmith who worked at the Indian agency. The elder Edwards and the handful of other whites who had come to the Coate's Bluff area were enthusiastic at the arrival of the quiet, confident captain and amazed at how he and his crew, with the *Archimedes*, were changing the Red River. The fact that steamboats were reaching Coate's Bluff meant that their hopes for growth would be fulfilled.

Among the first to act upon the rumors that the Great Raft would be removed were two enterprising New Englanders, William Bennett and James Cane. The two had come two or three years earlier from Montgomery, Alabama, after emigrating from New Hampshire. They left their wives at Montgomery while they went ahead to establish a business, building a double log cabin on a bluff just upriver from Coate's. The firm of Bennett and Cane was doing well enough that by 1832 it had issued paper currency to facilitate trading at the post. In 1833 they were sending for their families.

Shreve was pleased that the opening of the river to steamboats was already showing results and arousing confidence in the future of the upper Red River valley. He assured all the people he met that he would be back to finish the job. But for the summer of 1833, he could no longer keep his crew working. Too many were in ill health, and all were complaining of the great difficulty of working in the oppressive heat. Shreve realized they would walk out on him if he did not call a halt for the season.

Around June 20 they were working directly opposite Coate's Bluff. Shreve announced that this would be the stopping place and that camp would be set up among their new friends when they returned to resume work. On June 23 he ended operations, packed up equipment, and leaving behind whatever would not be needed in working other locations, set off down the Red River.

Shreve was busy again with observations and notations as they went along. He was particularly interested in how the riverbed and current had been altered by the removal of the raft for the estimated seventy-one miles already cleared. He saw that the increased current had washed out the channel to a depth of at least ten feet, adequate for navigation of all but the largest steamboats. Forty miles below the former foot of the Great Raft, he found that silt removal was still going on. The current had definitely increased to at least three miles per hour from the almost still water encountered in April. He saw that follow-up work would be needed because there were still some snags in the river, revealed when the water level had dropped. He also felt that he still needed to do timber clearance along the banks to maintain an open river.

When the fleet reached Natchez on June 27, Shreve wrote out his observations in a letter to General Gratiot. He also expressed his continued confidence that the raft could be completely removed and steamboat navigation far up the Red made possible. He was very optimistic about the economic benefits that would result from opening the river since the land was already being settled along the cleared area. Soon the newcomers would be marketing agricultural products that would make the expense to the government pay off handsomely. The land would also be of increased value when the government offered tracts for sale. These were advantages in addition to making Fort Towson and other frontier military posts more accessible, along with improving the prospects for the United States in relation to Texas.

Before he broke camp, Shreve had been thinking of his financial needs for the next season. He was aware that all the funds allotted by Congress for the Red River project had been spent and that before work could continue, there would have to be another appropriation. On June 5 he had written: "As relates to the expense to the United States, it will be no cost, but a large profit on the expenditure. The land on the immediate line of the raft will doubtless reimburse the Government four fold in a short time, the whole of which will be settled with cotton plantations in a very short time."[10] He later drew up an estimate for the cost of completing the removal of the raft, assuming that a minimum of seventy miles was yet to be done.[11]

10. Hardin, *Northwestern Louisiana*, 257.
11. *Ibid.*, 260.

Estimate of the probable amount of funds required to remove the remaining balance of the great raft in Red river.

300 men, including officers, mechanics, and laborers, from the
    1st October to 31st May, 8 months $44,000.00
Subsistence of 300 men 8 months, at $7.50 per month each 18,000.00
6,000 cords of wood for steamboats, at $2.25 per cord 13,500.00
Tools, cordage, &c 10,000.00
Wear and tear of steamboats 14,500.00
                                                   $100,000.00

Henry M. Shreve, Sup't &c.

Getting Congress to appropriate sufficient funds turned out to be a major part of Shreve's work. He had to haggle over items in his expense reports and put up with criticism from those who knew nothing of the problems he was encountering. The investigating committee of engineers had suggested, before Shreve tackled the removal of the Great Raft, that the job probably could not be done at all and that if, by some means or other it could be accomplished, the cost would be about three million dollars. But when Shreve proposed that one-thirtieth of this amount be appropriated to remove the remaining half of the Great Raft, the outcry was loud and indignant. Committees of men ignorant of the conditions Shreve was facing pronounced his demands outrageous and postponed any appropriation at all.

When Shreve arrived home in Louisville, his wife, Mary, greeted him in tears. The household was in mourning, because their elder daughter, Harriet, was dead. Harriet Louise Shreve had married John W. Reel of Louisville in 1830. The young couple's only child did not arrive until almost three years later, while Shreve was in the wilds of Louisiana doing battle against the Great Raft. He had hoped to come home to a happy meeting with his first grandchild and possibly a second one as well (daughter Rebecca was also expecting). The baby, a little girl named Harriet after her mother, was born on April 26, 1833, and was doing quite well. But her mother had not recovered. John Reel turned his baby daughter over to her grandmother Mary for care as he saw his wife failing. While Shreve was en route home, his elder daughter died at the age of twenty-one. Little Harriet Reel made her home with her grandparents until her own marriage in 1852, when she was nineteen.

At this time there was also another infant in the family. In 1832 Rebecca Shreve had married Walker Randolph Carter, whose home was just north of St. Louis. Two weeks after baby Harriet's birth, their first baby arrived—a boy named Henry Shreve Carter, born on May 9. Rebecca had come home to Louisville for the baby's birth.

For the rest of the summer, spirits were lifted somewhat by the presence of the babies. Mary, accustomed to doing without her husband for more time than she had him at home, had plenty to do that summer. For his part Shreve spent quite a bit of time on the multitude of paper work involved in his supervision of all the engineering projects under his control. One of his first obligations was to write a report of the progress thus far on the Red River.

He hoped to return there to continue the raft removal as soon as the hot weather had ended, about October 1. But controversies arose over his expense estimate. His report had been submitted on July 30. Two months later no appropriation had been voted. He sent in his map of the river segment, explaining that the sketch of the area upriver from Coate's Bluff was based on the "best information I could obtain. It is by no means strictly correct, but will convey a more correct idea of the country than can be otherwise given."[12]

All hopes of an October departure were abandoned, and Shreve turned to his Ohio and Mississippi river projects. In December he was still without approval to go on with the raft removal project. He wrote to General Gratiot from Louisville on December 19, 1833. He had not given up on the Louisiana work and was still sure that eventually Congress would settle down to action and approve his budget. He pointed out that delay was costly, since nature would make additional clean-up work necessary because of the lost season. He also stated the appropriation would have to be increased. His letter showed that his mind was on the Red, even if he could not be there in person. He was envisioning the flow of driftwood down the river and foresaw that it would collect at a place about fifty miles up from its mouth, where there was a shoal, a lake branching off, and the mouth of a tributary—the Black River—just a few miles below. He recommended that the lake be separated from the river by means of a dam of earth, brush, and log piles. An alternative was to open a wider passage.

12. *Ibid.*, 263.

One of these plans, Shreve insisted, must be followed to avoid a blockade of accumulated driftwood at that point in the Red River. He estimated the cost for either plan at about five thousand dollars.

He also suggested that the idea of hiring slave labor to work on the raft clearance should be explored because he was finding it difficult to get his regular employees to agree to return to that arduous and unhealthful work. He believed that slaves could be hired from their owners for twelve dollars each per month and offered a revision of his labor calculations based upon hiring two hundred blacks. He saw this as almost his only hope of getting a working crew. Over the months, he wrote, he had made it his business "to sound the men, and find an almost universal determination among them not to risk an expedition to that river. The existing prejudice has been created by the men employed in that river during last spring, many of whom came home sick, but few of whom died; still they have given out the opinion that the climate is extremely fatal to the health of laborers. The severity of the service is also a very material objection among the laborers."[13]

The rest of the winter, Shreve awaited a response from Congress. In the spring, he took the first of many steps to have payment by the United States government made to him for the use of his invention of the steam snag boat. He wrote out a petition to Congress, dated May 1, 1834, and may even have appeared before the House of Representatives in person, as "Washington City" appears alongside the date in the records. He offered testimony of the value of his invention as it was being used by the government on the Mississippi, Ohio, Arkansas, Missouri, and Red rivers and added, "With the aid of said snag boats, thirty-two men can perform as much labor in a day, as can be performed by five hundred men without such boats."[14] After enlarging on the income that would come to the government upon completion of the Great Raft's removal, he suggested that he be paid not in money but in land along the Red River, asking for 25,000 acres that the government then priced at $1.25 per acre.

Representative William H. Ashley of the Committee on Public Lands wrote an enthusiastic report on the merits of Shreve's request. His report was placed in the records as of June 5, 1834. Ashley recommended that the work on the Great Raft be completed and gave high commendations

13. *Ibid.*, 264.
14. *Congressional Record*, 24th Cong., 1st Sess., 3–4.

to Shreve, acknowledging the validity of his request for payment for the use of his invention. And yet he proposed a cut in the amount of land to be granted to Shreve from 25,000 acres to 11,250.[15] At the $1.25 price, this would amount to only $14,400 for all rights, past and future, to the use of Shreve's snag machine.

Shreve must have been shocked. He felt his request was reasonable. He could hold the land for a period of time, and when the river was opened and land values had risen, he could sell it for a price in line with the value of his invention. This would minimize the cost to the government. He was no doubt angered at having the validity of his claim acknowledged only to have payment downgraded. He apparently withdrew his offer to take payment in land.

As he waited for Congress to act on the Great Raft appropriation, Shreve pondered his situation. His appointive position offered no security, for he could be replaced at a shifting of the political winds. The snag boats were government property and would continue in use under future superintendents. The machines would be replaced, as they wore out, with replicas built on Shreve's designs. He would not give up on getting Congress to make suitable payment for rights to the invention. It was saving the government untold dollars each year in labor outlay, aside from other benefits.

Eventually, Congress acted on Ashley's strong recommendation that the Red River raft work be funded. The report was indeed convincing, for Ashley pointed out that the cost of freight shipments up to Fort Towson was expected to be reduced from three dollars per hundredweight to seventy-five cents. He stated that completion of the raft removal was not only "highly desirable in a military point of view, but . . . it will add some eight or ten millions to the value of the public domain on the waters of Red river, and eventually be productive of incalculable agricultural and commercial advantages." The same congressional report acknowledged widespread use of Shreve's snag boats on the upper Mississippi and the Missouri and its tributaries. The report stated that the snag boat could make even the distant Yellowstone River navigable for steamboats for "five or six hundred miles, almost to the eastern base of the Rocky mountains."

15. Shreve, *Memorial*, second part, 3–5. This part consists of the report of the Committee on Public Lands, reprinted from *Congressional Record*, 23rd Cong., 1st Sess.

The matter of payment for the invention was unsettled, but at last the appropriation and orders for continuation of the work on the Great Raft came through. Shreve was to plan to return to Louisiana in the autumn of 1834, about fifteen months after he left Coate's Bluff with promises to return soon. He had not been idle, of course. He had been supervising projects on the Mississippi, the Arkansas, and the Ohio and was personally involved in Ohio River improvements above Louisville. He finished this work on November 13, 1834.

Again he prepared for a long period away from home. At least now Mary would not be lonely. In about six weeks Rebecca was expecting her second child and was in Louisville with her mother, awaiting the birth. The house was lively with the presence of little Harriet and Henry. Although his departure must have been like that of a husband going off to war in a foreign land, Shreve saw that this time he need not worry that his wife would be brooding over his absence. He looked ahead with great interest to the work that awaited him at Coate's Bluff.

13 / **A City Founded, a Challenge Met**

On November 14, 1834, the working fleet again started down the Ohio bound for the Red River. Since the men were going to work in the comparative cool of the winter season, Captain Shreve was able to persuade his usual labor force to volunteer for the expedition. He reported taking three hundred men with him and apparently had abandoned the idea of employing slaves from the Louisiana plantations. He agreed to end the working season somewhat earlier than he had in 1833.

As they ascended the Red River, a disadvantage of starting at that season became evident. The water level was so low that the rock ledges that caused the rapids at Alexandria were scarcely covered by the water. Shreve grew impatient as the supplies, tools, and anything that added weight to the vessels had to be removed and carried to a point above the barrier. Even with minimal weight the situation was too precarious to use steam power. They hauled the boats with cables over the reefs by the old method of warping. Shreve saw how easily the riverbed could be engineered to completely eliminate the troublesome reefs, knowing he dared not spend time doing it then without congressional approval.

December 10 saw them about forty miles below Loggy Bayou, where they had found the foot of the Great Raft in the spring of 1833. The Red River narrowed at that place, "at the mouth of the Coshada chute," to a width of about two hundred feet. There they found so many trees growing in and near the water that Shreve decided to begin a clearance project, working on upriver and taking advantage of the low-water conditions. Snags and remnants of the raft were cleared away as the fleet progressed, and as before, they were forced into bayous. This work occupied the men until January 20, 1835.

As the men proceeded upriver toward Coate's Bluff, it was cheering to note the visible changes, mostly attributable to the opening of the waterway. More and more cabins appeared along the river. A strong influx of families, principally from the southeastern states, was taking place. Shreve foresaw that returns from the products of the farms would indeed soon compensate for the costs of clearing the Great Raft, as he had maintained in his letters to General Gratiot.

The crew set up camp near the growing settlements at Coate's Bluff and at Bennett and Cane's. The men quickly learned from the residents that a meeting was planned between agents of the United States government and representatives of the Caddo tribes. The purpose of the meeting was to be the signing of a treaty whereby the Caddos would give up all claims to this Red River valley land, now viewed as valuable and potentially very productive. Their cession, however, would exclude the section they had chosen to give to Larkin Edwards, a section whose location was to be specified by Edwards himself. It was rumored that Edwards' choice would be the land along the Red just downriver from Bennett and Cane's trading post.

On January 20, the crew resumed work on removal of the Great Raft below Bennett and Cane's bluff. At that segment of the Red River, it was difficult to determine which had been the main channel. The sluggish waters formed a network of inlets, bayous, and swampy lakes. The river was serpentine, doubling back in one loop after another. One of those loops, a short distance above the Caddo agency, almost made a complete circle, with its ends separated by a neck of land about an eighth of a mile wide. Shreve had noted on his sketch map that in all likelihood he would eliminate this loop, cutting a canal where the river completed its bend. The distance around the bend was at least eight miles, and to cut a canal of 260 yards length seemed a sensible step to take. After his experience with the cutoff near the mouth of the Red, however, he knew that the river could be somewhat unpredictable in its behavior when man interfered with its natural flow.

He took time to study the situation thoroughly and decided that the probability was that the results would be more beneficial than harmful. The crew of the *Archimedes* and fifteen extra hands began the cutting of a canal twenty-four feet wide and nine feet deep through most of the neck of land but wider and deeper through a timbered low area. Work on this cut began in March and was completed by a crew working with the *Archimedes* on April 2. On May 13 water was let into the canal. In three days' time, the flow had widened the canal to about two hundred feet and deepened it to about thirty feet. The *Java* and the *Souvenir* passed through it with no difficulty.

So badly clogged had the river been above this canal that formerly the water oozed rather than flowed, spreading into Bayou Pierre and the smaller Sand Beach Bayou. The men closed off the mouth of the latter with sections pulled from the Great Raft, and the openings into the old loop of the Red were also blocked with timber for some distance from either end. The flow of the river increased to an average of three miles per hour when the work was finished. Shreve felt that this cutoff was gratifying in its results.

Work continued that spring only until April 13, with progress to the entrance to Soda Bayou, marked "Lake Soder" on Shreve's rough map. The extra projects had slowed the work on timber removal, and the Great Raft was a solid, resisting mass in this part of the Red River. The men complained of ill health and the increasing heat and objected to continuing work into the summer steaminess. Shreve saw that to insist on a longer work season would be to invite mutiny. Agreeing to renew work the next season, the crew headed downriver to the Mississippi and thence up to the Ohio.

Shreve was in Louisville on July 1, 1835, writing his report. In it he expressed a conviction that one more season could see the work completed. He was less confident than formerly about exactly how long the season would have to be, for experience had taught him that weather conditions and other factors made this Red River job different from all others he had tackled. He added a recommendation that engineering work be done at the rapids near Alexandria, where he and his men had been de-layed in December. He suggested that the removal of the two reefs of rocks that stretched across the river there could be done with pick and shovel since the rock was of soft sandstone.

Congress was in a more giving mood that summer, and in the autumn Shreve was again heading for Red River. Most of the winter months were devoted to actual work on the Great Raft, for the previous season's snag and growth removal along the river had greatly improved the approach to the thirty miles of raft that remained. But progress was slow, for the tim-ber that had to be removed was tough and often covered with thick, grow-ing vegetation, unlike the looser, rotted character of lower segments of the raft.

While work was proceeding, Shreve became deeply involved in hap-penings in the area. Soon after his departure in the spring of 1835, a meet-ing between the Caddos and the government agents had taken place. The government offered goods in exchange for land, hardly a good trade for the Indians, it was later reported, for the goods were estimated to be worth scarcely a tenth of the value the agents stated. The Caddo chiefs signed the papers, however, and the land was surrendered. The formal ceremony had taken place on July 1, 1835, while Shreve was in Louisville writing his reports to General Gratiot. The Caddo Indians forfeited their entire reserve in that transaction, with the one exception of their gift to Larkin Edwards, the 640 acres considered by many to be the choicest site for the location of a settlement that would be sure to grow.

Larkin Edwards, who had lived there since 1803 in peace with the In-dians, found himself the center of attention. Word had spread far and wide that the Caddo lands would be available, and settlers flocked in like flies to a honeypot. Not all of them intended to farm. Some were shrewd men looking for ways to deal in land and thus become rich. Most promi-nent and perhaps the shrewdest of these was Angus McNeil. McNeil had migrated from North Carolina to Natchez in the 1820s and had become involved in banking there. He was doing well until the 1831 panic began. Debt-ridden, he headed west, thinking to go to Texas. This was just as the Caddo cession was taking place, however, and he glimpsed a dawning op-portunity in the neighborhood of Bennett and Cane's. His scheme had its inception when he learned that old Larkin Edwards had been given the choice block of land. He got in touch with an old associate in Natchez who owned a plantation and had financial resources, a man named Sturges Sprague. Then he began sidling up to Edwards to induce him to sell his land. He was successful. Edwards sold the land to McNeil in January, 1836, for five thousand dollars. This land would become the heart of the city of Shreveport.

There seems to be no record of why or when McNeil and Sprague drew Shreve into plans for forming a town company or why the settlement was to be named Shreve's Town, for the captain. But Shreve was never a man to miss an opportunity for a good business deal, and he became a member of the group formed to plat a town on Edwards' land.

While his crew was working on raft removal in the winter and early spring of 1836, Shreve spent quite a bit of time with the people of the growing settlements at Coate's Bluff and at Bennett and Cane's. He entered into long conversations with John Edwards, Larkin's son, who had acted as interpreter for the Caddos in their meeting of July 1, 1835, with the government agents, at which the principals were twenty-five Caddo chiefs and Jehiel Brooks, acting as commissioner for the United States. Edwards confided to Shreve his suspicions that the Indians had been hoodwinked. First of all, he claimed, they had agreed to sell for thirty thousand dollars, and the goods they had accepted had nowhere near that value. Also, Edwards said, a large tract of land other than the section reserved for Larkin Edwards had already been separated from the Caddo reservation, withdrawn by none other than the commissioner himself. Edwards said that the commissioner had stopped downriver to make a deal with "a half-breed Caddo, or his heirs" and bought from them the land starting at Pascagoula Bayou and going along Red River for about 36 miles of riverfront and including 34,500 acres (about 54 square miles) of choice land.

Shreve also heard much talk of Angus McNeil's schemes to make a big profit on the Edwards land. McNeil was scurrying about to find more people to invest in the development of a town on the land he had bought at such a low price from Edwards. By April, Shreve felt he should do something about the situation. On April 29, 1836, he addressed a letter to his old friend, Andrew Jackson, who was at that time president of the United States. Shreve believed the president should know of the alleged duplicity of the commissioner. The land Brooks had bought for himself, Shreve believed, could have been sold by the United States to individuals for "upwards of $150,000, if not double that amount." He also told President Jackson that the principal chiefs of the Caddos were ignorant of this tract having been removed from their reservation. "The opinion that prevails here is, that it was a premeditated plan to defraud the Government," Shreve wrote.[1]

Whatever the reason, and perhaps simply because he was known as a shrewd businessman, Shreve was invited by McNeil to a meeting on May 24, 1836, to participate in the formation of the new town. It was acknowledged that there would most certainly have been no town with good prospects for growth without the removal of the Great Raft and that the new community was to carry Shreve's name. The meeting of the Shreve Town Company was to be at Bushrod Jenkins' home, just below Coate's Bluff. Jenkins was among the earlier settlers and was in the business of buying and selling slaves. A fourth member of the group was Thomas Williamson, a man with good financial connections, from South Carolina by way of Arkansas. A wealthy friend of Williamson's, James Pickett, also from South Carolina, was the fifth.

McNeil, who could not finance the development of a town alone, was ready to sell the Edwards tract (at a profit, of course) to the Shreve Town Company. As a lever to get McNeil to make a concession or two, the men proposed to build their town on Jenkins' claim if the terms for the Edwards tract were too steep. Rather than be left without backers, McNeil chose to share some of his potential profits. He was elected president and Bushrod Jenkins treasurer of the Shreve Town Company. Three days later the articles of incorporation were ready. A meeting was called at Bennett and Cane's store, which was on the tract to be developed. The partners in the trading post were cut in for one share of stock. McNeil got in touch with his friend Sturges Sprague, then of Natchez, for more capital, and Sprague also became a shareholder.[2]

There was great enthusiasm for the new town, for it was on the only good route from Louisiana to Texas, where exciting events were taking place. The Texas Revolution had been in progress since November of 1835. San Antonio had been taken by the revolutionaries (mostly trans-

1. J. Fair Hardin, "The First Great Western River Captain: A Sketch of the Career of Captain Henry M. Shreve . . ." *Louisiana Historical Quarterly*, X (1927), 37–38. The case was later brought to trial but was won by Brooks.

2. Henrici, *Shreveport Saga*, 2.

planted Americans) on December 11, 1835, just before Angus McNeil made his deal with Larkin Edwards—and this event was probably a precipitating factor in McNeil's decision to buy the land. The Alamo fell on March 6, 1836, and McNeil may have had second thoughts about his investment. However, even if the land remained in Mexican hands, a city on the Red River would be a port of entry and bound to thrive.

News from Texas was eagerly awaited at Bennett and Cane's, and the cheering was loud when word came late in April that the defeat at the Alamo had been avenged at San Jacinto on April 21. Prospects looked good, and McNeil called his meeting for the formation of Shreve Town Company. Of course, ultimate success depended upon Shreve's completion of the task of removing the Great Raft. If the Red River was not opened all the way up for steamboat navigation, the company's plans could fail.

Shreve did his best. His crew labored on until the weather became too hot and humid for his men to work and until fever had laid low a large number of the men. The season was costly in time lost through illness. In his report, dated July 6, 1836, and written upon his return to Louisville, Shreve reported that 9,006 man-days were lost through illness, with additional loss of time sustained through having to assign some of the crew to tend those who were ill. Yellow fever had made one of its periodic appearances in that subtropical area.

When the season's work ended, there was still nine miles of raft formation left out of the thirty that had been there when the year's work began. Nine miles seemed very little, but the task had become more difficult than ever. Shreve described this segment of the Great Raft in one of his letters: "A deposit of mud had accumulated to such extent as to cover a large portion of the timber, on which the willow and cottonwood had sprung up and taken root on the logs of which the raft was composed. Many trees were found growing in that manner as large as eighteen inches in diameter."[3]

Experience had made Shreve a bit more cautious in his statements. He was wary of changes he would find when he again returned to work, wrought by the action of the river—clogged areas, new accumulations of

3. Hardin, *Northwestern Louisiana*, 267.

driftwood and snags—all of which would have to be cleared away before those final nine miles could be tackled. He was hesitant in 1836 to make definite statements of the amount of additional money that would be needed and of when the work would be completed. He knew the Red River better now and was wary of what new surprises—usually unpleasant—would await him upon his return. He was also a little uncertain about congressional reaction to the need for another season of work, and yet he knew that all so far accomplished would be wasted if he could not return to complete the task. In addition, he wrote in his letter of July 6 to Gratiot, "I am of the opinion . . . that to make the improvement permanent it will be necessary for the government to keep one boat at work for several years after the raft has been removed."

The *Archimedes*, which was used the year round, serving in the Ohio and the Mississippi when not on the Red River project, had taken a beating. As the 1836 Red River season drew near its close, it was obvious to Shreve that his principal working steam snag boat would have to be replaced. In his budget request for the next season of Red River work, he asked for forty-five thousand dollars, which included funds for construction of a new snag boat.

Congress would probably drag its feet again, Shreve thought as he wrote his requests. But what would the Corps of Engineers do without more snag boats? Again his thoughts turned to his personal situation. The political winds were shifting; his reappointment might not come through given a change of administrations. With his family's financial needs in mind, he renewed his effort to gain fair payment for his invention. He spent his evenings in the spring of 1836 making detailed drawings of the snag boat. He also began to draft an application for a patent on it. With a patent, he would have more leverage in his requests to Congress for reimbursement for the use of his invention in government work. The patent application was almost ready when he arrived back in Louisville in June of 1836. On the same day that he mailed his annual report to General Gratiot, July 6, he also mailed his letters of patent and drawings.[4]

Another item of business upon arrival in Louisville was to go across the Ohio to the boatyards at New Albany to arrange for the construction of a

4. Shreve, *Memorial*, 6.

new steam snag boat. This proved a fortunate move, for on November 14, 1836, while still in use on the Ohio River, the *Archimedes* tried to remove a large snag once too often and the boat's rotted hull gave way.

The summer turned out to be a busy one. A letter arrived in Louisville with a request from General Gratiot for Shreve to go to St. Louis immediately. Gratiot was a Missouri citizen, a native of St. Louis, and he was deeply concerned about a threatening situation that was developing there. In recent years St. Louis had become the neck of a giant funnel through which poured the multitudes of people and goods heading to the rapidly expanding West. Nearly all the goods and most of the people arrived at the city via steamboat; a long row of docked steamboats at the riverfront was testimony to this. But now the capricious Mississippi River was threatening to block this steamboat traffic. A new sandbar was forming near the St. Louis side of the river, forcing the channel toward the Illinois side, and a second sandbar between that one and the levee was growing. Soon, people feared, St. Louis would no longer be on the river at all. The closer sandbar already reached from the city's southern limits to a point halfway along the levee.

Shreve agreed to go to St. Louis to study the situation and make recommendations for a plan to remedy it. He boarded a steamboat for the trip, and in all likelihood his wife Mary and little granddaughter Harriet Reel went with him, to visit the Walker R. Carter home in St. Louis. Standing on the deck of the steamboat as it approached the city that had played so important a part in his own career, Shreve must have felt a surge of pride at the sight of the line of steamboats docked there. Each was built in the fashion of his own *George Washington*, changed only in minor details, such as increased use of gingerbread trim and use of hulls even broader and shallower than those he had designed.

St. Louis was growing rapidly, largely because of the tremendous increase in steamboat traffic. The unpredictable whims of "Ole Mississip'" could not be allowed to interfere with this progress. Gratiot had urged Congress to take action immediately, and for once there had been a quick response. It made an appropriation of fifteen thousand dollars "with which to build a pier to give direction to the current of the river near St. Louis."[5]

5. Richard Harwell, *Lee* (New York, 1961), 36.

Shreve measured and checked and then drafted his plan. It was to build up a "pier"—actually a log and rock dam or barricade—from the Illinois shore to divert the current toward the St. Louis side and thus begin river action to carry away the accumulating silt and sand. He also recommended that a channel be cut through some rocks along the western bank near the Iowa-Missouri line to result in safe passage for steamboats and added current impetus. He estimated the cost for these improvements would be at least sixty-five thousand dollars and recommended that Congress appropriate the additional fifty thousand dollars. There would be no opportunity to commence work that fall of 1836 under his own direct supervision, for even if Congress acted quickly, he had every intention of returning to the Red River to finish his work there as soon as the new snag boat was completed. His experienced assistant, Captain Israel S. Moorhead, who had been master of the snag boat *Heliopolis*, would be available. Shreve also thought the Corps of Engineers should send an officer to supervise the carrying out of his recommendations. Subsequently, a thirty-year-old engineer, First Lieutenant Robert E. Lee of Virginia was assigned to the project and went to St. Louis in 1837 to oversee it.

While he was working on his proposals for the project in St. Louis, Shreve was also attending to some matters of personal importance. An advertisement appeared in the city's newspapers stating that tracts of land of the old "Grande Prairie," the pastureland northwest of the city held in common by citizens of early French St. Louis, were open to bids for purchase by the public. Shreve immediately placed a bid upon three hundred acres of the land and succeeded in acquiring it. The tract today is in a crowded part of St. Louis, between Euclid and Taylor avenues. In 1836, it was four miles outside the city limits and had returned to a rather wild state after years of neglect.

Shreve and his wife saw no reason for them to be tied to Louisville in the future, now that their only living child, Rebecca Shreve Carter, was a St. Louis resident. He envisioned creation of a productive farm on his three hundred acres, and he and Mary planned a spacious home there for the years after his work with the United States government came to an end. President Jackson's second term was ending; if his party's candidate, Martin Van Buren, did not win the presidency in 1836, it was likely that the end of Shreve's employment was not distant. Van Buren, vice-president under Jackson, was the Democratic candidate. He was running against General William Henry Harrison of the Whig party, the hero of Tippecanoe. Jackson's popularity was spilling over to help Van Buren, and it appeared that he had a good chance to win the coming election. Shreve felt certain that Van Buren would confirm his continuation in office. But a man needed to look ahead. There was such bitter political rivalry between the Whigs and the Democrats that if the Whigs should win, there would probably be a clean sweep of all appointive offices.

This thought and his conversations with others led Shreve to consider his financial position and future prospects. His salary was still three thousand dollars per year; no doubt he could have been much better off financially had he remained in the business of operating steamboats. Other men whom he had known from early days had done very well indeed, while he, the man who designed a practical steamboat, had stayed with the thankless task of clearing the rivers of vicious snags and other impediments to navigation. Compliments on his work and expressed appreciation, which might have helped compensate for the low financial return, were rare, unlike the carping comments of those who criticized every step he took. He also had to put up with a constant struggle to get Congress—whose members sitting in Washington had no concept of the conditions under which Shreve worked, especially in the Red River raft clearance—to appropriate sufficient funds. The congressional committees haggled over every nickel, scrutinizing his expense reports as if convinced he was out to line his own pockets. Sometimes he wondered if he should continue in this thankless labor—and the summer of 1836 was one of those times. And yet, he felt that he simply had to see the Great Raft project to its conclusion.

With his work in St. Louis completed, he returned to Louisville and found construction of his new steam snag boat progressing fairly well. He named it the *Eradicator*, picturing how its first work, he hoped, would be to complete the eradication of the Great Raft. Congress obliged by appropriating sixty-five thousand dollars for the rest of the task, and he began to round up a crew for the winter's work.

With his thoughts returning to Louisiana, he attended to a matter he had promised to accomplish for the Shreve Town Company. He had brought home with him rough sketches of a proposed plat for Shreve Town that the company members had agreed upon. When it was time to board the new *Eradicator* in November and head for the Red River, he had a neatly drawn map of Shreve Town with him, with the street names lettered in. Some carried the names of heroes of the Alamo, so much in the news that year. But the Caddo Indians, former owners of the tract, and Larkin Edwards, their longtime friend, and even Angus McNeil (perhaps at his own insistence) were also honored with streets named for them—Caddo, Edwards, and McNeil streets. Shreveport today in its downtown section is built upon this plan conceived in 1836, with its commerce centering in Texas Street, and the Alamo heroes honored on Crockett and Milam to one side of Texas and Travis and Fannin on the other.

As the working fleet again made its way up the Red River, the boats were once more delayed at the rapids at Alexandria. Congress had not yet seen fit to allocate funds for the removal of the rock ledges, and the water level was again low. The *Eradicator* was tied up there, awaiting the time when the water level would be higher. The other steamboats and keelboats went on to Shreve Town. Clean-up work occupied the crews until the *Eradicator* arrived to attack that remaining nine-mile solid mass of raft, plus a collection of looser snags for several more miles up the river. There were also difficult problems in water-flow diversion, since most of the river was leaving the main channel and going into Soda Lake and Bayou Pierre.

Shreve was determined to get the job finished this season but not at all sure that the sixty-five thousand dollars would be adequate to do the work properly—stowing the snags and raft logs, clearing the banks, and doing all possible to insure a clear, open channel for the Red River. To urge Congress to keep funds coming he sent to Washington a copy of a journal kept by one Robert Peebles, aboard a small steamboat named *Rover* en route to Fort Towson. Making the trip in the 1835–1836 season, the *Rover* had progressed smoothly and with good speed up the Red River until it reached the place where Shreve's men were working on the raft. From there on, the little steamboat had to maneuver as best it could through the bayous, and progress was slow and difficult to the point of being torturous. The crew had to warp the boat along as if it were a keelboat and free it from limbs that entrapped it, often having to chop trees growing in the water to widen a passage. They even built small dams in two locations to make deeper pools in which to float the *Rover*, unloading the cargo, taking it ashore, moving the boat onward, and then carrying the cargo on their backs or on crude rafts before reloading it. Surely, Shreve thought as he dispatched the journal, anyone reading it would realize the necessity of completing the work so that a steamboat could go on to Fort Towson for the good of the people of the United States. He forwarded the journal to Gratiot in February, 1837.[6]

That was the month in which the founding fathers of Shreve Town called a meeting at which the name of the new city was changed. So many steamboats were arriving there that it was decided that a more appropriate name would be Shreveport. It was no doubt with great pride that Shreve began to use the new name in his communications to the War Department.

Congress sent a government engineer, Lieutenant A. H. Bowman, to check the progress of the project on the Red. On his return he wrote a report to Washington from his office in Memphis, on April 16, 1837, saying that no one could imagine without seeing it in person how spectacular was the work Shreve had been overseeing. He revised the estimated length of the Great Raft to 214 miles instead of the 160 Shreve had stated, and he also estimated that removal of the upper reaches of the raft was four times as difficult as the lower had been. He wrote to Brigadier General Gratiot: "It is difficult to form a just conception of the magnitude of this work, or fully to appreciate the important results that are to flow from it. . . . The indefatigable industry, zeal and perseverance of the superintendent have triumphed over difficulties well calculated to intimidate him; bayous have been closed by masses of timber, islands made of huge logs, for centuries embedded together, and covered with silt and living trees have been removed. . . . Indeed every mile in ascending bears evidence of immense labor bestowed upon its improvement."[7]

Shreve talked with Lietuenant Bowman about a second cutoff he had contemplated, in the river near Shreveport as shown in his rough sketch of 1833 and also mentioned as part of his future plans in his report of July 6, 1836, to General Gratiot. Bowman agreed that cutting the second canal would be beneficial since the 160-yard cutoff would save at least seven miles of winding river. He would see no adverse effects from it, and the job could be quickly accomplished.

However, Shreve did see an adverse effect—not in the action of the

6. Dorsey, *Master of the Mississippi*, 198–200.
7. *Ibid.*, 201.

river this time but in the actions of the people. Shreve was a quiet man, forceful with his employees and demanding of them but not inclined to involve himself in the petty rivalries and quarrels that went on among the several factions of Shreveport and its environs. The principal rivalry was between Coate's Bluff people and those of the new town growing around Bennett and Cane's. Each settlement was determined to be the nucleus of the growing city. Shreve realized that if he cut the canal as he had planned, which was a most sensible move, Coate's Bluff would be left high and dry, back from the river with no chance to develop as a river port.

He could not help but favor Shreveport. Its future would be assured— he envisioned it as a city like St. Louis, with a levee stacked with cargo from arriving boats and with bales of cotton awaiting shipment, grown on the plantations already showing signs of development. He could see the rows of business houses growing in support of the new commerce. But cutting the canal would most certainly make all the people of Coate's Bluff unhappy as the loop of the river became only a little lagoon that went nowhere.

He hesitated, resisting the prodding of McNeil and his fellow Shreveport investors. But Bowman had urged that the work be done, and on a Sunday in May, he brought the *Eradicator* back down the river and put it into position to cut the canal. The work was soon done. The waters of Red River entered the narrow ditch to continue the work of carving a new channel. As predicted, only disconnected arcs of water were left where the riverfront of Coate's Bluff had been. Bitter feelings among the handful of residents there were just as inevitable, and some never forgave Shreve for this bit of engineering work.

Later that month as hot weather began, Shreve faced bitter disappointment. He had to accept the fact that again he would have to stop work with tag ends left to be done in another season. The men slapped at mosquitoes and fought the lethargy of the fetid air, heavy with steamy heat and the odor of rotting vegetation, until they could endure it no longer. Illness had taken a heavy toll by mid-May. Only a handful of men were willing to continue to work, although there were only 440 yards of the Great Raft remaining. The crew of the *Eradicator* was transferred to the steamboat *Java* on May 25 to do some clean-up work; all the rest of the men headed down the Red and then up the Mississippi and Ohio rivers.

The *Java* remained on the job until June 25 and arrived at Louisville on July 12, 1837.

If Shreve had been a man of less will power, he might have shrugged his shoulders and turned away from the Red River. A financial panic had hit the United States, and Congress made Shreve scrap for every nickel that was spent. Even Lieutenant Bowman's strong support did not stop all the carping criticism. It was a constant burden to explain the delays and the problems peculiar to this subtropical river-clearance project. Writing his report to Gratiot on August 2, Shreve must have felt weary of having to admit that his hopeful estimates had fallen short in terms of time and money spent. Three seasons of work had gone into this seemingly endless task that he had originally thought might be done in three months.

Again he wrote a plea to Congress to appropriate funds—another fifty thousand dollars—to complete the work. Again he emphasized the importance of the work and the returns to the government in land sales and production, already much in evidence, from the land along the Red River open to steamboat traffic. The Indian lands and Fort Towson must be made accessible for the welfare of all, he maintained. Delay now in completion of the task would be expensive in terms of additional accumulation of snags and silt to be removed. Congress must come through with the means to go on as soon as workmen could be persuaded to return to Louisiana in the fall of 1837.

He wrote to General Gratiot, "I can now make a calculation, that I am willing to stake my reputation on, that the whole obstruction can be removed in three months after an appropriation is made, if done in the ensuing fall; but if it is postponed till the regular session, the appropriation, if then made, would be too late to admit of executing the work during the ensuing winter and spring, and consequently, must lie over till the fall of 1838."[8] He went on to urge that the appropriation be made at a special session of Congress in September, stating that delay would be sure to add another twenty thousand dollars to the costs.

Disappointment was the captain's lot once more. He was still at home in Louisville on November 8, 1837, writing a new estimate of costs, up to seventy thousand dollars as he had predicted.[9]

8. Hardin, *Northwestern Louisiana*, 272–74.
9. Maude Hearn-O'Pry, *Chronicles of Shreveport* (Shreveport, 1928), 21.

ESTIMATE OF FUNDS REQUIRED FOR REMOVING THE GREAT RAFT IN RED
RIVER FOR THE YEAR 1838

1. For one steamboat, fitted up with machinery and tools,
   complete $15,000
2. For salary of two assistant superintendents, at $125 each for
   6 months 1,500
3. Salary for three assistants and one physician, six months, at
   $100 per month 2,400
4. Four steam engineers, six months 1,500
5. For two carpenters, six months, at $50. 600
6. For two blacksmiths and four overseers, six months, at $45 per
   month each 1,620
7. For 175 men, six months, at $20 per month 21,000
8. For subsistence for 195 men, six months, at $8.50 per month each .. 9,945
9. For cordage, lumber, iron and steel 5,000
10. For wood for two boats (same time) 4,000
11. For engine stores for same 635
12. For two keel boats fitted up for quarters for men 1,000
13. For repairs and additions to tools, etc 1,800
14. For contingent expenses 4,000

$70,000

Louisville, Kentucky, November.   Henry M. Shreve, Superintendent, Etc.

With this report went a letter to Brigadier General Gratiot. In it Shreve
told the Corps of Engineers that in March, 1837, the *Heliopolis* had been
taken up to the boatyards at New Albany, "where her engines were thoroughly repaired and removed from the old hull to a new boat built by
authority of the Department." As a salute to the old snag boat and a reminder to the officers sitting in remote Washington offices, Shreve wrote,
"It will be seen that 1,894 snags have been removed from the bed of the
Mississippi River, and that 18,141 trees have been felled from its caving-in
banks during the year ending the 30th of September, 1837."[10]

The rebuilt *Heliopolis* had remained at New Albany for the hull replacement and engine renewal work until July 22, when she returned to
work in the Mississippi River under a Captain Smith. Shreve reported
that the improvements in the snag boat allowed it to increase efficiency
by 25 percent in the last two months of the reporting year. In the mean-

10. *Ibid.*

time another new snag boat was under construction, and Shreve expected it to be ready for work early in December.

His official patent on the steam snag boat had not yet been granted as he wrote his letters late in 1837. The commissioner of patents had ordered an investigation to make certain that Shreve's snag boat was of original design and not a copy of the earlier snag boats produced when Congress issued its call for someone to clear the rivers in 1824. Specifically, plans by John Bruce, who had been assigned to the work, and by another river-man, David Prentice (in all likelihood the same Captain Prentice who built the steamboat *Pike*), were being investigated. Government officials appear to have been reluctant to grant recognition to Shreve, perhaps as part of the political in-fighting. Many complaints were aired. Even Representative Ashley of Missouri, who had written the committee report giving high praise for the work of Shreve's snag boat, brought before the House a petty grievance about the removal of trees from the riverfront land of one of his constituents. Citizens complained of the expense of operating the snag boats but accused Shreve of wastefulness in letting them stand idle when floods forced a work stoppage. In 1836 a Representative W. C. Dunlap had questioned Shreve's long employment as superintendent, occasioning a reply highly supportive of Shreve from General Gratiot.[11] Through it all, Shreve had no choice but to wait for the congressional wheels to grind, and continue with his usual duties in the meantime.

In 1838, while still awaiting funds to continue with the Red River work, he became a resident of St. Louis. He so describes himself in the introduction to "Letters Patent No. 913," dated September 12, 1838. For the questioning had ended, and a patent was issued to Shreve for an "Improved Machine for Removing Snags and Sawyers from the Beds of Rivers." The letters patent furnish a detailed description, with diagrams, of the construction and operation of the steam snag boat. The document closes with Shreve's description of the particular innovations he was responsible for.[12]

The invention claimed and desired to be secured by Letters Patent consists in the manner in which I have combined and connected the mechanical power

11. *Congressional Record*, 24th Cong., 1st Sess., 3–4.
12. Shreve, "Letters Patent," 3.

of the windlass and the pulleys so as to operate with the momentum given to a twin steamboat and with the continuous action of the paddle-wheels, so as to break off, uproot, and raise snags and sawyers, as above set forth.

I however, particularly claim as new—

1. The application of the forward or snag beam D for the purpose of raising or breaking the snag or sawyer preparatory to its being lifted on board the boat by the apparatus constructed for that purpose.

2. The manner of connecting together the two boats by means of the upper and lower tier of beams, diagonal braces, bulk-head, and forward beam D.

Now Shreve had solid legal grounds for his requests to Congress for compensation.

In St. Louis, he found himself hearing complaints from the citizens about the remoteness of the young Virginian who was in charge of the river current diversion and especially about how slowly the work was proceeding while the riverfront was blocked by the sandbars. Lieutenant Lee spent the 1837 season surveying and mapping the site, with the assistance of Shreve's longtime fellow worker and friend Israel Moorhead and a young civilian, Henry Kayser. They had determined that Shreve's plan was excellent but that the dike should be built farther upriver where the water was more shallow. Before actual work began, they had increased the cost estimate to $150,000 in order to include other improvements. Meeting with the usual deliberate pace of Congress in supplying funds, Lee had to keep the impatient people of St. Louis waiting throughout a whole working season. The city fathers, anxious to get work started, guaranteed the funds, and General Gratiot, vitally interested in this project, urged a speedy start. But Gratiot's term as chief of engineers ended in that year of 1838, and there was little he could do. He was succeeded by Colonel Joseph G. Totten.

Eventually both the St. Louis and Red River appropriations came through. Shreve was not free to go to the Red River himself that autumn of 1838, but in November he sent the *Eradicator*, with a keelboat in tow and a work force of seventy-four men, to start on the work under Captain Abram Tyson. The water was so low that once again the *Eradicator* was held up at Alexandria's rapids. A crew for the snag boat was left there while the rest of the men took the keelboat on up to the remnants of the Great Raft above Shreveport. It was January before the water was high enough for the *Eradicator* to go on upriver. Hearing of this added expensive delay, Shreve was justly upset. (In 1840, the work to break up the rock ledges at Alexandria was finally approved in Washington.)

The delay in resumption of work on the Great Raft had resulted in still more accumulation of driftwood, as Shreve had predicted. The 440 yards that had been left in May of 1837 had grown to nearly 3,000 yards. But this was loose accumulation, not yet rooted in the river bottom, and the work went rapidly. The last of the raft was pulled away and stowed in a bayou entrance on February 15, 1839. Navigation by steamboat to Fort Towson was at last possible, although the steamboats had to proceed with care. The military post was nearly 1,200 miles up the Red River from the Mississippi and approximately 800 miles above what had been the foot of the Great Raft.

When the cheering ended, the crew settled down for less dramatic clean-up work. They cut trees from the banks, trees that were liable to drift down and start another raft at the first bend, and they pulled up snags and worked in various other ways to improve the channel on up toward Towson.

In April, Shreve himself arrived in Shreveport to inspect the work. All was not as open and clear as he had hoped. The spring freshets had come, bringing with them the nucleus, one mile long, of another raft. Forty-five miles above Shreveport, two steamboats were unable to get through with their cargoes of cotton, and five other steamboats, carrying government stores to Fort Towson and cargo for the increasing numbers of residents on the farmlands, were unable to proceed. Three other steamboats had stored their freight at Shreveport and returned to New Orleans. Obviously, the new accumulation must be attacked and cleared away. But the available funds were exhausted; in fact, Captain Tyson had run up a deficit.

Shreve was as discouraged as he had ever been in his entire career. He had repeatedly warned the Corps of Engineers that the nature of the upper Red River was such that there would be a need for permanent engineering work when the raft itself was gone and that a snag boat would be needed on the river for some years to come. He had stated in his letters that Congress could not really afford to ignore this need and must set aside funds to cover it. Otherwise all that had been expended to date would soon be wasted.

But this did not take care of the immediate emergency. He decided to take action without awaiting the slow grinding of congressional wheels. On the very day of his arrival at the site of the new river obstruction, he commandeered a horse and rode north to the town of Washington, Arkansas. The next day, April 16, he sought to obtain the funds from a bank there.

Washington, Ark. 16 April, 1839

To the President and Directors,
Branch Real Estate Bank, of Arkansas,
Washington.

Gentlemen:

On my arrival at this place, yesterday, I was informed that there was a late re-formation of timber near the head of the great raft in Red river, obstructing the channel nearly one mile in extent, and being anxious to remove that obstruction before the force now employed by the government under my charge is withdrawn, I am induced to apply through you to the people whose interest it is to have that work completed, for a sum of money sufficient to work that force up to the 1st day of June . . . all the available funds heretofore appropriated by Congress for removal of the raft, having been expended. . . .

To continue the operations with the force now at work in the raft of the 1st of June will require at least seven thousand one hundred and forty-seven dollars, fifty cents ($7,147.50). If that sum can be furnished by the citizens interested, I will take the responsibility of continuing the operations to the time for which the laborers now at work in the raft are employed (1st June next). But under the express condition that the parties making such advance take the entire responsibility of being reimbursed by Congress, my engaging only to apply the funds to removal of the raft, and calling on the Engineers Department for appropriations sufficient to repay the amount at as early a day as such appropriation can be obtained, but not being liable on my own responsibility in any shape for the repayment of the funds except as agent of the government as herein before expressed.

I am Gent. Very respectfully
Your Obt. Servt.
Henry M. Shreve, Supt.[13]

The bank obliged, rounding out the amount by $2.50 to make it an even $7,150. Shreve hurried back to the Red River with the funds in hand and ordered the work to continue. The force, knowing that they would be paid, obliged and attacked the newly formed raft. It proved to be more than the estimated mile long by about a thousand feet.

13. Hardin, *Northwestern Louisiana*, 275–76.

The river flowed freely by May 4. The men worked on until May 21, opening the width of the river, and then headed down the Red and up the Mississippi to St. Louis. There they arrived on the last day for which Shreve had guaranteed payment—June 1, 1839. The task was finished at last. The Great Raft was removed.

14 / **The River Eternal**

A burden was lifted, but not entirely. On June 12, 1839, Shreve sent off a long letter to Colonel Totten. In it he made it clear that he expected Congress to act quickly to appropriate not only the money owed to the bank at Washington, Arkansas, but also money that apparently had come from his own personal funds. He was most exact in reporting, down to the fractional cent.

> On settling the accounts for the work during the season since the 31st December, 1838, the expenditure has been $18,985.03 ¾; the available funds at that time amounted to $7,815.88½, to the amount received from the Real Estate Bank of Washington, Arkansas, $7,150.00, making an aggregate sum of $14,965.88½, which leaves a balance due me of $11,019.15½ which is the amount I have exceeded the available fund from former appropriations and the loan from the people of Arkansas and which, under the existing circumstances was not in my power to avoid.[1]

He was quite put out with the failure of Congress to provide funds for the year's engineering projects. He urged that the deficits be repaid and that further appropriations be made to prevent the undoing of all his work by the actions of the rascally Red. He wanted more work done to insure

1. Hardin, *Northwestern Louisiana*, 276.

the carrying away of the immense quantities of driftwood that would float down each spring for some years to come and more work on closing up the remaining open bayous and building of levees along low banks. He went into great detail to explain precisely what needed to be done and why, as if he sensed he might be charging a new superintendent with maintaining the good he had done.

To inspire Colonel Totten to fight for congressional backing as General Gratiot had, Shreve again went over the ways in which all that was spent was returned to the government multiplied. He pointed out that the land opened to cultivation was as fertile as any that could be found and that "instead of the operation being a charge to the government, it must result in a large profit in the value of the land that will be dried which is now flooded one-half of the year."

He spoke of changes already evident—new settlements where in 1833 there had been only the Caddo agency, Coate's Bluff, and Bennett and Cane's trading post. He wrote, "There are now many flourishing cotton plantations on that part of the river where the raft was located and where the lands were then nearly all inundated by the back water caused by the masses of timber which formed the raft. There has also a town sprung up equal in population and surpassing any on Red river in amount of business transactions." He was referring to Shreveport, but modesty kept him from naming it in his letter. He closed with a glowing recommendation for the area's agricultural future.

Eventually, Congress acted to take care of the expenses of this last part of the Red River work, but it held back in providing for the continued annual work Shreve recommended to prevent the buildup of another raft. When the river was in danger of having to be closed again, a snag boat was sent. But now and then there would be a buildup of driftwood. After 1875 such major accumulations were quickly broken up with dynamite, following Nobel's work to make dynamite usable underwater.

In 1840, President Martin Van Buren, blamed for the Panic of 1837 and other national ills, failed to be reelected to a second term in office. The Whigs' rallying cry of "Tippecanoe and Tyler too!" brought in the votes and on March 20, 1841, a cold, rainy day in Washington, General William H. Harrison was inaugurated as president of the United States. But his time in office was very brief, for he died on April 4 of complications resulting from the cold he caught on Inauguration Day. His vice-president,

John Tyler, succeeded him and began a clean political sweep in which Shreve was among those removed from appointive offices.

The notice arrived in September, 1841. It was not a complete surprise, nor could it have been a major disappointment to him. He had put in approximately fifteen years as a government official, serving under Presidents John Quincy Adams, Andrew Jackson and Martin Van Buren. For all of that time, he had been forced to plead with the War Department to get congressional appropriations for the work that needed doing and to justify the expenditure of every nickel, while being paid three thousand dollars per year, far less than he could have earned had he stayed in private enterprise. Now there would be no more long reports to write to convince those from whom he took orders that he was handling his responsibilities properly. His only pleading with Congress henceforth would be to get proper remuneration for the invention of the steam snag boat, which would continue in use under the new superintendent of western river improvements.

His official notice of the end of his government responsibilities came in a letter from Washington dated September 11, 1841.[2] He was instructed to "transfer the public property under his charge" to his successor, a Captain Russell. The letter's closing paragraph read: "In concluding this communication which finally dissolves your connection with the Government as an Agent of this Department, I take the occasion to say, that the zeal you have manifested for the public interests, the ability you have displayed in conducting your operations, and the faithful manner in which for a series of years, you have executed the various and important trusts committed to your charge, entitle your conduct, (so far as is known to this Department,) not only to an avowal of satisfaction, but also to an expression of high approbation."

Had General Gratiot still been chief of engineers, the tone of the letter would no doubt have been less cautious. Shreve must have felt some gratification at a tribute from those in the new administration, but words of praise did not make up for the lack of more concrete expression of appreciation—payment for the use of his invention. That apparently was again stalled in Congress.

Should he return to steamboat building and operation? This was a

2. [Treat (?)], "Henry Miller Shreve," 248.

temptation. Back in the years following the success of his *Washington*, the future as a steamboat owner and merchant had been bright for young Captain Shreve. Now he saw steamboats up and down the rivers built upon the very plans he had originated but failed to patent. Many were the men who had profited from his ideas. But should he venture back into the field? Costs were higher now. The competition would be keen, but that had never bothered Shreve. A challenge had led him into each phase of his career. He had been a keelboat merchant who gambled on new markets, a steamboat builder when a legalized monopoly sought to thwart his efforts, an improver of the steamboat when people ridiculed his novel ideas, and then, with a successful career in his pocket, the inventor of a snag boat that had made the rivers safe for nagivation and even removed the Great Raft.

But now he was no longer a young fellow with his life ahead of him. He was almost fifty-six years old when he received his official notice of dismissal. At that time, when life expectancy for an American man was around forty, that was old age. But he felt hale and hearty, and he could not sit around in idle retirement. He had his fine new home named Gallatin Place in St. Louis County on a tract of good land. He decided to develop the land into a farm that would be a model of efficiency.

This he set about doing, putting all the energy he had formerly put into his life on the rivers into making his tract of the Grande Prairie into a flourishing farm. It must have been quite a change for Mary Shreve to know that her husband was at home to stay for the first time in the thirty years of their marriage. But except for sharing her bed at night, he was gone from her almost as much as before.

He spent his time supervising the farm work and, of course, in frequent visits to the riverfront where steamboats brought his old friends to St. Louis. The actual labor on the farm was done, as was the custom around St. Louis in that era, by slaves and hired men. Shreve purchased slaves and hired several young immigrants from Ireland and Germany. He built houses for all, and the big house became the center of a small community. The household was managed by Mary with the help of slaves and servant women, mostly the wives of the farm laborers. Soon the fertile land was producing well; the big Shreve farm prospered. He bought additional acreage plus some lots in the city as the years went on.

Harriet Reel, eight years old when her grandfather retired, lived at

Gallatin Place until her marriage in 1852. Her cousin Henry Shreve Carter, just a month younger than Harriet, was at his grandfather's home as much as at his own home in St. Louis. Grandpa Henry hoped that his young namesake would take over the operation of the farm eventually, and the two walked the fields often, closely trailed by a dog or two.

The spare bedrooms at Gallatin were seldom unoccupied. Mary Shreve had nieces and nephews, as well as grandchildren, who loved to come to stay. Henry, Callie, and Amelia Blair were frequent visitors. Henry was a mischievous boy who helped keep life from growing dull. One winter he broke his leg while ice-skating. It did not heal, and there was a sad day when the boy lay stretched out on the big dining table while doctors amputated the leg. Besides these older youngsters there were the others of the growing Carter family, since Rebecca gave birth to nine children in all. There was always a baby around to keep things lively, and the older children often took turns riding on the back of the horse, old Rock. Rock, loved for many years by Shreve, was a gift from President Jackson. At Gallatin Place, as he grew old, he became a favorite and was often brought out for riding by the smallest of the grandchildren without fear of his endangering the child. The hair was gone from the top of his tail, and there were those on Gallatin Place who swore that this was because of a brush with a cannonball at the Battle of New Orleans.[3] Especially when the clan gathered for Christmas and New Year's at the big house on the high ground above the river, grandparents Mary and Henry Shreve realized their contentment with their new life.

But when his farm was being tended satisfactorily by the young men who worked for him, the old riverman returned to his first love as much as he could without actually taking charge of a steamboat. He bought into the shipping business and warehouses along the levee. This gave him a good excuse to be near the action when steamboats arrived and departed and to talk with the younger captains. They, in turn, delighted in knowing the Father of the Mississippi Steamboat himself. Often they would join him on the veranda at Gallatin Place. Son-in-law Walker Carter became involved in a steamboat company, a fact that pleased Shreve.

Although Gallatin Place was outside the city limits of St. Louis in the 1840s, it was but a short carriage ride to an old military road that ran

3. Dorsey, *Master of the Mississippi*, 222.

southward to the city from Fort Bellefontaine on the Missouri River. Even then there were suburban settlements, and the Shreve farm was close to them. St. Louis itself, reaching eighteen blocks in from the river at its heart and stretching about three miles in length, had a population of 16,291 in 1840, with enough people in the environs to make the population of the metropolitan area 22,640. "It is not unreasonable to suppose," a city guidebook said in 1840, "that at the end of another ten years, the city will number between 40,000 and 50,000 inhabitants and will take rank among the first cities of the Union."[4]

The commerce of the city supported this projection. In 1840 there were 1,721 steamboat arrivals with an aggregate tonnage of 144,193. Shreve, noting this data, could not help but think back to his first arrival there from New Orleans with the *Washington*, the first steamboat to make the voyage upriver between those two cities. He had departed New Orleans on February 1, 1819, he recalled, and arrived at St. Louis four weeks later, on March 1.[5] The young captains of these big steamboats, coming up in a week or less, would laugh at that record—but never at Captain Shreve, whose ingenuity and labors made possible the faster runs.

The *Washington* had had plenty of room to dock on that day in 1819, Shreve remembered. But in the 1840s the steamboats were lined up so thickly that it seemed it would be almost impossible to get a skiff between them, and the levee was crowded with cargo. The threat to the riverfront had been handled well, Shreve observed, and he had high praise for Robert E. Lee, now promoted to a captaincy. Lee's supervision of the work had ended rather abruptly late in 1840, before completion of the project, but Moorhead and others had seen it through to the finish. Lee, "basically adapting Shreve's and Gratiot's plans (after satisfying himself they were the most practical) . . . had broken the back of the work and won the lasting respect of riverman Shreve. St. Louis was saved as a port."[6]

It was fortunate that this engineering work was well carried out, for the life of the city revolved around its function as a river port—the Gateway to the West. The 1840 guidebook played up the city's commercial prospects: "There is on the Mississippi, above the mouth of the Ohio, no spot where a city could be located with so many advantages in its favor, as St.

4. Charles Keemle (ed.), "Sketch of St. Louis," in *St. Louis Directory, 1840–41* (N.p., n.d.), 6.

5. Billon, *Annals of St. Louis*, 308.

6. Clifford Dowdey, *Lee* (Boston, 1965), 66.

Louis. To it Missouri, Iowa, Wisconsin, a large part of Illinois, and a portion of Arkansas, already look for a market. . . . The commercial relations of the city are extended over the entire west, and it will not be considered exaggerative, or more than what is admitted by all who visit it, that St. Louis must, at no distant day, be the commercial emporium of the valley of the Mississippi."[7]

The guidebook went on to enumerate the city's industries. The fur trade had given rise to St. Louis and was still of great importance to its economy. Manufactures in St. Louis, the guidebook admitted, were still on a "limited scale"—two foundries for castings, two white lead mills, a "Bagging and Bale Rope Factory," a type foundry, two planing machines, nine sawmills, and a variety of processing mills and plants for agricultural products. Culturally, the city was also still in its infancy, although the Jesuits had established St. Louis University, which was flourishing. There were also several newspapers; two public schools, "in which between two and three hundred scholars are taught by respectable and efficient teachers;" some private academies; and a medical college and an academy of natural sciences, each newly opened. But had it not been for the busy riverfront, St. Louis would have amounted to little.

Shreve found that the winter months, when ice blocked the traffic, were dull, and he was not alone in that reaction. John James Audubon, writing a letter from the city on March 28, 1843, reported that the ice had not yet broken on the Missouri River above the city and commented, "Business is extremely dull here, and will remain so until the Upper Rivers are open. . . . There are great numbers of Steamers at the Levee for the Wharves are much like that at N. Orleans. They are bound for all portions of the Western World, but the River is too low at present for most of them."[8]

Spring brought a dramatic change. In 1843 Matt Field arrived in St. Louis immediately after the opening of the rivers and wrote an account of what he saw for the New Orleans *Weekly Picayune*.

> The expansive Levee is so narrowed by the rising river that the boats stand opposite to the store doors, so near as to present the singular appearance of a contracted street with very queer houses, having tall chimneys all along one

7. Keemle (ed.), "Sketch of St. Louis," 5–6.
8. John James Audubon, *Audubon in the West*, ed. J. F. McDermott (Norman, 1965), 36–39.

side. What is left of the Levee is literally piled up with produce and merchandise. It is with the utmost difficulty that drays can move about, and passengers have enough to do to elbow their way along the sidewalk. All is bustle and activity. The steamer Eclipse, I am told, went off the other day with a freight barge in tow, and the value of the cargo taken down was estimated at the enormous sum of seventy-five thousand dollars! Boats are starting now every day loaded down with produce, and yet the Levee continues heaped up with it. . . . The town seems to have jumped out of passive slumber into raging excitement.[9]

Shreve set a task for himself to attend to in the winter months. He was determined that Congress should take action on the question of compensating him for the use of his invention. The engineering work on the rivers was continuing under the new superintendent, and from time to time he saw his *Archimedes* and its sister snag boats being put to good use. By the spring of 1842, another congressional committee had completed its study of his case and prepared another long and commendatory report. The conclusion was that both justice and policy dictated that Shreve should be paid for his invention and that if he were paid on the basis of one year's savings through the use of the snag boat, he should receive between $50,000 and $200,000. But the committee fixed upon a recommendation of only $40,000.

This committee report stated positively that the snag boat was vital to the Corps of Engineers in keeping the rivers open, and it included a table showing the great quantities of farm produce shipped via riverboats and imperiled by neglect of the rivers. It stated that in military supplies and Indian goods alone, there was $2,000,000 worth of shipments annually that could be lost if snags were struck. A single steamboat had recently lost arms valued at $700,000 when it struck a snag.

And yet the haggling went on over payment of the committee's recommended award of $40,000 to Shreve, an amount far less than what was reported as paid to the heirs of Robert Fulton, who made a highly questionable claim for government use of steamboats in the defense of New Orleans in the War of 1812. Despite the unusable condition of the *Vesuvius* during most of the period of martial law and despite the fact that the *Aetna* and the *Buffalo* did not arrive in New Orleans during that time, the Fulton heirs sued for wartime services of these three steamboats. Congress passed a bill in 1846 awarding them $76,000.

9. Quoted in *Ibid.*, 38n, 39n.

Congress resumed discussion of the Shreve award in its 1843 session, but again postponed action. Another select committee was assigned in 1844, and this time the report included a recommendation from Shreve's successor in the office of superintendent of western river improvements, Captain Russell.

> I have witnessed the progress of the great and important improvement made in that river by the operations of the snag boat, the benefits of which are of so much importance that it is difficult to estimate the value of them. The Mississippi river, that was formerly a forest of snags, is now comparatively free from that dangerous obstruction. The effect produced on the navigation by the removal of the snags, has been of vast importance to the navigation in many respects. It has almost done away with the risk of snags, and has evidently been the means of shortening the passage of steamboats on the Mississippi about one-half. For example: the boats that now run from New Orleans to St. Louis and Louisville in six to seven days, could not have made the passage . . . in less than twelve to fifteen days; for the snags were then so numerous that it was impracticable for any boat to make a passage without striking snags frequently, which must have been fatal to them at the high speed they now run. . . . I am also of opinion that the Government is indebted in a large sum for the patent-right of the snag-boat. . . . As to the value of the patent, I could not estimate it at less than one hundred thousand dollars, as it has evidently been the means of saving many millions of dollars of property to the citizens of the United States, the many lives that must have been lost, had not that invention been put in operation. Besides, it is a machine of such vast importance that it cannot be dispensed with, as it is necessary to continue its operation in all our great rivers for many years to come.[10]

Shreve's old friend, Captain Israel Moorhead, who had operated the *Heliopolis* for years, stated his opinion that $200,000 was "as small a compensation as the Government could expect to get so valuable a patent right for." The report also pointed out that the Red River improvement alone was saving the government $85,000 every year on its shipments to Fort Towson.

The new committee agreed that the patent right was worth between $100,000 and $200,000. But once again, even while admitting that this was less than half its value, they recommended payment to Shreve of $40,000.

Shreve was incensed. That was less than half of what he had been told the government was saving in one year alone just on the Red River raft

10. Shreve, *Memorial*, 9–10.

removal! Policy, he had also been told, was to award the inventor half of a year's profit made by the United States through the use of an invention. But $40,000 was far below that amount. He refused the payment on the grounds that it was inadequate. He entered another petition, maintaining that the offer of $40,000 was "utterly unworthy of an invention which . . . has poured millions into the coffers of the nation, and the benefits of which to the western country, present and future, are only inferior in point of importance to those of the application of steam." But Congress ended its session without settling on an amount larger than the rejected $40,000.

In that year of 1844, Shreve had other problems. Great floods hit St. Louis. The Mississippi widened out to six miles in some places and interfered with spring planting. Even the fields of Gallatin Place were "waterswept and gullied."[11] Steamboat traffic suffered badly as the entire riverfront disappeared underwater. Shreve went down to see the warehouses in which he had an interest as soon as he could get there. With others, he suffered losses.

But financial losses were as nothing when compared with a personal one. Mary's health was failing. As 1844 drew toward its close, she did not plan the usual Christmas festivities, and the big parlor did not take on its holiday gaiety. As 1845 began, she was obviously weakening, and the doctors could not help her. On February 25, five days after her fifty-fourth birthday, she died.

Shreve wandered about the house like a lost soul. Rebecca did her best to help her father, but she had her hands full with her own family and was expecting another baby—her sixth child—in November. Friends suggested that he find a person to look after his home, and by some chain of circumstances Lydia Rodgers of Boston came to be the housekeeper at Gallatin Place.

Lydia's presence cheered the aging riverman. She was not quite thirty years of age and, though not beautiful, was considered "quite distinguished looking." She was a woman of culture, and Shreve found she could converse with him intelligently. Before she had been in his home a year, they were married.

Shreve's step was quicker and his eyes brighter, especially when a baby

11. Dorsey, *Master of the Mississippi,* 227.

daughter was born to Lydia and him. They named her Mary. Baby Mary saw far more of her father through the months of infancy than had his other daughters.

With a new companion and new young life about him, Shreve emerged from the sadness of the months following Mary's death. His life outside his home also was good. He was the acknowledged authority on steamboats and the rivers, a subject of great importance in St. Louis. He took part in many of the civic concerns of his day. One of them that threatened economic conditions was the growing abolitionist movement. To most landowners in the southern states, the use of slaves for farm labor was considered the customary solution to a need for workers, and the St. Louis area was in a state where slavery was lawful. Shreve was so far removed from his Quaker roots that he joined with his neighbors in this custom. Like his neighbors, he felt threatened by the abolitionists when they began to work in St. Louis in 1846, aiding many blacks to escape to the neighboring free states. A mass meeting was called in September after several such escapes had been arranged, and a committee of one hundred was formed "for the protection of slave property against the evil designs of the abolitionists and others."[12] John O'Fallon, a civic leader and friend of Shreve's, was president, and Shreve's name appears in a list of members of the organization's finance committee as a representative from St. Louis township. The city council was petitioned to institute curfew regulations for all slaves except when they were in the company of their owners.

Besides bemoaning the work of the abolitionists, the leading St. Louis citizens were often embroiled in hot discussions over the events leading up to the Mexican War and the progress of the war after it was formally declared on May 13, 1846. The trade with New Mexico had begun in 1821 with a caravan of pack animals organized at Franklin, Missouri, and St. Louis merchants had been deeply involved in it during the twenty-five years since that first trading venture over the Santa Fe Trail. Most St. Louis citizens agreed that it would be a great advantage to the United States to have its territory enlarged to include the Southwest. When an attempt to purchase this land failed, the Manifest Destiny enthusiasts were ready to back military expeditions against the Mexican owners of

12. Scharf, *History of St. Louis,* 585.

the land. Soon companies were in drill formation frequently on St. Louis streets. A call had gone out for three thousand volunteers, and the young men of St. Louis responded heartily. Shreve regretted that he was too old to join them, but he helped cheer on the sons of some of his friends when they drilled with Battery A of the Missouri Light Artillery.[13]

The steamboats in and out of the St. Louis riverfront were even more numerous than before with the additional military cargo and transport of soldiers. There were also supplies to be shipped to the new settlements around the big bend of the Missouri River to fill the needs of the wagon caravans starting westward across the plains from that area in the 1840s. Most of the supplies were sent by steamboat from St. Louis.

At that time people were also dependent upon the steamboat for much of their communication from a long distance. The telegraph wires that connected most eastern cities following a congressional appropriation for that purpose in 1843 were a long way from St. Louis. But in 1847 it appeared that there would be connections to Washington, D.C., from St. Louis before long, since poles were being set and wires run west of the Appalachians.

Before the wires crossed the Mississippi, however, steamboats brought news to St. Louis of the progress of American troops in Mexico. The Fourth of July parade of 1847 in St. Louis along Market Street in response was impressive indeed, and Shreve was among the leading citizens taking part in the festivities. Some of the troops were already returning home victorious, and their arrival via Mississippi River steamboats was timed to coincide with the July 4 celebration. Along with the throaty steamboat whistles, all the bells in St. Louis pealed out a clangorous welcome. The volunteer fire department was out in full force for the parade, with more bells to clang and whistles to blow. Special noise effects came with the soldiers from Jefferson Barracks (located south of the city limits), who brought along cannons. These were fired to reverberate back and forth across the Mississippi River.

That year the people of St. Louis were eagerly following the approach of the telegraph poles and wires to the Mississippi River. As the crossing of Illinois was completed, a tall mast was set up on the riverbank opposite a shot tower 185 feet high on the Missouri side. An intermediate pole to safeguard against sag (the wires had to be held higher than any steamboat

13. Dorsey, *Master of the Mississippi*, 229–30.

stack) was positioned on Bloody Island, named for the many duels fought there. Workers in boats carried the wires across the water, and the connection was made. St. Louis could at last be in instant communication with most of the eastern cities, a wonderful step forward. On December 23, 1847, a St. Louis newspaper announced, "The first streak of lightning passed through the wires yesterday." Captain Shreve was selected for a great honor in the ceremony opening the telegraph service since he was still recognized as the one man who had contributed most to the growth of the city. He was chosen to send the first message from St. Louis to Washington, D.C., a greeting to President Polk.[14]

Around this time Shreve also went back to his long struggle to get compensation from Congress for his steam snag boat. In 1846 another committee report was made, this time by the Committee on Patents. The report concluded with a new amount of remuneration recommended, after substantially agreeing that the steam snag boat had saved the United States government millions of dollars. The committee suggested that Congress should appropriate, to pay for past use of and future rights to the patent, the amount saved "in the expense of transportation of supplies to the single post of Fort Towson, on Red river, to wit: the sum of eighty-five thousand dollars, ($85,000)."

This was a sum worthy of consideration, Shreve thought. But the rest of 1846 brought no appropriation. In the winter that followed, he pulled together all the reports and data, wrote a review of the situation, and took all these materials to a printer and binder to be made into a pamphlet. The pamphlet began with a summarizing statement by Shreve, titled "A Memorial." As was the current custom, he wrote it in the third person, referring to himself as "your memorialist," and addressing it to "The Honorable Senate and House of Representatives of the United States of North America, in Congress assembled." He reviewed the terms of his employment by the government and described how he had designed the snag boat because all other means of snag removal were slow and far from efficient. His invention, he wrote "was a combination of several mechanical powers, not only entirely new in itself, but applying one power in said combination which no one supposed previously could be successfully used, viz: Percussion."[15]

14. *Ibid.*, 234.
15. Shreve, *Memorial*, 4.

He recounted how he furnished an estimate of the probable cost of building a machine according to his plans and received the approval of the secretary of war. He was authorized to build the steam snag boat *Heliopolis*, "which was finished on the 22d of July, 1829, and the department duly notified of the fact. With that boat your memorialist broke off and raised snags—consisting of trees sixty feet long and three feet and a half in diameter, implanted twenty feet in the bed of the river,—with the greatest ease. The department were so well satisfied with the result of the experiment and the great service performed by the Heliopolis, that in 1831 he was instructed to build another boat, and in 1836, two others."[16]

He continued with a review of the scope of work done with the snag boats, including the removal of the Red River raft. He recalled: "That river was opened for twelve hundred miles inclusive of the raft region, and an immense quantity of most valuable land worth millions to the Government, reclaimed. Although thus engaged upon that most important work, he did not permit it to interfere with the improvement of the Ohio, Mississippi and Arkansas rivers. His labor and responsibility was however greatly increased as he had often the management of seven distinct appropriations, of the disbursement of which he had to keep separate accounts. His salary was not increased nor was he allowed more than one clerk."[17]

Following a reminder of the committee's recommendation for payment of $85,000, he asked for compensation for past and future use of his patented invention. Then, to save further congressional searching of records, he included all the significant reports, including a copy of his patent. The final report was that of the 1846 committee. This was followed by a linen sheet about eighteen by twenty-four inches, bound into the book and folded to page size, on which was reproduced a lithograph in stone of his last snag boat (see Figure 15). The drawing was by a St. Louis artist, August A. Von Schmidt. No doubt the little volume was prepared at some expense to Shreve. Hoping to reach a settlement at last, he sent copies to the appropriate individuals in Washington. But this effort also failed to bring the money, though the Corps of Engineers continued to use Shreve's invention in its river clearance work.[18]

16. *Ibid.*, 5.
17. *Ibid.*, 5–6.
18. Dorsey, *Master of the Mississippi*, 248. The case was still pending at Shreve's death. The suit was continued, and the final settlement was $50,000.

The great additions to United States territory that followed the conclusion of the Mexican War brought even greater shipping activity to St. Louis. The discovery of gold in California set off a veritable fever of emigration to the West Coast, and steamboats up to Independence and Kansas City were constantly booked with both passengers and cargo headed westward across the plains. Only land travel could carry on from there. Slow, plodding draft animals pulling heavy wagons were scarcely efficient, and the talk of railroads took on a note of urgency.

First the tracks had to be laid westward to the Mississippi, and they were not yet that far. Nevertheless, Shreve and his St. Louis friends saw the building of a railroad as an immediate need, not just a dream for the future. If the tracks began at St. Louis instead of farther north, the steamboat port would continue to be vital, with the railroad supplementing river transportation rather than replacing it. Carrying freight via railroad would be far more expensive than via riverboat, so despite some predictions there was really no reason to fear an end to steamboats. Shreve was an enthusiastic supporter of the idea of a railroad to the Pacific coast that led westward out of St. Louis.

He met with a group of other interested citizens throughout the year 1848 to discuss possibilities. Early in 1849 they were ready to incorporate for the construction of the first section of a railroad headed toward California. In February, Senator Thomas Hart Benton of Missouri introduced a bill in Congress. His concept was a combination wagon road and railroad—"an iron railway where practicable and a wagon road where a railway was not practicable."[19] Benton was opposed in his plans by the powerful Stephen A. Douglas of Illinois, who wanted the railroad to begin at Chicago. Nothing came of Benton's bill, but in March the group of St. Louis citizens took action. They would start a railroad without government aid, if necessary, and thereby influence the government to continue the laying of tracks and clinch the matter for St. Louis. They optimistically named their railroad-to-be the Pacific Railroad and drew up an act of incorporation approved on March 12, 1849.[20] The incorporators included, besides Shreve, some men of St. Louis families prominent in the fur trade—Pierre Chouteau, Jr., and Bernard Pratte—and several civic lead-

19. *Ibid.*, 241.
20. *Pacific Railroad Records* 1849–50, p. 41, in Missouri Historical Society Library, Jefferson Memorial Building, St. Louis.

ers whose names have lived on in St. Louis history, including Thomas Allen, James H. Lucas, Edward Walsh, Wayman Crow, and John O'Fallon.

But soon afterward Shreve ceased his active participation in the affairs of the railroad because of difficulties that overcame him. May 17, 1849, was a day of double tragedy for him. In the spring there had been an outbreak of cholera in the city. Shreve's little granddaughter, Virginia Carter, six years old and adored by her grandfather, had fallen ill, and on that day she died.

On that same day, down at the riverfront the steamboat *White Cloud* burst into flames from some unknown cause. A strong wind fanned the flames, and soon other steamboats were also ablaze. Whipped along by the hot draft and wind and fed by dry timbers, the fire spread along a half mile of docked steamboats within a half hour. Some of the steamboats were empty of cargo, but several had just arrived or were taking on goods for the next voyage. In all, twenty-three steamboats burned to the waterline. A few others were saved by being set adrift in the river.

The levee was, as usual, stacked with freight of all sorts awaiting loading onto, or just unloaded from, the steamboats. The sparks fell on the goods, and bales of cotton began to smolder while other loose materials sent up new tongues of flame. The several volunteer fire companies of the city dragged their pumping carts hastily to the riverfront and hooked up their leather hoses to try to contain the flames. Others filled and passed leather buckets of water in a bucket brigade that seemed futile as spring winds fanned the flames even higher up the levee. A row of old frame shacks blazed up, and then all of downtown St. Louis was in danger. The warehouses, including those in which Shreve had an interest, were lost in the conflagration as the flames swept up from the levee. Before the fire was extinguished, four hundred businesses and homes in fifteen blocks had burned.

The day of the fire and of his granddaughter's death marked the beginning of a decline in Shreve's health and activity. There were still a few occasions for joy, such as the birth of another granddaughter, little Elizabeth Carter, in August, 1849, and soon afterward of his own last child, Florence Shreve. Watching little Florie, as she was called, brightened the year 1850. But as the year wore on toward its close, the dread fevers again swept through St. Louis. This time they struck the Walker Carter family, and two more of Shreve's grandchildren died, a five-year-old boy and the infant Elizabeth. Shreve had been spending his days sitting in his comfortable armchair at home, but with the death of his two grandchildren, he seemed to grow weaker. Then, in January, 1851, he and Lydia lost their darling little Florie, a final blow.

Henry Miller Shreve had fought many battles, and fought them well. But after the passing of little Florie, he lay quietly. On March 6, 1851, he could faintly hear the mellow tones of the steamboats announcing their approach to the landings. He is said to have remarked, "When it reaches you from somewhere in the distance, a steamboat whistle is the sweetest music in the world." Hearing that sweet music, he died peacefully. The St. Louis *Republic* reported his death in its issue of March 7, with a brief tribute.

> He was for nearly forty years closely identified with the commerce of the West, either in flat-boat or steamboat navigation, During the administration of Adams, Jackson and Van Buren, he filled the post of United States Superintendent of Western River Improvements and by the steam snag-boat, of which he was the inventor, contributed largely to the safety of Western commerce. To him belongs the honor of demonstrating the practicability of navigating the Mississippi with steam-boats. He commanded the first steamboat that ever ascended that river, and made several valuable improvements, both of the steam-engine and of the hull and cabins of Western steamboats.
>
> When the British were threatening New Orleans in 1814–15 he was employed by Gen. Jackson in several harzardous enterprises, and during the battle on the 8th of January, served one of the field-pieces which destroyed the advancing column of Gen. Keane.
>
> His name has become historically connected with western river navigation, and will long be cherished by his numerous friends throughout this valley.[21]

They laid him to rest in the new Bellefontaine Cemetery, opened in 1849, when the cholera epidemic made its need evident, on the Hempstead family farm, near his own lands. For weeks, there had been about thirty funeral processions each day to this resting place on a bluff overlooking the Mississippi River. A tall monument marks the place where Shreve lies, facing toward the river that had been his life. Mary Shreve's body was brought from its first burial site and placed to his left; to his right is Lydia, who outlived him by forty-one years.

One can no longer decipher the four-line verse that once was on the

21. Gould, *Fifty Years on the Mississippi,* 111.

captain's monument. But this does not matter, for Shreve has other monuments. A street leading into the cemetery from where Gallatin Place once stood bears his name. Children play on the grounds of the Henry M. Shreve Public School in St. Louis, many not knowing the story of the man for whom the school is named. Shreveport, Louisiana, has grown to become the second-largest city in the state. There, too, many citizens are vague about the lifework of the man for whom their city is named.

It may not really matter that so little is remembered of the man who was called the Father of the Mississippi Steamboat and of whom it was said many years ago that he was "a man whose name will be remembered as long as Fulton's." His true monuments are still with us—the cities that prospered along the rivers he opened, the farmlands that grew to productivity because he opened the way to marketing their output, and the American hearts in which there still lives the indomitable spirit that moved Henry Miller Shreve to rise to challenges to make our lives better. And most of all his monument is the busy riverway that flows below the bluff on which his body lies—the river eternal.

Bibliography

BOOKS

Allen, L. P. *The Genealogy and History of the Shreve Family from 1641*. Greenfield, Ill., 1901.

Ambler, Charles Henry. *A History of Transportation in the Ohio Valley*. Glendale, Calif., 1931.

American State Papers: Documents of Congress of the United States. IV, *Commerce and Navigation*; V, *Military Affairs*; VIII, *Public Lands*. Washington, D.C., 1834.

Athearn, Robert G. *Forts of the Upper Mississippi*. Englewood, N.J., 1967.

Audubon, John J. *Audubon in the West*. Edited by J. F. McDermott. Norman, 1965.

[Baird, Robert (?)]. *View of the Valley of the Mississippi; or, The Emigrant's and Traveller's Guide to the West*. Philadelphia, 1834.

Baldwin, Leland D. *The Keelboat Age on Western Waters*. Pittsburgh, 1941.

Banta, R. E. *The Ohio*. Edited by Hervey Allen and Carl Cramer. New York, 1949.

Billon, Frederic L. *Annals of St. Louis in Its Territorial Days from 1804 to 1821*. St. Louis, 1888.

Bradbury, John. *Travels in the Interior of America, 1809–1810*. 1817. Reprint. New York, 1966.

Brooks, Charles B. *The Siege of New Orleans*. Seattle, 1961.

Brownsville Historical Society. *The Three Towns: A Sketch of Brownsville, Bridgeport and West Brownsville*. 1883. Reprint. Brownsville, Pa., 1976.

Carter, Hodding. *Lower Mississippi*. New York, 1942.

Carter, Samuel III. *Blaze of Glory: The Fight for New Orleans, 1814–1815*. New York, 1971.

Chittenden, Hiram M. *The American Fur Trade of the Far West*. Vol. II of 3 vols. New York, 1902.

————. *Early Steamboat Navigation on the Mississippi*. Vol. I of 2 vols. Minneapolis, 1903.

Churchill, Winston, *The Crisis*. New York, 1901.

Coates, Robert M. *The Outlaw Years*. New York, 1930.

Comstock, J.C., ed. *West Virginia Heritage Encyclopedia*. Richwood, W. Va., 1976.

Congressional Record. 1832–36, 1843, 1855.

Cramer, Zadok. *The Navigator: Containing Directions for Navigating The Monongahela, Allegheny, Ohio and Mississippi Rivers*. 1814. Reprint. New York, 1966.

Dayton, Fred Erving. *Steamboat Days*. New York, 1925.

Dennett, Daniel. *Louisiana as It Is*. New Orleans, 1876.

Dorsey, Florence L. *Master of the Mississippi*. Boston, 1941.

Dowdey, Clifford. *Lee*. Boston, 1965.

Drago, Harry Sinclair. *The Steamboaters: From the Early Side-Wheelers to the Big Packets*. New York, 1967.

Dunbar, Seymour. *A History of Travel in America*. New York, 1937.

Ellis, Franklin. *History of Fayette County, Pa*. N.p., n.d.

Eskew, Garnett Laidlaw. *Pageant of the Packets*. New York, 1929.

Faris, John T. *The Romance of the Rivers*. New York, 1927.

First National Bank of Wheeling. *Wheeling in West Virginia*. N.p., 1974.

Flexner, James Thomas. *Steamboats Come True*. New York, 1944.

Flint, Timothy, *Recollections of the Last Ten Years in the Valley of the Mississippi*. Edited by George R. Brooks. Carbondale, Ill. 1968.

Foreman, Grant. *Adventure on the Red River*. Norman, 1937.

Frazer, Robert W. *Forts of the West: Military Forts and Presidios and Posts Commonly Called Forts West of the Mississippi River to 1898*. Norman, 1965.

Freeman, Douglas S. *Washington*. Edited by Richard B. Harwell. New York, 1968.

Fuller, Myron L. *The New Madrid Earthquake*. 1912. Reprint. Cape Girardeau, Mo., 1966.

Gould, E. W. *Fifty Years on the Mississippi; or, Gould's History of River Navigation*. St. Louis, 1889.

Hamlin, Talbot. *Benjamin Henry Latrobe*. New York, 1955.

Hardin, J. Fair. *Northwestern Louisiana: A History of the Watershed of the Red River, 1714–1937*. Louisville, 1937.

Harwell, Richard. *Lee*. New York, 1961.

Havighurst, Walter. *River to the West: Three Centuries on the Ohio*. New York, 1970.

———. *Voices on the River: The Story of the Mississippi Waterways*. New York, 1964.

Hearn-O'Pry, Maude. *Chronicles of Shreveport*. Shreveport, 1928.

Henrici, Holice H. *Shreveport Saga*. Baton Rouge, 1977.

Hollon, W. Eugene. *The Southwest: Old and New*. New York, 1961.

Houck, Louis. *A History of Missouri*. Vols. I and II of 3 vols. Chicago, 1908.

Huber, Leonard V. *Advertisements of Lower Mississippi River Steamboats, 1812–1920*. Barrington, R.I., 1959.

Hunter, Louis C. *Steamboats on the Western Rivers*. Cambridge, Mass., 1949.

Johnston, J. Stoddard. *Memorial History of Louisville*. Vol. I of 2 vols. Chicago, 1896.

Keemle, Charles, ed. *St. Louis Directory, 1840–41*. N.p., n.d.

Knox, Thomas W. *The Life of Robert Fulton and a History of Steam Navigation*. New York, 1890.

Latrobe, Charles Joseph. *The Rambler in North America*. London, 1836.

Latrobe, J. H. B. *The Journal of Latrobe, 1796–1820*. New York, 1905.

Lavender, David. *Bent's Fort*. New York, 1954.

Lloyd, James T. *Lloyd's Steamboat Directory and Disasters on the Western Rivers*. Cincinnati, 1856.

Lorant, Stefan. *Pittsburgh: The Story of an American City*. New York, 1964.

McDermott, John Francis, ed. *Before Mark Twain: A Sampler of Old, Old Times on the Mississippi*. Carbondale, Ill., 1968.

McLure, Lilla, and J. E. Howe. *History of Shreveport and Shreveport Builders*. Shreveport, 1937.

McMurtrie, H., *Sketches of Louisville*. Louisville, 1819.

Montule, Edouard de. *A Voyage to North America in 1817*. London, 1824.

Moore, Edith Wyatt. *Natchez Under-the-Hill*. Natchez, 1958.

Morison, Samuel Eliot. *The Oxford History of the American People*. New York, 1965.

National Bank of West Virginia at Wheeling. *Wheeling's First 250 Years*. Wheeling, 1975.

Ogg, Frederic A. *The Opening of the Mississippi*. New York, 1904.

Parrish, Randall. *Historic Illinois*. Chicago, 1906.

Quick, Herbert, and Edward Quick. *Mississippi Steamboatin'*. New York, 1926.

Read, Frederick Brent. *Up the Heights of Fame and Fortune and Routes Taken by the Climbers to Become Men of Mark*. Cincinnati, 1873.

Roosevelt, Theodore. *Winning of the West*. Vol. II of 6 vols. New York, 1889.

Roush, J. Fred. *Chalmette National Historical Park*. Washington, D.C., 1958.

Samuel, Ray, Leonard V. Huber, and Warren C. Ogden. *Tales of the Mississippi*. New York, 1955.

Saxon, Lyle. *Father Mississippi*. New York, 1927.

Scharf, John Thomas. *History of St. Louis City and County*. 2 vols. Philadelphia, 1883.

Schneider, Norris F. *Blennerhassett Island and the Burr Conspiracy*. Columbus, Ohio, 1966.

Shreve, Henry M. *A Memorial: Official Evidence in Support of the Claim of Capt. Henry M. Shreve on the United States Government for Its Use of His Patented Invention of the Steam Snag Boat*. St. Louis, 1847.

Thwaites, Reuben G. *Early Western Travels*. Vols. IV and XIX of 32 vols. Cleveland, 1904–1907.

————. *How George Rogers Clark Won the Northwest and Other Essays in Western History*. Chicago, 1904.

Trollope, Frances. *Domestic Manners of the Americans*. Edited by Donald Smolley. New York, 1949.

Tyson, Carl Newton. *The Red River in Southwestern History*. Norman, 1981.

Veech, James. *The Monongahela of Old*. N.p., 1858.

Vestal, Stanley. *Mountain Men*. Boston, 1937.

Vogt, Helen. *Westward of Ye Laurall Hills*. Parsons, W. Va., 1976.

Way, Frederick. *Way's Directory of Western River Packets*. Sewickley, Pa., 1950.
Williams, Walter, and Floyd C. Shoemaker. *Missouri, Mother of the West*. Vol. I of 5 vols. New York, 1930.
Works Projects Administration Writers' Program. *Kentucky*. New York, 1939.
——. *Louisiana*. New York, 1945.
——. *Missouri: A Guide to the "Show Me" State*. New York, 1941.
Wright, Margery Daily. *Mary Cane: A Chronicle of Caddo and Bossier*. Baton Rouge, 1979.

ARTICLES

Atherton, Lewis E. "Missouri's Society and Economy in 1821." *Missouri Historical Review*, LXV (1971), 450–77.
DeBlieux, Robert B., comp. "Excerpts from Correspondence Between Captain Henry Miller Shreve and His Superior, Brigadier General C. Gratiot, 1832–33." *North Louisiana Historical Association Newsletter*, April, 1966.
Dos Passos, John. "The Conspiracy and Trial of Aaron Burr." *American Heritage*, XVII (February, 1966), 4–9, 69–84.
Evans, Nelson. "The First Steamboat on the Ohio." *Ohio Archeological and Historical Publications*, XVI (1907), 310–15.
Foreman, Grant. "River Navigation in the Early Southwest." *Mississippi Valley Historical Review*, XV (1928), 34–55.
Hardin, J. Fair. "The First Great Western River Captain: A Sketch of the Career of Captain Henry M. Shreve . . ." *Louisiana Historical Quarterly*, X (1927), 25–67.
Huber, Leonard. "Heyday of the Floating Palace." *American Heritage*, VIII (October, 1957), 14–25, 96–98.
Hunter, Lloyd A. "Slavery in St. Louis, 1804–1860." *Bulletin: Missouri Historical Society*, XXX (1974), 233–65.
Pfaff, Caroline S. "Henry Miller Shreve: A Biography." *Louisiana Historical Quarterly*, X (1927), 192–240.
Phillips, Josephine E. "Flatboating on the Great Thoroughfare." *Bulletin of Historical and Philosophical Society of Ohio*, V (June, 1947), 11–32.
Rickey, Don, Jr. "The Old St. Louis Riverfront, 1763–1960." *Missouri Historical Review*, LVIII (1964), 174–90.
Sampson, Francis A. "Glimpses of Old Missouri by Explorers and Travelers." *Missouri Historical Review*, LXVIII (1973), 74–93.
Shreve, Israel. "Israel Shreve's Diary and Letters." *Magazine of American History*, II (1878), 743–48.
——. "Journal from Jersey to Monongahela." *Pennsylvania Magazine of History and Biography*, LII (1928), 194–202.
Shreve, John. "Personal Narrative of the Services of Lieutenant John Shreve." *Magazine of American History*, III (1879), 546–79.

Speck, Robert M. "200 Years Under the Sea: The Connecticut Water Machine Versus the Royal Navy." *American Heritage*, XXXII (December, 1980), 33–39.

[Treat, Samuel (?)]. "Henry Miller Shreve." *U.S. Magazine and Democratic Review*, XXII (1848), 163–71, 241–51.

Vesilind, Priit J. "River with a Job To Do—The Ohio." *National Geographic*, CLI (February, 1977), 245–73.

"Washington's Real Estate." *Magazine of American History*, II (1878), 623–26.

NEWSPAPERS

Allen, Billy. "Shreveport's 125th Birthday." Shreveport *Times*, June 26, 1960, Sec. D, p. 1.

Franklin *Missouri Intelligencer*, May 28, 1819, April 30, 1821.

Niles' Weekly Register (Baltimore), 1814–20.

St. Louis *Enquirer*, 1819.

Sarrazin, Jean Fairly. "Story of Shreve Family Reveals Character of Shreveport's Founder." Shreveport *Times*, August 24, 1941, p. 13.

Webber, Everett. "Cap'm Shreve vs. the Red River Raft." Shreveport *Times*, March 15, 1959, Sec. F, p. 1.

UNPUBLISHED MATERIALS

Fayette County Land Records. Book I, 381–82; Book K, 346–47. Fayette County Courthouse, Uniontown, Pa.

Funk, Margaret Jean. "Henry Miller Shreve: His Contributions to Navigation on the Western Rivers of the U.S." M.S. thesis, Texas Tech University, 1971.

Pacific Railroad Records, 1849–50. Missouri Historical Society Library, Jefferson Memorial Building, St. Louis.

Shreve, Henry M. "Specifications Forming Part of Letters Patent No. 913, Sept. 12, 1838." U.S. Patent Office, Washington, D.C.

U.S. Census of 1790. Fayette County, Pa. Microfilm copy, Brownsville Public Library, Brownsville, Pa.

U.S. Census of 1840. St. Louis and St. Louis County, Mo. Microfilm copy, Missouri Historical Society Library, St. Louis.

U.S. Census of 1850. St. Louis and St. Louis County, Mo. Microfilm copy, Springfield Public Library, Springfield, Mo.

Welch, Lowry H., to the author, March 20, 1980 (letter providing information on the Benjamin Shreve House).

Index

257